To mitchell —
a brilliant n
who was a pleasu
work with on Beyond the Basics!

Jim Kobs

Second Edition

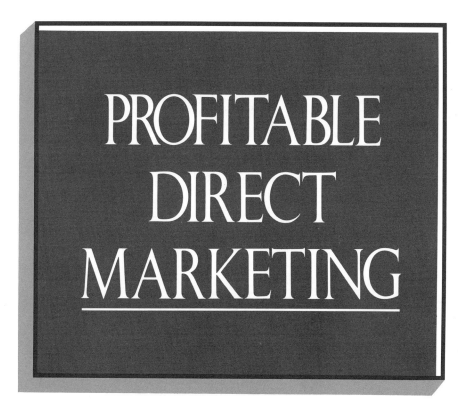

PROFITABLE DIRECT MARKETING

Jim Kobs

NTC Business Books

a division of *NTC Publishing Group* • Lincolnwood, Illinois USA

To Karen,
Ken, and Kathy, who
were there when I wrote
the first edition.

And to Nadine,
who provided much-needed
support and companionship
while I finished the second edition.

Library of Congress Cataloging-in-Publication Data

Kobs, Jim.
    Profitable direct marketing / Jim Kobs. — 2nd ed.
        p.   cm.
    Includes index.
    ISBN 0-8442-3029-4
    1. Direct marketing—United States.   2. Direct marketing—United
States—Case studies.   I. Title.
    HF5415.1.K58   1991
    658.8′4—dc20   91-9010
                                                                                        CIP

Published by NTC Business Books, a division of NTC Publishing Group
4255 West Touhy Avenue
Lincolnwood (Chicago), Illinois 60646-1975, U.S.A.

1 2 3 4 5 6 7 8 9 BC 9 8 7 6 5 4 3 2 1

Critics welcome Kobs' new edition

"I know of no one who is better qualified to write a book on direct marketing than Jim Kobs. He lectures, he teaches, he writes, but most importantly, he does. When we need a new, clear insight for a new program, we turn to Jim. He has the down-to-earth insight and approach that work."

Jack Miller,
President,
Quill Corporation

"Jim Kobs shows us how profit is the final result of market analysis, careful planning and flexible execution. . . . An important study for current direct marketers and those considering entry into the business."

Frederick J. Simon,
President,
Omaha Steaks International

"One book I will always have at hand for a quick and truly usable reference."

Katie Muldoon, Author of Catalog Marketing

"Jim Kobs puts together all the ingredients for a successful competitive strategy. Anyone seeking a leadership position in this growing market will find *Profitable Direct Marketing* an indispensable guide."

Robert Teufel,
President,
Rodale Press

"With a real slowdown in growth of traditional market segments projected over the next 20 years, savvy marketers will want to pay close attention to what Jim Kobs has to say. He talks direct marketing but it's really marketing. And he's the consumate strategist. A must read!"

John J. Flieder,
Vice President,
Allstate Insurance Company

"For anyone considering direct marketing as an element in the marketing communication mix, Jim Kobs' *Profitable Direct Marketing* is must reading."

Ted Spiegel,
Northwestern University

"This new edition is practically a new book. It's 'beyond the basics.' It is the mature Jim Kobs with all the new experience of a past master of direct marketing."

Robert F. DeLay,
Editor,
The DeLay Letter

"Jim Kobs' welcome book will certainly increase the understanding of the direct marketing concept among consumer and industrial advertisers worldwide. His intimate knowledge of applying principles of direct response advertising to a wide variety of marketing problems makes this text an important business tool."

Pete Hoke,
Publisher,
Hoke Communications, Inc.

CONTENTS

♦

FOREWORD

♦

I CONSIDER IT A PRIVILEGE TO WRITE the foreword to Jim Kobs' great new book.

Memories of Jim's growth go all the way back to 1966 when Stone & Adler was launched. He was, in fact, the first account executive that we hired. (I still compliment myself for having recognized a great talent at an early age.) He was involved in every presentation at the outset and our success rate was phenomenal. Jim was a key player in making it happen.

As Jim traveled the road towards superstar status, two tenets developed above all others: the importance of the offer and a keen grasp of strategy. His checklist of 99 Proven Direct Response Offers, found in this text, has long been the standard reference for direct marketers around the world. And his ability to plan and create strategically have accounted for scores of direct marketing breakthroughs.

In 1978 my protege—Jim Kobs—became an entrepreneur, combining his wealth of knowledge and experience to launch Kobs & Brady. His was not a fledgling agency for long. Instead, the new agency enjoyed as meteoric a rise as Stone & Adler some ten years earlier. The culmination was a multimillion dollar sale of his agency to Ted Bates in 1986. But, still young, he has reentered the direct marketing scene as a principal of Kobs, Gregory & Passavant.

I'm proud of Jim Kobs' business accomplishments, but more proud of his willingness to share his knowledge and experience with others. Jim has spoken frequently at direct marketing conventions, direct marketing days and at seminars. He has given freely of what he has learned. I've always felt that "giving back" is the true gauge of a successful person.

All Jim Kobs has learned reaches a climax in this second edition of *Profitable Direct Marketing*. He has stopped the clock, as it were, to put a focus on direct marketing as it is today.

And a different direct marketing world it is from the time Jim first viewed it with eyes of wonder. In the earlier days direct marketing was a myth to most, a discipline with rules that were unique unto itself, a discipline which, when practiced as the rule-makers intended, promised riches beyond wildest dreams.

The 1980's especially was a time of acquisition mania, big general agencies taking title to much smaller direct marketing shops. Fortune 500 companies acquiring direct marketing operations and setting them up as separate profit centers.

Well the myth has pretty much evaporated. The merger mania has subsided. Many of the acquired direct marketing operations, even though they have been profitable, have been spun off, mostly because they didn't serve normal channels of distribution of major marketers. Direct Marketing hasn't been abandoned by major marketers, to the contrary, its principles have been applied to their total marketing mixes. And they are the better for it.

In the early days direct marketing had to be "sold." Today that is not the case. It is no longer a case of whether or not a firm, large or small, will use direct marketing. The only question to be decided is how best can direct marketing be used. *Profitable Direct Marketing* provides all the answers to that question. This is truly a book for our times!

> Bob Stone, Chairman Emeritus
> Stone & Adler, Inc.
> Professor, Northwestern University

AUTHOR'S PREFACE

◆

When the first edition of this book appeared in 1979, there were only a handful of books devoted to direct marketing. Today there are over 200 books on the subject.

When the first edition was published, direct marketing was relatively unknown to the general public. It was an accidental career choice for most people. And when someone asked you what you did at cocktail parties, it was standard practice to give a five-minute explanation. Today, a mere mention of direct marketing is likely to be greeted with approving recognition. And there are over 100 college and university courses devoted to this specialized discipline.

When the first edition came out, most large firms were just discovering what direct marketing was all about. AT&T, for example, had just hired a direct marketing consultant to do private seminars for its senior executives. Today, one of the Bell System operating companies I talked to recently spends over one-third of its total advertising budget on direct marketing.

I could go on, but I'm sure you get the idea. Telemarketing, infomercials, 900 numbers, home shopping TV shows, and databases have all emerged or exploded in the past dozen years since *Profitable Direct Marketing* was written. It was clearly time for an all-new edition.

As I planned and developed this volume, I saw both how much has changed and how little has changed. There have actually been very few modifications to the basics of product selection, offers, and testing. For instance, I only found three new offers worth adding to my list of 99 Proven Direct Response Offers.

On the other hand, strategic planning is here to stay. And, perhaps the biggest change I've seen is how direct marketing has moved from a tactical tool to a strategic weapon. Instead of jumping right into the tactics of creative execution, it's becoming commonplace to first lay the groundwork with a solid creative strategy. Likewise in the marketing arena, where not too many years ago a marketing plan was a fancy term for "how many pieces do we mail next year?"

Today, a sound marketing plan examines strategic planning issues and lays out key growth strategies. I think you'll find the new chapters on Creative Strategies and Marketing Strategies as valuable as anything in this book.

But there are also a lot more additions to this second edition. New chapters on the major media for direct response advertising, including telemarketing. Separate chapters on creating mail, print, and broadcast. And an expanded look at direct marketing applications—which include the business market, catalogs, package goods, fundraising, retail, and financial services.

From the first edition, I've retained and updated the section on *launching a new direct marketing program*. It covers basic questions to consider, selecting a product or service, creating an effective offer, and testing different facets of your program. There's also a new chapter on research to reflect the growing use of this decision-making tool.

The section on *improving an already successful direct marketing program* is another popular carryover. It shows how to boost results with new creative ideas, management and marketing techniques, and back-end marketing. And I've added extensive information on databases.

Throughout the entire book, I've tried to go one step beyond most others by not merely telling you about something, but also providing examples. You see how to develop a test matrix, take the risk out of a new product development program, and apply an RFM formula to maximize repeat sales from customers. I've also scattered mini case studies throughout the book to show how the principles are applied in real world situations. In the same vein, there are more than 100 illustrations and charts to amplify the text.

I've also tried to avoid handing down hard-and-fast rules like tablets from the mountaintop. While you will find various lists of numbered techniques, please consider them as guiding principles that can be adapted to fit your own marketing situation. In fact, one of my rules in Chapter 15 is "don't be afraid to break the other rules" we've covered.

In total, *Profitable Direct Marketing* is a distillation of my 30-year career. I've been fortunate to be involved during direct marketing's greatest growth period. I've also been fortunate to meet or work with most of the direct marketing giants of yesterday. . . to serve some of the nicest clients in the business . . . and to work side-by-side with many of today's smartest direct marketing professionals.

This new edition is dedicated to all of them. And to the bright, young direct marketing leaders of tomorrow who soak up knowledge like a sponge. I hope you find this ever-growing field as stimulating, challenging, and rewarding as I have.

ACKNOWLEDGMENTS

"This is the best direct marketing book yet written," one of my editors said to me when she finished reading the final chapter. I don't know if it is or not, but I do know it was harder the second time around. And it wouldn't have gotten done without the help of many people.

Special thanks go to Anne Basye, a freelance editor who was my sounding board, researcher, and rewriter. This second edition is much better than the first one because of her dedicated professionalism.

Thanks, too, to Pete Hoke, whose *Direct Marketing* magazine continues to monitor and measure the evolution of direct marketing. I don't always agree with him, but I'm glad to have him as a conscience. The staff of the Direct Marketing Association's Information Central was also helpful in providing statistics and background material. And John Reebel of Bayer Bess Vanderwarker supplied media rates and data.

The 100 or so illustrations, charts, and captions in this book were carefully assembled, typed, and retyped by Barbara Nagucki. Nikki Hanna was able to track down many illustrations used in the first edition, and Carolyn Williams added a creative flair to a number of new illustrations in this edition.

Finally, thanks go out to all the fellow workers and colleagues who helped me build the knowledge and experience this book represents. While I've had the opportunity to work with and for some fine people, I'm especially grateful that I had the opportunity to share most of my agency career with Bill Gregory. And more recently, to have Pierre Passavant as a partner. Many others, who I equally respect, are quoted throughout the text.

Jim Kobs

PART I

HOW TO START A DIRECT MARKETING PROGRAM

1

A MATURING MARKETING DISCIPLINE

♦

IN 1923, THE GREAT ADVERTISING pioneer Claude Hopkins called it *scientific advertising*. It's had other names and nicknames through the years. Today it's called *direct marketing*.

Regardless of the nomenclature, this marketing technique has caught the fancy of everyone from individual entrepreneurs to bottom-line executives in giant corporations. And in the years since its introduction, the buying public has voiced its approval by responding with orders and dollars.

Maybe that's why the American business community embraced this new marketing discipline so enthusiastically during the seventies and eighties—and why direct marketing continues to grow at a dramatic rate.

Of course, the direct marketing explosion didn't happen overnight. The basic techniques have been around for decades. They've been used successfully, but quietly, by scores of firms seeking to generate sales and leads—while simultaneously reducing selling costs. But the spectacular growth of direct marketing during the last two decades has made these techniques seem "revolutionary." That growth has also transformed direct marketing from a little-known technique into a reliable, effective, and maturing discipline that can help sell almost any product or service.

DIRECT MARKETING TODAY

SOMETIMES DIRECT MARKETING EXPERTS invent their own terms and definitions, while newcomers use terms like "direct mail" and "direct marketing" interchangeably. Everyone has a favorite way of defining things. But here's how to distinguish between direct marketing and some similar terms.

Direct mail is simply an advertising medium, like magazines or television, except that it uses the mail to deliver its message. That message can have a wide variety of objectives, from making a sale to changing opinions or providing information.

Mail order is a way of doing business. It is a distribution channel in which the customer's order is received by mail or phone and delivered through the mail or a similar direct-to-the-buyer shipment method. Of course, the order can be solicited by any advertising medium.

Direct response is an advertising technique. This is a specialized type of advertising that solicits an immediate action or response. The action requested might be an order, an inquiry, or even a store visit.

Direct marketing is a term that embraces all of the above—direct mail, mail order, and direct response. Direct marketing uses media to deliver the message; it calls for action on the part of the message recipient; and it often provides its own distribution channel. Direct marketing, however, is also a method of promotion that can be employed with traditional distribution channels, such as providing leads for a sales force. While there are many more elaborate definitions floating around, I prefer to define it in simple terms:

Direct marketing gets your ad message direct to the customer or prospect to produce some type of immediate action. It usually involves creating a database of respondents.

The two key words are *direct* and *action*. This is because direct marketing is really the straightest line between you—the advertiser—and the action you want those who receive your message to take. You bring your message direct to customers or prospects, and you direct them to take a specific action. The respondents might be consumers or businesspeople and their actions are normally captured on a database to enhance and refine future marketing efforts.

The flow chart in Exhibit 1.1 illustrates this process. The top half represents the advertising media that deliver messages to customers and prospects; the bottom half shows the distribution channels used to place orders. Those orders are captured by your database and flow back to the top to influence future advertising decisions.

A couple points on the chart are worth noting. All the media alternatives can be used for prospecting. But only two, direct mail and telemarketing, can be used to target customers and inquiries with no waste circulation. I like to call these *database media*.

EXHIBIT 1.1   Kobs' direct marketing flow chart

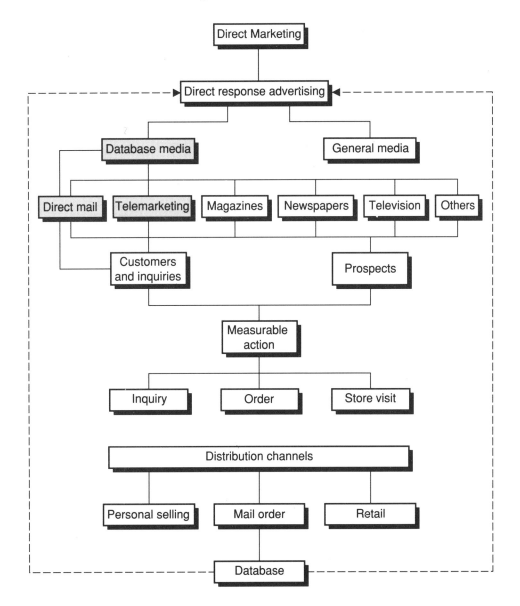

Source: Adapted from "Direct Marketing Model" by Jenkins and "Direct Marketing Flow Chart" by Baier, Hoke, & Stone.

Other than vending machines, there are only three distribution channels—mail order, personal selling, and retail. Direct marketing supports personal selling when you provide inquiries for a sales representative or agent. Likewise, direct marketing impacts the retail channel when a consumer visits a store location with a coupon or certificate.

Finally, it should be noted that some large advertisers, like AT&T and IBM, use direct marketing in all three of their distribution channels.

Dollar Volumes and Percentages Document Growth

What does the "action" add up to in consumer purchases? The direct marketing field is still playing catch-up with meaningful statistics, but here's some key figures from leading industry sources.

♦ An estimated 98.6 million Americans made shop-at-home purchases in 1990.

♦ Annual sales of goods and services through direct marketing now top $200 billion.

♦ Seventy percent of consumers used an 800 number for home shopping in the past 12 months.

While direct marketing's growth rate showed some signs of slowing down as we entered the nineties, it's projected to gain six to ten percent annually. This is still strong growth for a maturing category and remains somewhat higher than the growth in the retail sector. Growth rates vary by product category, of course; in some, direct marketing sales are growing at a rate almost double the increases stores are posting.

How much do advertisers spend to make these increases happen? Plenty, as direct marketing has burgeoned. One of the big phone companies hardly knew what direct marketing was ten years ago, yet today direct marketing activities get a third of its total advertising dollars. Similarly, in just five years, Home Box Office's direct marketing budget grew from $1 million to $35 million. By 1990,

Hyatt Hotels Corporation was spending one of every two advertising dollars on direct marketing.

Direct mail continues to get a large share of direct marketing expenditures. In 1980, $7.6 billion was spent on direct mail advertising. By 1990, direct mail dollar volume had topped $23 billion, representing about 18 percent of all advertising dollars.

Other media not only get their share of direct marketing expenditures but have also shown strong growth. Mail order expenditures in magazines, for example, increased from $86.2 million in 1977 to $530.8 million in 1990. Newspaper preprints of all types reached $6.9 billion in 1989, while mail order advertisers spent $71.8 million on run-of-press space ads in newspapers. Moreover, direct response TV has shown similar spending increases.

THE POWER OF DIRECT MARKETING

Most mail order activity is not geared to selling the necessities of food, clothing, and shelter. It's directed toward what some have called *marginal luxuries*. Yet everything from books, magazines, and sportswear to phone systems, copiers and office supplies can be promoted via direct marketing. Sales figures in selected categories are impressive.

> ♦ About 68 percent of all magazine subscriptions are sold by mail, accounting for $193 million in annual sales.

> ♦ Premiums of $10 billion were paid in 1989 for all kinds of insurance bought through the mail.

> ♦ The Home Shopping Network, which didn't exist when the first edition of this book was written in 1979, had sales of over one billion dollars last year.

> ♦ Americans now order everything from pears and fruitcakes to steaks and clambakes by

mail—a category likely to increase from $1.2 billion to $3 billion between 1990 and the year 2000.

♦ In 1989, nonprofit organizations (religious, educational, charitable, and public interest) raised $29 billion through the mail, or 25 percent of all charitable contributions.

♦ Bertelsmann sells more than $3 billion Deutsch marks in books to its 22.2 million book club members in 26 countries—5.5 million of them in English-speaking countries.

MAJOR CORPORATIONS NOW USING DIRECT MARKETING

Firms using direct marketing can be classified in two broad categories: Those who use it as their primary selling and distribution method; and those who are not primarily in direct marketing, but do use it for certain divisions, subsidiaries, or marketing situations.

The first category includes some mail order firms that have been around for years, as well as newcomers who have built "kitchen table" success stories. Some of these are still run by their founders; others by the founder's family; and still others have brought in professional managers or have been sold outright. Most of them pay more attention to costs and results than they do to image, and usually develop their own creative capabilities or rely on a single direct marketing agency for help.

I regard the giants in the field as those doing $100 million or more in annual sales. These include traditional firms like J.C. Penney, Fingerhut, and L.L. Bean, along with newer companies such as Lands' End and Lillian Vernon. (See Exhibit 1.2.)

The second category is somewhat harder to identify. It consists primarily of medium-size to large corporations that have entered direct marketing fairly recently, either by acquiring an existing business or developing a new one. Some promote under their own names; others under the names of subsidiaries. Some have entire divisions devoted to direct marketing; others integrate direct marketing techniques into their total marketing programs.

EXHIBIT 1.2   Selected top U.S. direct marketers

COMPANY	BUSINESS	MAIL ORDER SALES
J.C. Penney	General merchandise	$3.315 billion
Time Warner	Books, magazines, cable TV	$2.784 billion
Reader's Digest	Books, magazines, collectibles	$1.757 billion
Fingerhut (Primerica)	Merchandise	$1 billion
Home Shopping Network	Apparel, health, jewelry, general merchandise	$1 billion
Lands' End	Apparel	$575 million
L.L. Bean	Sporting goods, apparel	$528 million
Prudential Insurance	Insurance	$350 million
Quill Corporation	Office supplies	$289 million
Bradford Exchange	Collectibles	$284.5 million
Dreyfus Corporation	Financial services	$179 million
Lillian Vernon	Gifts, housewares	$165 million
Walt Disney Company	Records, books, children's gifts	$105 million
Garden Way	Gardening equipment	$100 million

Source: Adapted from *Direct Marketing,* July 1991.

This second category is *very* concerned with image, and often uses direct marketing to support another main activity, like building customer relationships or selling aftermarket products. It normally uses multiple agencies to develop its many campaigns.

Not all of these companies are "blue chips"; today, direct marketing is embraced by all sizes and types of firms. In fact, the largest direct marketers in the U.S. include a mix of traditional mail order firms and giant corporations like AT&T and Time Warner. The latter now earn a surprisingly large portion of their revenue through direct marketing.

WHY DIRECT MARKETING KEEPS ON GROWING

Everybody has a pet theory that explains the explosive growth of direct marketing. While it's possible to list many contributing factors (as Exhibit 1.3 does), I think the following are the most significant.

1. CHANGING LIFESTYLES Between 1980 and 1990, the number of women working outside the home jumped from 42 to 58 percent. More than 70 percent of women with children under six hold jobs. With everybody working, these dual-income households have more money to spend, but hardly any time for conventional shopping. And, according to the *Wall Street Journal,* more people hate browsing in stores than hate housework. So it's only logical that by letting consumers select and examine merchandise in their own homes, whenever they find it convenient, direct marketing fits today's lifestyles like a glove.

2. DECLINE AND COST OF PERSONAL SELLING A lot has been written about the growing cost of business sales calls, which now exceed $250 per call, as Exhibit 1.4 documents. At the same time, there's been a steep decline in the kind of personal selling that takes place in a retail store. Self-service discount stores have eliminated scores of salespeople, and those remaining are often uninformed and overworked.

3. TECHNOLOGY The increased sophistication of computers and the constantly decreasing cost of using them have made direct marketing a more exact science than ever. Computers provide tremendous list selectivity and personalization for direct mail. Also, the computer plays a key role in everything from program planning and analysis to fulfillment and database management. It's

even influenced the production process, so that ads and catalogs can be designed, illustrated, color separated, proofed, and in part even printed by computers.

4. PRODUCT PROLIFERATION The tremendous growth in the number of products available means that many highly specialized items and services are aimed at relatively small market segments—segments that can often be targeted better with direct marketing than with mass media.

5. TELEPHONE ORDERS AND FASTER FULFILLMENT In an era that values almost-instant gratification, "Allow four to six weeks for delivery" is a phrase that's becoming extinct. Thanks to 800 numbers and United Parcel Service, consumers can confidently expect to have merchandise delivered in less than two weeks or,

EXHIBIT 1.3   Factors contributing to the success of mail order catalogs

SOCIOECONOMIC FACTORS	EXTERNAL FACTORS	COMPETITIVE FACTORS
More women joining the work force	Rising cost of gasoline	Inconvenient store hours
Population growing older	Availability of 800 lines	Unsatisfactory service in stores
Rising discretionary income	Expanded use of credit cards	Difficulty of parking, especially near downtown stores
More single households	Low-cost data processing	"If you can't beat 'em, join 'em" approach of traditional retailers
Growth of the "me" generation	Availability of mailing lists	

Source: Harvard Business Review, July–August, 1981, "Non-store marketing: Fast track or slow?" by John A. Quelch and Hirotaka Takeuchi.

Exhibit 1.4   Cost of a business-to-business sales call

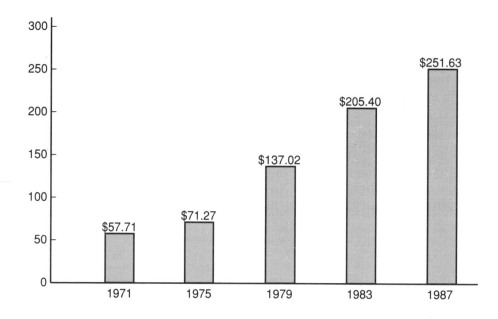

Source: Adapted from McGraw-Hill Research, 1988.

for a premium, two days. (Given the choice, which would you prefer—schlepping to a crowded mall, or ordering a gift that will be delivered via Federal Express to the address of your choice almost overnight?)

Some top advertising executives have predicted that direct marketing will be advertising's biggest growth area over the next 15 to 25 years. But what will direct marketing be like in the next century?

Direct Marketing in the Year 2000

It's always fun to try to predict the future, especially in a dynamic field that is the focus of plenty of technological attention. I'm not sure how good my crystal ball is, but I think two of the things that will have the biggest impact on direct marketing in the year 2000 will be *integrated marketing* and *the human element.*

I believe we'll see more direct response techniques incorporated into regular advertising and traditional distribution channels. *General advertising* will make greater use of 800 numbers and coupons to call for action; *direct marketing ads* will be developed with an eye to creating a favorable image, brand awareness, and future sales. Catalog firms will continue to open retail stores, while retail stores will use direct marketing to build loyalty and store traffic. Interactive videotex systems that use a computer and modem to connect consumers with vast sources of data, goods, and services will offer marketers a whole new marketing medium.

At the 1990 annual meeting of the American Association of Advertising Agencies, Chairman Glen W. Fortinberry commented, "Integrated marketing is where we believe, and where the analysts tell us, the business will be in the nineties. It's where the industry is shifting to and that reflects the mindset of our customers."

Finally, I think the *human element* will play a key role in the direct marketing efforts of the next century. The direct marketing field has been developed by creative executives who recognize important changes in the marketplace, adapt them to their own selling situations, and produce improved results. And that's one thing I *don't* expect to change, regardless of how much technological progress we make.

HOW DIRECT MARKETING COMPARES TO GENERAL ADVERTISING AND MARKETING

IF YOU COMPARE A DIRECT MARKETING ad to a general advertising ad, you'll notice a couple of differences right away. The general advertising ad will focus on image and awareness. The direct marketing ad will feature product benefits and reasons to buy now. It will also include a response vehicle such as a prominently displayed 800 number, a coupon to be clipped, or a separately bound reply card.

These differences stand out, but they're superficial compared to the deeper differences between the two disciplines, summarized in Exhibit 1.5. The

♦

comments in the left column apply mainly to mail order, but the chart highlights some important distinctions. We'll discuss some of these.

DIRECT MARKETING RE-PERSONALIZES THE COMMUNICATION PROCESS

Australian Vin Jenkins, author of *The Concept of Direct Marketing,* believes that the fundamental characteristic that distinguishes direct marketing from general advertising and marketing is the creation of a direct relationship between the marketer and the consumer. In effect, it's like reviving the old days, when door-to-door peddlers and general store owners knew the preferences and habits of their customers.

Instead of following the mass marketing strategy of trying to make a lot of people purchase a product, direct marketers endeavor to create a base of customers who buy often. To court regular customers and encourage their loyalty, they personalize their companies and their approaches. Catalogs from companies like Sharper Image and Lillian Vernon routinely feature a photo and a message from their founders. And databases containing meticulous customer records let marketers tailor their offers to a particular customer or group of customers. In the best direct marketing relationships, the customer feels known and valued by a firm—a quality that has all but vanished in most retailer/ customer exchanges.

SERVICE CONCEPT ADDS VALUE TO PRODUCTS

Les Wunderman of Wunderman Worldwide gets the credit for advancing this concept. He once said, "I believe direct marketing has the unique ability to convert products to services and satisfactions. It's built into the way we sell."

For example, the sale of individual books at retail can become a book club when offered by mail. Likewise, a magazine: Buy one at the newsstand and you're buying a product. But a year's subscription, delivered to your door, is a service. Even a direct marketing merchandise offer becomes something of a service by offering convenient monthly terms, home delivery, a free trial, and/or easy return policies.

EXHIBIT 1.5   Comparison of direct marketing and mass marketing

DIRECT MARKETING	GENERAL ADVERTISING AND MARKETING
♦ Selling to individuals with customers identifiable by name, address and purchase behavior	♦ Mass selling with buyers identified as broad groups and sharing common demographic and psychographic characteristics
♦ Products have the added value of distribution to the customer's door as an important product benefit	♦ Product benefits do not typically include distribution to the customer's door
♦ The medium is the marketplace	♦ The retail outlet is the marketplace
♦ Marketing controls the product all the way through delivery	♦ The marketer typically loses control as the product enters the distribution channel
♦ Uses targeted media	♦ Uses mass media
♦ Advertising is used to generate an immediate inquiry or order, with a specific offer	♦ Advertising is used for cumulative effect over time for building image, awareness, loyalty and benefit recall. Purchase action is deferred
♦ Repetition is used within an ad or mailing	♦ Repetition is used over a period of time
♦ Consumer feels a high perceived risk—product bought unseen, recourse is distant	♦ Consumer feels less risk—has direct contact with the product and direct recourse

Source: Adapted from DMA's Basic Direct Marketing Institute

THE MEDIUM IS THE MARKETPLACE

General advertising transmits ideas about products and services. But the actual sale of those products and services happens somewhere else—in a retail store or a person-to-person selling situation. Mail order, on the other hand, combines the advertising and sales function into a single ad, mailing, or commercial.

♦

One result of this combining of activities, of avoiding a separate sales function, is that a larger percentage of gross sales is spent on advertising. Mail order firms usually spend between 15 and 25 percent of sales on advertising . . . versus only two to four percent for mass marketers. This means you get to work with relatively larger ad budgets and have more opportunity to leverage sales.

Direct Marketing Generates an Immediate Inquiry or Order

Various studies have shown that the majority of retail sales are planned purchases. Direct marketers know that most customers aren't sitting home waiting for an attractive ad or mailing to land in their laps. So direct marketers concentrate their efforts on stimulating unplanned purchases or impulse sales. And everything they do is geared toward making it as easy as possible for the prospect to place an immediate order.

Here's how my former partner Tom Brady explains the difference: "Basically, the general advertiser attempts to build brand or name awareness—*image,* if you will—so that when a customer is ready to buy, he or she will be favorably inclined toward the advertiser's product. Thus, the general advertiser may have to wait months or even years before the full effects of today's ad dollars are realized.

"The direct response advertiser, on the other hand, wants to sell his product *right now!* And he uses all the salesmanship techniques at his command to persuade the reader to act immediately."

That's why we try to make it as easy as possible to order, prepaying postage on reply cards and envelopes or offering 800 numbers or FAX order service.

Built-in Result Feedback

But based on my experience, the main difference between direct marketing and general advertising and marketing is *built-in result feedback*. The reply cards, coupons, and phone calls that come back—the inquiries, orders, and payments—give you an opportunity to measure virtually every element of your marketing program.

Bob DeLay, editor of the *DeLay Letter,* agrees: "Every next move is based upon feedback—the instant replay—available from the marketplace." As a result, direct marketing is the most scientific method of advertising. You can find out which creative approach motivates the most people; if a laser-personalized letter is better than a printed one; whether a premium is cost effective; or whether a particular list or publication delivers an acceptable selling cost.

In short, you know what's producing and what isn't. And that scores big points with advertisers who want to make sure their advertising and marketing investments pay off.

Add up these unique characteristics and I think you'll see why I like to describe direct marketing as a marketing discipline. It requires a special discipline, in many specialized areas that we'll be discussing throughout this book, to maximize revenue and profits.

FROM THE CONSUMER'S VIEWPOINT

WHY CONSUMERS LIKE SHOPPING BY MAIL

The amount of research that's been done on why consumers purchase by mail is relatively limited, and those studies that have been done are often difficult to compare because questions are not standardized. Despite these limitations, let's look at two research studies that bring out some interesting comparisons.

The first was done some years ago by *Better Homes & Gardens* to measure reader attitudes and buying habits from its mail order shopping section. Readers were asked: "Why do you purchase items by mail?" The responses (in percentages) came out as follows:

Can't find items elsewhere	33%
Convenience	27%
Fun	7%
Price	5%
Better quality	1%
Other	1%
Don't purchase items through the mail	32%

(Note that total exceeds 100 because of rounding.)

The second study was done more recently by a leading direct marketing catalog house and was limited to its own customer list. One question asked: "Why do you buy from (firm name)?" Here's how the answers (in percentages) came out:

Convenience 49%
Items not found elsewhere 37%
Variety 16%
Price 14%
Service 12%
Desirability for gifts or personal use 11%
Quality 10%
Other (e.g., free gifts, utility of items) 10%
(Note that total exceeds 100 because of multiple answers.)

While there are some obvious differences in the figures, the similarities are worth noting. Both studies put "convenience" and "can't find elsewhere" at the top of the list. While the latter points out the importance of offering items that are not readily available at retail, I suspect that many of the items consumers had in mind *were* available at retail. But the consumer was not aware of them and a direct marketing ad or catalog was needed to bring them to his or her attention.

Moreover, in both studies, price and quality were rated much lower. It should be mentioned, however, that the merchandise most commonly found in this magazine's shopping section and this particular catalog tends to be low-priced. Direct marketers offering more expensive or upscale merchandise might find these factors are more important with their customers.

THE CONVENIENCE OF ARMCHAIR SHOPPING

What about the convenience cited by consumers? If one thinks about it, convenience actually covers two areas: Avoiding the problems and frustrations of retail shopping and taking advantage of the particular benefits of direct marketing. Who wouldn't forsake traffic congestion, parking problems, incomplete stock, and invisible clerks in favor of mail order's broad product selection, completely flexible shopping hours, free product trials, and home delivery?

Balanced against the convenience of direct marketing is its major drawback. In the past, many consumers have been reluctant to order an item that they can't "feel and touch." But this reluctance is fading, as consumer confidence in direct marketers grows. Martin Baier, author of *The Elements of Direct Marketing,* reasons that today's consumer is more self-reliant. He or she has been made so out of necessity by the trend toward discount stores and the decline in personal selling. And it's this growing self-reliance, he feels, that makes a consumer more likely to shop on his or her own from a catalog, ad, or mailing.

FROM THE ADVERTISER'S VIEWPOINT

FIVE INHERENT ADVANTAGES

THROUGH THE YEARS I'VE BEEN able to talk and work with many large advertisers who were exploring direct marketing for the first time. Of all the advantages the field offers, five seem to be most universally significant. The first three are unique to direct marketing's most common distribution channel, mail order.

1. YOU CAN ESTABLISH A SEPARATE AND SUBSTANTIAL PROFIT CENTER   It's no surprise that the profit motive heads the list. Many firms reach the point of near saturation through existing channels and believe they must explore new areas to maintain their growth. What may be a surprise is that mail order often provides the opportunity for higher profit percentages than other distribution channels.

One reason for this has been called *profit dynamics.* When the manufacturer is selling through traditional channels, the firm may gross only about 50 percent of the retail sales dollars its items generate. Therefore, it takes a substantial increase in sales for the manufacturer's profits to increase dramatically. With mail order, by contrast, 100 percent of the retail sales dollars usually accrue to the manufacturer. The manufacturer is not sharing profits with distributors or retailers. And even a relatively small increase in results or response rates has a much more dynamic effect on the firm's bottom line.

2. YOU CONTROL THE DISTRIBUTION CHANNEL   General advertisers often spend many months in filling the distribution pipeline. Much of their marketing effort

is directed toward moving the product along from various wholesalers through distributors to the retail shelf. Because the advertiser doesn't control the distribution, getting enough shelf or display space becomes very important.

When you are in the mail order business, the product usually moves directly from the manufacturer to the consumer. You decide when and where to move out your product, what market segments to go after, how much advertising support the product should have in the marketplace. And the whole process is geared toward making things happen much faster.

3. You can maximize market penetration Mail order offers the opportunity to "fill the gaps" in an existing distribution system. It's an excellent way of reaching into unrepresented markets where you lack a sales force or retail distribution. (In some cases, the people in such markets may already be pre-sold on your product or service by the national advertising you've done.) You may be able to maximize market penetration by developing new products and services that for one reason or another don't result in profitable sales through other channels. Mail order and retail distribution can even be used simultaneously to allow customers to purchase in the manner most convenient to them.

The next two advantages apply to all areas of direct marketing.

4. You control the risk All direct marketing expenditures are measurable and projectable. By studying your test results, you should know what to expect in the way of total revenues, returns, and repeat purchases. You know what to anticipate for every media investment. And again, through testing, you know exactly what to expect from a price increase or what a free gift will do to your variable costs.

5. Your marketing program is completely accountable This is what it all adds up to. You improve the return-on-investment of your advertising budget because you know exactly what results are produced. Your advertising dollars are no longer an unmeasurable expense item. They not only pay their own way— in terms of traceable responses or orders—they provide self-funding ad exposures to those who see your ad or mailing but don't respond.

♦

Can Your Firm Benefit from Direct Marketing?

It's tempting to suggest that direct marketing makes sense for everyone. Fact is, it doesn't. There have been some notable failures: where the product concept wasn't sound, where advertisers didn't want to believe their test figures, or where direct marketing simply didn't fit a particular marketing situation.

Factors to Help You Decide

In an *Advertising Age* article entitled "Should Mass Marketers Go into Direct Marketing?," consultant Robert Kestnbaum suggested three criteria for determining whether to use mail order to sell goods and services. First, he noted, a company should have a unique product or service. It should also have a market of prospects with some highly recognizable or definable characteristic, and there must be lists or other media that can match this characteristic. Also, the product should require a complete and careful explanation.

I'd also add the following questions to think about when considering any direct marketing program. What resources does your firm have for starting a direct marketing operation? Do you, for example, have a substantial customer list or database? Or, can you perhaps build one easily and inexpensively by using product warranty cards or inserts in your retail packages? Perhaps your resources include particular manufacturing skills, editorial expertise, or a strong consumer identity with a particular product area.

The conclusion, I think, is a rather obvious one: The more resources you can bring to bear on a direct marketing program, the more sense it makes. And the more likely it will work.

How to Cash In on It

If you're still unsure whether direct marketing is logical for your operation, let's look at what I call the "big opportunity areas." These are areas in which direct marketing is already being used successfully by numerous other firms.

Opportunity #1 Use mail order as an *alternate distribution method* for specific products, types of customers, or geographic areas. Perhaps your small accounts can be sold more cost efficiently via direct marketing. Or, perhaps your present distribution method fits your product line like a glove—except for one product you've been holding back on.

Hewlett-Packard's first pocket calculator was priced well under most of its other products—but its sales force was geared to big-ticket sales. It substantially expanded its market by using mail order to generate individual orders, while letting its sales force concentrate on quantity sales.

OPPORTUNITY #2   Use *lead generation systems* to lower the growing cost of personal sales calls and increase the effectiveness of your sales force.

Lanier Business Products designed a program that helped its sales force close 25 percent of all the leads it generated, with sales that averaged $800. By including its dealers and sales force in planning the campaign, Lanier helped them "buy into" the program and secured their enthusiastic participation.

OPPORTUNITY #3   Use direct marketing to test or expand into *new product and service concepts*. You may have a great idea for a new product, but it's too expensive to launch through traditional channels, or even to "tool up" and manufacture it until you're sure the market is viable. You can often test a product or service concept less expensively via mail order, sometimes without even having the product finalized.

Before it launched its auto club, Montgomery Ward carefully pretested the concept to determine whether a club would appeal to Ward customers, which offer would attract the most members, and which name would be most appealing. Not until after its seven-way test had answered those questions did it move forward with a marketing strategy, and its auto club is now one of the largest in the U.S.

OPPORTUNITY #4   Use a specialized program to maximize profits on *aftermarket sales*. In some firms, aftermarket sales account for 50 percent or more of total revenue. Regardless of the percentage, if you can handle them economically, these sales can be quite profitable.

———

EXHIBIT 1.6   When should you use direct marketing?

---

1. *When you can identify and also reach your target audience.* (For example, you can target lawyers in rural areas, but there's probably no list or publication to pinpoint left-handed lawyers.)

---

2. *When you have a lot to say about your product or service.* (Or when it's expensive and you need to say a lot to justify the buying decision.)

---

3. *When your product or service has continuity, repeat sales or follow-on sales possibilities* to justify building your own database. (Most successful direct marketing businesses are built on repeat sales; many times the initial sale is less profitable than subsequent sales, or even not profitable at all.)

---

4. *When the product or service is purchased infrequently,* and you can use direct marketing techniques to identify who's currently in the market to buy. (Like cars or major appliances.)

---

5. *When you want to control the selling message or process.* (This can be particularly desirable if sales are being made through a wholesaler/dealer network.)

---

6. *When you want to build a predictable model that you know can be repeated to achieve pre-set sales objectives.* (Direct marketing is ideal because it is measurable and repeatable.)

---

7. *When you have a product that really doesn't fit other distribution channels.* (Isn't glamorous enough, too complicated, doesn't sell itself, needs lengthy explanation.)

---

8. *When you want less visibility than space or broadcast provide.* (Such as in a test market situation or in launching a confidential new product.)

Many large corporations, like AT&T and Xerox, have developed a direct marketing program for aftermarket sales to low-volume customers, freeing its sales force to focus on more profitable accounts.

OPPORTUNITY #5   Use direct marketing techniques to improve the performance of your *regular advertising.* Some common offers used in direct response, such as a free gift, can be applied to many sales promotion programs. You can even design tests to find out which gift is strongest. Or simply use some type of "send for" offer to measure the readership of your ads. Many direct marketing techniques can successfully be transferred to general advertising.

Breakfast cereals often include inexpensive trinkets in the package to attract kids. Instead of arbitrarily selecting an item to offer, Quaker Oats produces prototype TV spots for a number of different premiums and tests them to select the winning item.

These opportunities are pretty neatly summarized in Exhibit 1.6, which I developed some years ago. You might find it a handy checklist when exploring alternatives for direct marketing.

The Last Word on a Maturing Marketing Discipline

In its earliest days, direct marketing tended to be applied as a tactical tool. The "Let's try an ad" or "Let's try this mailing" approach was often successful, but it didn't capitalize on the full potential of this powerful discipline.

As direct marketing has grown, so has the sophistication with which it's applied. Now, with bigger budgets and greater internal expertise, we're seeing more people approach it from a strategic standpoint, making a greater effort to integrate it into a complete advertising and marketing program. It's not only gratifying to me personally to see this maturization, but it bodes well for direct marketing's continued growth.

2

LAUNCHING A NEW DIRECT MARKETING PROGRAM

♦

LET'S ASSUME YOU'VE MADE the decision to go into direct marketing—or at least to investigate it. You understand what's different about it. You appreciate the advantages it offers. You think your firm can benefit from direct marketing. So now you're ready to wrestle with some of the basic, but important, questions almost every direct marketer before you has faced in launching a new program. You want to know what major problems to anticipate. What essential factors have to be covered in planning a successful program. And finally, how to get started.

BASIC QUESTIONS TO CONSIDER

NOT NECESSARILY IN ORDER of importance—because they're all important—here are some key questions to ask yourself. (And if you don't ask them, your management probably will.)

DO WE HAVE A SOUND CONCEPT FOR DIRECT MARKETING?

It is surprising how many firms decide to go into direct marketing simply because their executives see others promoting a similar product or service via direct marketing. And because direct marketing is considered a "hot growth area" in many management circles, they decide it's the thing to do. But a good marketing person does more than that. He or she studies the direct marketing competition to see how well they're covering the market. He or she tries to find opportunities either to improve on what the competition is doing or to zero in on areas they seem to be overlooking. And in so doing a good direct marketer tries to develop a unique concept or idea for his or her direct marketing program.

♦

Is the Profit Potential Big Enough to Justify the Test Investment?

Very few direct marketing programs show a profit on the initial test. This is primarily because of the start-up expenses for finished art and production, plus the premium one pays for small-run printing of a mailing package or a regional test in a magazine. But most firms are willing to make the test investment if the down-the-road profit potential is substantial enough. So you should look at similar programs and make some profit and loss projections. It's difficult to come up with precise figures until you make a test and get actual experience under your belt. Use the best estimates you can arrive at and look at what your direct marketing sales volume and profit picture might be a couple years after the test.

Do We Need Professional Help?

Having spent most of my career with a direct marketing agency, I may not be totally objective about this one. I do think professional help is important, whether you go to a direct marketing ad agency or consultant, or add an experienced direct marketing person to your staff. There are so many details and intricacies in direct marketing that professional help is essential to ensure a sound test program that will provide some definite answers. I guess I've seen too many examples of firms that tried to do it themselves or went to a general ad agency which had no real direct marketing experience. Not only is their test usually unsuccessful, they don't find out how well they *might* have done with a properly constructed direct marketing test.

Should We Use Our Own Firm Name?

This question is often asked because a firm is concerned about one of two things: direct marketing's effect on its image, or its effect on its dealers, distributors, or sales force. The assumption is that going out under a different name or brand name will allow the firm to enjoy "plus" business from mail order, without detracting from existing business.

The main thing that's overlooked here is the value of a firm's well-established name in building a direct marketing profit center. Yes, you can launch a successful program under a new unknown name. But that unknown name initially will not do as well. That happened to a Fortune 500 company that recently tested a consumer merchandise offer two ways. Half of the test mailing went out under its well-established firm name; the other half offered the same merchandise with the identical mailing package except that it was sent under an unfamiliar name. The test using the well-known name pulled 91 percent better! And I've heard of other tests where the well-known name has made an even greater difference.

If this isn't reason enough to go with your own firm name, it's also a fallacy to assume that your dealers, distributors, or sales force won't eventually discover your direct marketing effort regardless of what name you use. And by using an unknown name you may actually be deprived of some of the extra sales that will otherwise accrue to your normal distribution channels.

THE EFFECT ON OTHER DISTRIBUTION CHANNELS

WHEN A FIRM CONSIDERS SELLING by mail, executives usually worry that this "new" distribution channel will hurt other, established channels. Will it take sales away from the firm's dealers, distributors, or sales force? Will it upset the people involved? A typical dealer, for example, is concerned first with his or her own sales. So, if the dealer *thinks* a mail order program is going to rob him or her of sales, the company will surely hear about it.

FOUR OFTEN OVERLOOKED FACTS

Dealer reactions like this either overlook or ignore four key facts:

> 1. A percentage of any audience or group of prospects prefers to shop and buy by mail. The reasons for this were covered in Chapter 1. But various studies have shown that 25 to 35 percent of consumers fall into this category. If you don't offer them an opportunity to buy by mail, there's a good chance they'll do so from a competitor.

◆

2. Any direct marketing effort has a very high "failure rate." A direct response space ad will usually get less than 1 percent of the audience to respond. A mailing package can prove very profitable, even though only two percent of the audience respond. That's a 98 percent "failure rate." This means that if you make a mailing of one million pieces, 980,000 people will not respond or order by mail—truly a silent majority.

3. The direct marketing budget provides bonus advertising impressions at no extra cost. Most of those 980,000 people will receive an advertising impression, just as they do from a firm's regular TV, radio, magazine, or newspaper advertising. Research shows that 75 percent of all consumer mailings are at least opened and glanced at, and about half of these are read. Applying these percentages to our example, we find that 750,000 people will open and glance at the mailing, probably at least noting the advertiser's name and registering an impression of the product being offered. Of these people, 375,000 will read the mailing, and, in the process, they'll absorb a good amount of your advertising message. Best of all, if the 20,000 who do respond by mail make the mailing profitable, all these bonus advertising impressions cost you nothing!

4. A portion of your audience will buy through regular distribution channels. Just as there are those who prefer to shop and buy by mail, there is another large group that prefers to see a product first-hand or prefers to buy through a salesperson. Even if a direct marketing ad or mailing

doesn't suggest it, some of those 375,000 readers in our example will seek out a dealer, distributor, or salesperson who has the product. This is what I like to call the "echo response" of direct marketing. We understandably devote most of our attention to the *direct* response in the form of mail and phone orders and often forget the echo responses that accrue to other distribution channels.

THE POSITIVE EFFECT OF DIRECT MARKETING

All the available evidence I have seen points to the fact that direct marketing enhances other distribution channels. Let's look at some of that evidence.

When book clubs first arrived on the scene in the 1920s, bookstore owners were concerned that the clubs would steal their sales and put them out of business. But a McGraw-Hill Book Store staffer notes that, "Actually, clubs spur sales despite the lower prices of the offers. Remember, there are many people who would never join clubs and actually prefer to purchase from a retail outlet. Keep in mind that clubs—whether Book of the Month or Literary Guild—send people into bookstores, and this traffic is what we're after. Once they're in the store, we can take care of them."

Similarly, a company with an extensive chain of retail stores and a large mail offer catalog has proved that one-third of its retail purchases are pre-shopped in the catalog. The customer has made the purchase decision by reading the catalog and then has gone to a store to pick up the item.

A consumer electronics company with substantial mail order sales and a growing group of retail stores has found that, when a new retail outlet is opened, mail order sales fall off in that area for six months to a year. After that, mail order sales in the area resume their normal level, and the store provides additional sales. Eddie Bauer has experienced the same phenomenon, but has found that by the third year, both mail order and store sales increase over previous levels. A few years ago, Bloomingdale's reported that its average catalog produced $3.4 million in mail order sales and another $6.8 million in store sales.

EXHIBIT 2.1 Catalogs stimulate mail order and retail sales for multi-channel companies like Eddie Bauer and Bloomingdale's.

THE EFFECT ON THE SALES FORCE

When Allstate first began selling insurance by mail, its executives were naturally concerned about the reaction of their own agents. So they first assured agents that direct mail solicitations would not be continued if they took business away from the agents. The firm then asked a professional research center to conduct a series of tests to measure the effect of its direct marketing efforts. The research reports showed that one test after another produced similar results.

For a mailing soliciting auto insurance sales, two carefully matched groups of prospects were set up. One group was mailed. The other wasn't. Agent sales in the same areas were tracked, and it was found that the mailed group produced 29 percent more *agent sales* than the non-mailed group.

Two groups of 100,000 prospects were matched as identically as possible. Only one group received a direct mail solicitation on life insurance. But life insurance sales by agents were tracked to both groups. Forty-five days after the mailing, agents' life insurance sales to the mailed group were *double* the agent sales to the non-mailed group.

A similar test was set up on a small loan program. Total agent loans to the mailed group were 26 percent greater than to the group that did not get the mailing.

All these results are for agent sales only. And this "plus" business written by the agents was in addition to the significant revenue the firm produced on direct marketing responses.

HOW TO NEUTRALIZE NEGATIVE REACTIONS

This evidence certainly indicates that mail order advertising enhances sales through other distribution channels. The initial reaction of your dealers, distributors, and sales force, however, is still likely to be negative.

Informing your agents and *involving* them in the program will usually minimize or neutralize that reaction. Tell them that you're testing direct marketing. They're going to find out about it anyway, so you might as well explain it your way. Assure them that it should help rather than hurt their own sales results.

Try to find a way to involve them in the program. Some firms pay their salespeople a token commission on orders generated through mail order. Though the major thrust of your direct marketing effort should be toward producing orders by mail or phone, your advertising can mention that products are available through other sources. Or you might offer each dealer a small quantity of mailings to send out in his or her own area. Most won't take advantage of the offer, but at least you've made an effort to get them involved.

Mary Kay Cosmetics made partners of its salespeople when it launched its Direct Support program (see Exhibit 2.2). Beauty consultants were asked to contribute customer names with the assurance that the personalized mailings would help them increase their sales. About half the firm's consultants have participated in this highly successful program and Mary Kay now maintains a database of over eight million active customers. By contrast, Tupperware recently tried selling products in direct competition with its hostesses. Needless to say, the reaction from the Tupperware sales organization was negative—so negative, in fact, that Tupperware chose to abandon the program, despite having made a considerable financial investment in it.

EXHIBIT 2.2   Mary Kay mailings encourage customers to place orders with their local beauty consultant by mail or phone.

TEN ESSENTIALS FOR LONG-RANGE PROFITS

WHEN EMBARKING ON A NEW direct marketing program, you naturally want to build substantial sales and profits as soon as possible. But direct marketing should be looked upon as more than a one-shot program. If you are selling by mail, it should be viewed as a distribution channel that can provide steady growth in the years ahead. With that thought in mind, let's consider ten essentials that not only will help pay immediate dividends, but also will lay the groundwork for the success of future direct marketing programs.

1. Develop a Master Financial Plan

Success in mail order begins with the numbers end of the business. You must determine proper selling prices with adequate markups. You have to establish test budgets that are adequate to provide projectable results and know what your true breakeven points are on those tests. While it is not imperative, you can also develop cash-flow charts to project your peak investments and payout points.

Most large firms entering direct marketing like to develop a three- to five-year profit-and-loss projection. If this is done before the first test, the projection naturally has to be based on some assumptions. But it provides an indication of what can be expected. And, after the initial test, the plan can be revised to substitute actual test results for the assumptions.

Most management financial experts like to work with direct marketing programs. They know that sales and expense forecasts can be based on actual test results. And they like the idea of expanding a program step by step with an opportunity to review results and see if the program is on target at each stage. This provides a built-in safety factor because plans can be changed or altered as necessary.

The appendix of this book includes a handy worksheet that can be used for planning profitable mailings, and the same type of mathematics applies to print and broadcast media.

2. Select Products or Services Suitable for Direct Marketing

While you may have an extensive product line for other distribution channels, it's not necessarily true that all products will sell well by mail. I know of one large industrial company that had hundreds of products in its line. A new product that was ideally suited to direct marketing was used for an initial test. It produced very satisfactory sales and profits for many years. But a number of the company's other industrial products were later offered the same way, and none of the others did nearly as well.

Chapter 3 will go into more detail on product selection, but naturally you want to consider products that represent good quality, have broad appeal, and can be offered to the consumer as a sound value. It's nice to have a product or service that has a built-in repeat business factor, such as office supplies that are consumed or an insurance policy that will be renewed year after year.

3. MAKE YOUR OFFER IRRESISTIBLE

Some direct marketing newcomers are shocked to learn that the offer can make more difference in results than the copy that tells your story, the graphics that display your product, and the format you use for your ad or mailing. The offer is one of the most important factors for direct marketing success. It will be covered in depth in Chapter 4. For now, let's just say that the development of the offer or proposition you make to the customer deserves your best thinking. Your goal is to come up with an offer so appealing it's hard to resist.

4. USE LISTS OR MEDIA THAT ZERO IN ON YOUR BEST PROSPECT

Even a good product or service with a strong offer has little chance of success if your message doesn't get to the right prospects. In media selection and planning, your first job is to select the mailing lists, magazines, newspapers, or broadcast buys that are most likely to deliver the prospects you want. A general rule of thumb is that if you start with the best—and they don't pay out—your direct marketing effort doesn't have much potential.

Given some initial success, your second media job is to test enough different mailing lists, publications, or broadcast stations to determine how big a universe you can successfully sell. To a major degree, the potential profitability of your direct marketing program will be determined by the number and size of the lists and publications that will pay out for you. The chapters in Part II are devoted entirely to the media most widely used for direct marketing.

Of course, before you begin selecting media, you must determine whether the market you're seeking can be reached cost effectively. Some years ago, Hallmark tested a gift shipment service called Grandchildren U.S.A. But it encountered a major stumbling block when it discovered that there were no publications or mailing lists that targeted grandparents. Likewise, if you want to sell large-size clothing to men, you'll probably have to build your own prospect list through space ads . . . as King-Size has done.

5. Choose Formats That Fit Your Story and Objective

Almost every medium offers a wide variety of formats. Your direct mail efforts can range from an inexpensive two-color self-mailer to a 9 × 12 mailing package or a catalog with a hundred or more pages. Likewise, in print advertising, you can choose a small space ad, run a two-page, full-color spread with a bind-in card, or use a newspaper insert. Even on television, common spot lengths range from 30 seconds to two minutes.

Which format you use depends on several factors. Of course, you'll have to abide by any constraints of your budget. You'll want to consider how much copy and how many illustrations you'll need to adequately tell your story. And you'll want to keep your objective in mind. If you're soliciting inquiries rather than orders, you normally need a less-elaborate format because your goal is to tell only enough of the story to whet the readers' appetite for more information. And your audience is also important. Do you want a mailing package that will stand out among the many other mailings on a businessperson's desk, or is it designed for leisurely reading by the consumer at home?

6. Create Advertising That Sells

Unlike general advertising, the creative aspect of direct marketing usually is not intended to inform, entertain, or build brand awareness. The objective is to sell, to get an order or have the consumer take some other specific action. There's a lot more to the selling process than just combining nice-sounding words and pretty pictures.

Think about the creative strategy. Try to come up with a "big idea" you want to get across in each ad or mailing. Then get an experienced direct response writer to prepare copy that captures the prospect's attention, weaves a strong selling story, and calls for action. And don't be reluctant to use long copy. It often takes a lot of copy to get people to order a product, sight unseen, by mail. And, if it's sufficiently well written to hold their interest, prospects will read long copy.

Graphics are also an important part of the creative-selling process. Their job is to capture on paper the excitement of your product and the benefits of your proposition. Graphics should be in character with your firm's image, the nature of the product being offered, and the profiles of the markets being reached.

Creative suggestions for mail, print, and TV are covered in Part III, along with a discussion of creative strategies.

7. Plan for Prompt Fulfillment

If your creative effort is effective, prospects will often order on impulse and look forward enthusiastically to getting the product. But that enthusiasm can die quickly if it takes four to six weeks to get product delivery or get a response to an inquiry.

A good fulfillment program must be designed to handle orders promptly and economically. Many companies who enter direct marketing have a shipping operation that is geared to handle large orders, such as those from a wholesaler or dealer. And it's usually difficult for them to efficiently handle smaller volume orders for consumers. Fortunately, there are organizations that specialize in direct marketing fulfillment, who can be used at least until the proper internal capability is developed. The fulfillment operation is also responsible for capturing and recording the information needed for analyzing results.

8. Set Up an R&D Budget for Testing

Your testing budget is like the research and development budget for a manufacturing firm. Whether your program is a brand new one or one that's been going on for years, you never stop testing. This is simply because there are always new things to try, new things to learn, new ways to improve response.

The bulk of your testing budget should be directed to testing the big things that can lead to a major improvement in results. Just as a manufacturer's R&D department is often measured by how many new products it develops, the success of your testing program can be measured by how many breakthroughs you produce. Chapter 6 goes into more detail on testing, including the major areas where your testing should be concentrated.

9. Analyze Results Carefully

Direct marketing tests are often quite complicated with many different things being tested simultaneously. So you have to do more than just count the orders to see how a test comes out. Result reports should be studied, analyzed, and interpreted, taking into account the front-end response (orders or inquiries), the back-end results (conversions, pay-ups, and returned goods), and the lower costs anticipated for a rollout. Part of the job of analyzing results entails recommending the specific action that should be taken. Where you have some proven success, you would naturally recommend expanding the test to a bigger universe.

10. Maximize Customer Value Through Repeat Sales

If you look at the broad spectrum of products and services sold via direct marketing, you find that very few operations have become big simply by making a single sale to each customer. The classic formula for direct marketing success is to build a list of satisfied customers and then go back to them for repeat sales.

In some cases, you can sell your customers more of the same product, such as the renewal of a magazine subscription. In other cases, you can sell them accessories, supplies, or similar or related products.

It makes sense to have a structured program for getting repeat sales. Mail your customer list frequently. Use every customer contact opportunity to increase sales, such as including package inserts with your shipments. Have your customers help you find more like them by establishing a referral program in which they send in the names and addresses of friends who might be interested in your product or service.

The customer list you build becomes your greatest asset. If you send an identical mailing to a list of good prospects and a list of your customers, it's not unusual for the customer list to respond three to six times as well. In other words, a mailing that pulls a one percent response from prospects can pull a three to six percent response from customers. And, because your mailing cost per piece is about the same to either group, you don't have to be a super mathematician to figure out that the customer mailings will be much more profitable. Similarly, newsmagazines have found that they can renew a subscription at about 1/20 the cost of getting a new one.

Which of These Factors Is Most Important?

Baseball fanatics say that pitching is as much as 70 percent of the game. And although there is no universal agreement on which factor is most important, direct marketing has its rules of thumb for success, too. The late Ed Mayer, a pioneering teacher and consultant, developed his famous "40–40–20 rule" to predict the success of a direct mail program. He believed that:

◆ 40 percent depends on reaching the right audience,

◆ 40 percent depends on who you are and what your offer is,

◆ 20 percent depends on the format and creative execution.

My partner, Pierre Passavant, believes that Ed Mayer's dictum holds true for new programs. But the mix is somewhat different for an established direct marketing program, where you have already done a lot of testing to establish the best offer and find the right audience. According to Pierre, the odds to boost the response rate of an established program depend:

◆ 10 percent on list and media refinements,

◆ 10 percent on offer enhancements,

◆ 80 percent on changes or improvements in creative execution.

Since Pierre developed his formula some years ago, there's been a growing recognition of the importance of marketing strategy (a subject we'll cover in Chapter 5). And as direct marketing programs have become more complex, it's harder to ignore the role of proper analysis. So my own formula, which I call a *Simple System for Direct Marketing Success,* attributes results as follows:

◆ 20 percent—marketing strategy,

◆ 20 percent—lists or media,

◆ 30 percent—offer,

◆ 20 percent—creative execution,

◆ 10 percent—analysis.

BASIC DIRECT MARKETING MATH: MEDIA COST, RESPONSE RATE, AND COST PER RESPONSE

AS NOTED EARLIER, DIRECT MARKETING is a numbers-oriented business. To determine the success of any direct marketing program, you must be able to pinpoint how much you spent on media, how many responses you received, and how much each response costs you. Three simple formulas can help you keep track of these areas.

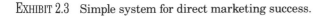

EXHIBIT 2.3   Simple system for direct marketing success.

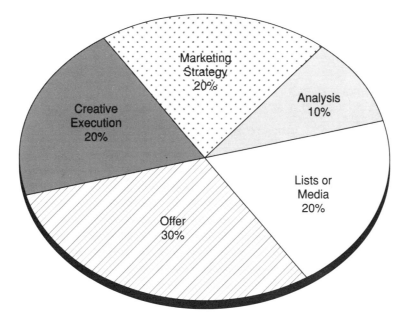

♦

Media cost can be determined by dividing the total number of dollars spent on promotion by the number of pieces mailed or circulated. $22,500 spent on a 50,000 piece mailing means that each piece costs 45¢ to print and mail. The formula is:

$$\frac{\text{Total promotion dollars}}{\text{Total number of pieces mailed (in thousands)}}$$

and is expressed as *CPM,* or *cost per thousand.* The CPM for the mailing just mentioned is $450.

The *response rate* can be determined two ways. First, dividing the total number of orders or inquiries received by the total number of pieces mailed yields *OPM* or *IPM, orders or inquiries per thousand.*

$$\frac{\text{Response Quantity (numbers of orders)}}{\text{Promotion Quantity (in thousands)}} \quad \frac{1000}{50} = 20/M$$

Second, to express the same results as a percentage, simply divide the number of orders by the total promotion quantity:

$$\frac{1000 \text{ orders}}{50,000 \text{ pieces}} = 0.02\% \text{ response}$$

By tracking the *cost per response,* you'll know quickly whether your promotion will pay off. Simply divide the total promotion budget by the total number of orders or inquiries received. The answer is usually expressed as the CPO (cost per order) or CPI (cost per inquiry).

$$\frac{\$22,500}{1000 \text{ orders}} = \$22.50 \text{ CPO}$$

Another way to compute this is to divide CPM by OPM or IPM:

$$\frac{\$450 \text{ CPM}}{20 \text{ OPM}} = \$22.50 \text{ CPO}$$

It's also possible to reverse these formulas and use promotion cost and cost per response to determine total response.

$$\frac{\$22,500}{\$22.50} = 1000 \text{ orders}$$

$$\frac{\$450 \text{ CPM}}{\$22.50 \text{ CPO}} = 20 \text{ OPM}$$

While a good grasp of these basic mathematical concepts is essential, direct mail math is by no means limited to these formulas. In later chapters we'll cover methods that will let you maximize the value of your customers and achieve your profit objective by determining an allowable order cost.

THE LAST WORD ON LAUNCHING A NEW DIRECT MARKETING PROGRAM

IT TAKES MORE THAN JUST A "good idea" to launch a new direct marketing program. There's a lot to think about. To sort out and organize your thinking, I strongly recommend you put your plan on paper. Your written plan doesn't have to be elaborate. But it should cover such things as the concept, rationale, market segment, competition, proposed operation, and problem areas. I like to think of this as a "mini marketing plan." It may only run two or three pages, but it can help clarify a lot of critical thinking.

3

SELECTING PRODUCTS AND SERVICES

♦

MOST THINGS ABOUT DIRECT MARKETING are pretty logical; some persons even call it scientific. You study audience demographics. You assemble your costs. You analyze test results. And you make decisions in an impartial, logical way.

But when it comes to choosing a product or service for mail order, perhaps selecting the most appealing of dozens of possibilities, there's something more to it. The best way I can think of to describe that "something more" is a combination of instinct and creativity.

Can any product or service be sold through mail order? Technically, I guess it can. But from a practical standpoint, a product can do well at retail and just "so-so" when sold by mail. Or be just fair at retail and be a big winner in mail order. Picking those big winners is where instinct comes into play.

THE "FOUR PLUS ONE" FORMULA FOR PRODUCT SELECTION

I'VE HAD THE PLEASURE OF WORKING with a few people who have a true instinct for picking and developing merchandise suitable for direct marketing. And most of them have trouble explaining exactly why they select one item or reject another. Bob Stone discovered this a few years ago when he did an *Advertising Age* column on the subject, but he still managed to suggest some helpful principles.

With Stone's article as a guide, I've developed a formula to help you select products suitable for direct marketing. It's no substitute for that magic intuition. But, if you aren't fortunate enough to be blessed with it, this list should be of help in evaluating products.

1. BROAD APPEAL Always look for an item that has universality or widespread appeal. That appeal can be to broad-scale lists and markets—something that virtually every man, woman, or household can use. Or it can have broad appeal to specific market segments which can be reached cost-efficiently. Such as

a book on engineering where you can direct your ads and mailings to engineers with very little waste circulation.

2. Unusual features in the basic product   Because of the growth of discount stores and self-service, little or no salesmanship is left at the retail level today. So, unusual features may not have much appeal unless the browsing consumer discovers them. But in direct marketing, those same unusual features can be highlighted with glamorous photography and skillful copy. So look for something different or unique that can be built up. That can create desire, that can get the consumer to order now.

3. Not readily available this way   This might seem like a catchall point because there are so many different situations it covers. But it zeroes in on one of the main things a good direct marketing offer can have going for it. Namely, that it's not easy to find the same product, offered the same way, somewhere else. For example:

> ♦ The product is a mail order exclusive—you won't find it in stores. Like a product you manufacture yourself or one made especially for you.

> ♦ Or it's perceived as hard to find. Brookstone built its reputation offering a large assortment of tools designed for special purposes (see Exhibit 3.1). These tools could be found at retail, if the consumer had any idea what sort of store would carry an aluminum can crusher.

> ♦ Or it's not readily available at retail at this price. Because you can offer a bargain by selling direct.

> ♦ Or it's not usually offered this way. Like a catalog which has a more complete assortment of the product line than a comparable retail store. Or a single mailing that lets you subscribe

to a wide assortment of magazines, as Publishers
Clearing House does.

♦ Or the offer itself makes it unique—like a
related free gift that's not available at retail.

It's important to realize here that you can often build this uniqueness
into a product by adding extras or accessories. Years ago, in selling a blender by
mail, I felt it needed something to make it more attractive. So I developed a deck
of blender recipe cards that could be included with the product. We tested with
and without this inexpensive addition and found it increased response 32 percent.

EXHIBIT 3.1   Brookstone catalog offers tools that are perceived to be unique and hard to
find.

4. Proper Price and Profit Margins   The starting point for any product or service being sold by mail is the right price. Most direct marketers require at least a three-time product markup. For example, if you're selling a home appliance for $59.95, your product cost should be around $20.00. Even though they spread out their promotion costs over a large number of products, catalog firms still try to get a three-time markup. Publishers usually work on a greater markup.

Naturally, in establishing the price for a new product, you'll want to consider your market and what's being charged for competitive products, making sure, of course, that you have sufficient margin for your offer to be profitable. Rather than make an arbitrary pricing decision, many direct marketing firms will do price testing on new products.

Bob Stone wisely points out that the price must *appear* to be the right price to the prospect you're going after. He or she must perceive your price as being a good value. And that perception will vary depending upon the item and the audience. For example, let's say you are selling men's ties. A price of $12.00 might represent a good value to a blue collar worker, but connote poor quality to a businessman.

Plus—The dream element   One person who had that instinct for picking products was Sam Josefowitz, the legendary European mail order consultant. At an international direct marketing conference some years ago, he was asked what he looked for in a mail order item. Josefowitz replied, "I look to products with a dream element. An exerciser, for example, which promotes the dream fulfillment of a better figure without putting forth much effort." It's interesting to note that items like this have also been successful in the United States, such as a pedal exerciser that was promoted as a means to pedal your way to a better figure, while watching television!

There's an alternative to the dream element that can be equally important. I call it the *story* element. Does the product have an interesting or appealing story behind it? Was it discovered accidentally? Does it use a technology that was actually developed for another purpose—like our space program—but has been adapted to an everyday household product? Such a germ of a story, placed in the hands of an experienced copywriter, can often blossom into a spellbinding selling message. In one of its letters, Thompson Cigar told how it smuggled Cuban cigar seeds out of Cuba and onto another Caribbean island, where they were jealously guarded until they were harvested for Thompson's products. The story lent a clandestine air to the company's products and considerable excitement to the sales message.

To see the "four plus one" formula in action, just take a look at the direct response ads in any Sunday newspaper supplement. In a recent issue, I found ads for products ranging from fishing rods and flower bulbs to shoes. Every single ad met at least three points of the "four plus one" formula. Some met four; one or two met all five. And, by the way, in addition to possessing the "dream element," the pedal exerciser mentioned earlier also happens to meet points 1, 2, and 4.

THE APPEAL OF A SERVICE

RECENT STATISTICS SHOW THAT services now account for over half of the U.S. economy. A much larger share of the consumer's budget goes for services today—from appliance and car repair to having someone maintain his or her house and lawn.

The same is true of direct marketing. Many successful offers are built around products that are readily available at retail, but are transformed into services by direct marketing. For example, when a customer joins a video club, he or she is buying a convenient service that reviews hundreds of new videos, offers the most appropriate ones on a set schedule with return privileges, ships them automatically, and allows delayed payment.

Some successful direct marketing services are not readily available at retail. One is the popular World of Beauty Club, which offers women a chance to sample a wide variety of cosmetics at bargain prices. Computer-based direct marketing, ranging from personalized children's books to investment advice, are another example. Since they take time to prepare, you can't just pick them off the shelf in a store and take them to the checkout counter.

PRODUCT DECISIONS TO CONSIDER

IN SELECTING AND REFINING the product for your direct marketing offer, there are many things to think about. We will cover the major decisions many firms wrestle with and then some of the details involved in product planning.

Existing Products, New Ones, or Variations?

Let's assume you already have a successful product line being sold through other distribution channels and you're trying to decide what product or products to use for your initial mail order offer. First, it's usually wise to start with the same type of products your firm is already familiar with, not go into an entirely new product area. This way, you're building on the product knowledge, strength, and consumer reputation you already have.

One large blue chip company that entered direct marketing a few years ago didn't follow this principle. The firm launched an entire new product line for direct sales. One major problem during the first few years was developing the product expertise to know what types of items to offer at what price points. The problem was sufficiently serious that it almost caused the entire direct marketing program to fail before it got off the ground.

An existing proven product is normally your best bet. But, if it's important to minimize comparisons with other sales channels, you can use a modified product that permits a "blind" offer. When Xerox sold reconditioned copiers by mail at discount prices, it didn't want them to be compared with new machines. So it changed the cabinet color and gave the reconditioned copiers a different model number. Changes like these can be made relatively easily and inexpensively.

New product development just for direct marketing, on the other hand, can be quite expensive. It's usually more practical to try to launch or test a new direct sales program with existing products. Once you've established an ongoing program, with a substantial number of members or customers, it's easier to justify the expense of new product development.

A couple of other considerations, however, are relevant. The product you're offering through retail may not be priced at the ideal level for mail order. You may want to develop a higher-priced or deluxe version of the same item.

With mail order, you usually don't have the same physical limitations as might be expected in retail product development. Let's say you've developed an inexpensive kit to help children learn to tell time. The kit includes a book, a clock with movable hands, and punch-out numbers. For retail, it would be essential to have all components fit together in a box or see-through bag for display purposes. And you would probably need colorful graphics on the package to show the product in use and do a selling job. In direct marketing, your main concern is that the product is easy to ship. So the same three components can be put in a shipping carton without a self-contained package. And, because your ad or mailing will do the main selling job, a colorful package is not essential.

ONE-STEP OR TWO-STEP?

A one-step offer—sometimes called a one-shot—is the approach you use when your ad or mailing aims for an immediate sale. This contrasts with a two-step offer where your ad or mailing is designed simply to produce an inquiry (the first step), and that inquiry is followed up to produce the sale (the second step). Naturally, the inquiries can be followed up any way you choose—by a salesperson, a series of mailings, or a telephone sales contact. Generally you're better off going with a one-step offer, especially on lower-priced products. But sometimes a product is too expensive or too complicated to aim for a one-step order. For example, while some encyclopedias have been sold successfully by mail, most require a two-step offer with a high-powered sales force to produce maximum sales.

Sometimes media limitations require you to use a combination of the one-step and two-step offers. You might have a complicated product that can be sold successfully with an elaborate mailing package. But, in space advertising where you're normally limited to a page or spread ad, you may not be able to tell enough of the story to do an effective selling job. You might be forced to use a one-step method in the mail and a two-step method in space advertising.

CONTINUITY, CLUB, OR SERIES?

Many advantages exist in a continuity product plan in which you ship the product in continuous installments. But they can only be enjoyed if the product or service is suited to a continuity, such as a series of books or cassettes.

If the product is suitable, the very nature of a continuity makes repeat sales to the same customer almost automatic. You also benefit from a larger unit of sale to the average customer. If the product and value you offer are good, the average customer might accept six to eight shipments before dropping out of the program. And, if the program sells for $10.00 a shipment, that brings your average order up to the $60.00 to $80.00 range.

Traditional book and music clubs are now being supplemented by clubs whose primary job is not to sell product, but to enhance or support a brand's image. Mattel's Barbie Doll Club is a good example. Its colorful mailings to young girls promote Barbie clothes and accessories. By charging a small membership fee, Mattel essentially gets consumers to pay for its advertising. And cruise clubs, recently started by some of the major cruise lines, promote and generate resales among customers who might otherwise overlook additional travel opportunities.

Start a Catalog?

A catalog provides still other product considerations. First of all, every catalog item doesn't have to have the broad appeal of items offered by themselves. A catalog is more like a department or specialty store. Although all the products might be selected to serve a particular interest, such as a catalog for golfers, some items will appeal to some customers and some to others.

Launching a full-scale catalog operation, however, can be expensive. Not only must you come up with enough products to offer a wide selection, your development expense for art and production can be substantial. Many mail order firms start with a smaller catalog and expand it in stages. Or some develop winning items through individual mailings and then use them as a nucleus to start a catalog.

And you must make sure that your product line is broad enough to sustain a catalog business. In general, the more items a catalog contains, the more sales it will generate. A product line that is too narrowly conceived—one that contains items like watches that are not replaced often, or promotes a single style of apparel that consumers may tire of—will restrict the growth of both catalog sales and the customer database.

Other Product Details

Finally, other product details to consider in your mail order offer are:

♦ Do we offer a choice of sizes? (If so, how does this affect inventory needs?)

♦ Should we offer a choice of colors? (Or do we want to adopt Henry Ford's famous stance: You can have any color so long as it's black?)

♦ Can the items be personalized? (Personalization usually enhances the sale of a mail order item.)

♦ Is the product relatively lightweight and easy to ship?

♦ Can you include any necessary accessories (like batteries or film) so the product will be ready to use when it's received?

♦ What will it cost to refurbish or restore returned goods to salable condition?

EXPERT VIEWPOINTS

I asked three international mail order experts what criteria they felt a mail order product must meet to be successful. One said that visual appeal is critical: Any potential product must photograph or illustrate well. Another felt that its benefits should not be obvious in a retail environment, but should require a detailed creative treatment to explain. One expert even suggested that consumers be able to operate the product without instructions because nine times out of ten, that's what they do when they open the package! But all three agreed on one vital criterion: The successful mail order product must fit the company's image *and* the customer's profile.

THE LAST WORD ON PRODUCT SELECTION

DON'T FORGET THAT EVEN THE MOST successful products have life cycles. (We'll discuss this in greater detail in Chapter 5.) While the ideal situation is to introduce tested new products just when the old ones are beginning to decline, life cycles can sometimes repeat themselves. One insurance company I know of has sold the same basic types of policies by mail for over 30 years. When one set of policies reaches the saturation point, management rests them, promoting other policies until it recycles the original policies a few years later.

If a successful product seems to be wearing out, don't give up on it. Just put it on the "back burner" for a while and test it periodically to see if it can be revived.

4

PROVEN DIRECT RESPONSE OFFERS

♦

PROBABLY THE MOST MISUNDERSTOOD concept in direct marketing is the offer. I've known persons who have been in the business for years but didn't really understand how to structure an offer. Some have made what they thought were very insignificant changes in an offer, and their response dropped 35 percent or more.

Yet the offer is one of the simplest and most dramatic ways to improve results. If the average direct marketer spent as much time testing, refining, and fine tuning his or her offer as editing and polishing a piece of direct response copy, the bottom line would look a lot better.

But let's start with the basics. What is the offer? It's simply your proposition to the prospect or customer, what you will give the customer in return for taking the action your mailing or ad asks him or her to take.

What does the offer include? Your product or service, the price and payment terms under which the customer can get it, any incentives you're willing to throw in (like a free gift), and any specific conditions attached to the offer. Sometimes the offer includes free literature or booklets as a first step toward selling the actual product or service.

Here's another way to think about the offer. It's whatever you physically get in the package or carton, plus the financial arrangement and any "strings" or commitments. The commitment might apply to the customer (such as when joining a book club) or to the advertiser (such as guaranteeing return privileges).

Don't confuse the creative presentation with the offer. It might make sense to add testimonials to a letter, or include a dramatic brochure, but these don't change the nature of your offer.

Why is the offer important? Because the right offer can sell almost anything. Because it can mean the difference between the success and failure of a promotion. Because it can make a successful promotion dramatically more successful! I've seen rather simple changes in offers that have improved results on the same product or service by 25 percent, 50 percent, and 100 percent.

Relate the Offer to Your Objective

THE FIRST STEP IN PLANNING an offer is to think about your objective. Are you trying to get orders by mail? Produce more sales leads? Sell subscriptions? Raise funds? If your efforts are designed to produce any type of immediate response, the offer should be carefully planned to help you accomplish that objective.

The more attractive you can afford to make your offer, the better your response will be. So your goal is to come up with the most attractive offer you can afford, one that will melt away human inertia and get people into action now. Please note that I didn't say the most attractive offer possible. I said the most attractive offer you can afford.

Before you get the impression that all good offers are expensive ones, let's spend a minute on the economics of the offer. Without going into great detail, I think it's important for you to realize that your advertising program includes both fixed costs and variable costs. Let's take direct mail as an example. Fixed costs are basic expenses like postage, list rental, and production of a given mailing package. Variable costs change according to the number of responses you get, such as merchandise, free gifts, and fulfillment.

You can often "sweeten" your offer and make it more attractive without increasing your fixed costs. On the other hand, the cost of an incentive (like a free gift) normally has to be applied to all orders. If a $5.00 free gift improves your results from 10 to 13 orders per thousand, you incur the free gift cost for all 13 orders, not just the three additional orders. So how does your profit come out? It depends on such things as your gross margin per order, what you spend on the gift, and how much it improves your response.

Let me just point out that the best or most successful offer is not necessarily the one that will be most expensive for you. Even if you do increase your variable cost, by throwing in an incentive like a free gift, your objective is to increase response more than enough to offset the added cost involved, so your cost per order or cost per inquiry is lower than it was without the free gift. If you plan your offers carefully with budget in mind, that's exactly the way they can turn out.

Basic Offers to Relieve Risk

Two basic offers have become real standbys. Both are designed to reduce the risk of ordering a product by mail.

FREE TRIAL If mail order advertisers suddenly had to standardize all their efforts on one offer, this would no doubt be their choice! Down through the years, it's proved to be effective time after time. Probably first used by book publishers, today it's also a favorite marketing tool for selling merchandise by mail.

When you think about it as a customer, you can recognize that the free trial offer is almost essential for mail order buying. You're dealing with a firm by mail, someone you probably don't know, and who is located hundreds of miles away. You've seen an attractive ad or mailing package, but you haven't had the opportunity to see a "live" product before buying, as you normally do in a retail store. So the free trial offer relieves the fear that you might get stuck. The advertiser is willing to let you try his product before he gets your money!

If your product or service is suited to a free trial offer, you'll want to think carefully about how long the trial period should be. Most trial periods are 10 or 15 days. But the trial period should fit the particular product or service being offered. How long will it take the prospect to be sold on your merchandise? If you don't allow enough time, you tend to force a "no" decision. On the other hand, allowing too much time can permit procrastination to set in and enthusiasm to wear off. Here are some guidelines to follow:

♦ Ten days is plenty of time to examine and make a decision about most book and merchandise offers.

♦ A trial period of 15 days or more may be necessary for a product that entails a habit pattern. In selling cigars by mail, for example, you want the cigar smoker to acquire the habit of smoking your brand.

♦ If you are selling something more complicated, such as a foreign language course, 30 days may be more appropriate. Where personal effort is required, a longer trial period is usually warranted.

Naturally, a trial offer will result in some returned goods from persons who decide for one reason or another not to keep the merchandise. This group

♦

will generally average 10 to 20 percent of those who accept the offer. But a trial offer will normally produce about *twice* as many orders as a money-back guarantee! So even with the added cost of shipping and processing the returned goods, the free trial offer should pay out better.

One word of caution: The free trial offer is so common to most direct marketing promotions that it's easy for the copywriter to take it for granted and not play it up enough. This was dramatically born out by a research study for Amoco Oil Company. The research disclosed that many of the firm's charge card customers, who had been exposed to a number of free trial offers from the company, didn't actually realize that the products were being offered on such an attractive basis. So future promotions were designed to play up the "no-risk trial offer" more strongly.

MONEY-BACK GUARANTEE This is an offer that has worked pretty well for Sears. For over 100 years Sears has guaranteed satisfaction on every item ordered from the company's mail order catalogs. And the technique has been duplicated by scores of mail order firms, large and small alike. When you sell a variety of items, as a catalog does, a money-back guarantee is the best way to show your firm stands behind its products.

With a single product, a free trial offer is usually your best bet. But if you can't use one, the money-back guarantee is the next best thing. The main difference is that you are asking the customer to pay part or all of the purchase price *before* you let the customer try your product.

This can be used to your advantage. Because the customer has already paid, inertia is on your side when he or she gets the merchandise. Unless the customer's really unhappy with the product, it's unlikely that he or she will take the time and effort to send it back. As a result, you can afford to be more generous with a guarantee period than with a free trial period.

PRICE AND PAYMENT OPTIONS

Price is an important part of the offer that's already been covered in the previous chapter. So let's concentrate on the payment options that go along with it. Exhibit 4.1 shows how these options relate to the basic offers just discussed.

EXHIBIT 4.1   Payment options for basic offers

BASIC OFFERS TO RELIEVE RISK	PRICE AND PAYMENT OPTIONS	CREATIVE MESSAGE
Free trial	Bill me later	Try my product before . . .
Money-back guarantee	Cash with order	Send your money and . . .

CASH WITH ORDER   This is the basic payment option used with a money-back guarantee. it's also commonly offered with a choice of other payment options. Incentives (such as saving the postage and handling charge) are often used to encourage the customer to send a check or money order when he or she orders.

Your credit and collection problems are minimized with this option. If you offer *only* cash terms, however, your response will be substantially lower. Because you are asking the customers to come up with the full price immediately, they may delay ordering until they're in a better cash position. And, of course, some people are reluctant to send any payment until they've seen the merchandise.

BILL ME LATER   This the basic payment option used with free trial offers. The bill is usually enclosed with the merchandise or follows a few days later. And it calls for a single payment. Because no front-end payment is required by the customer, it's easier for him or her to respond immediately, even on an impulse purchase.

Despite the fact that "bill me later" provides some collection and bad debt problems, it is usually one of the most profitable payment arrangements to offer. And these problems can be minimized by checking credit before you ship.

INSTALLMENT TERMS   This payment option works like the one above, except that it usually involves a higher selling price with installment terms set up to keep the payments around $10.00 or $20.00 per month. Installment terms are

♦

almost essential to selling big ticket items by mail to the consumer. They can boost response by 30 to 40 percent and usually pull better than "bill me," because the customer knows that he or she won't have to come up with the full purchase price at one time.

Charge card privileges This payment option offers the customer the advantage of "bill me later" and installment plans, but the seller doesn't have to carry the credit. It can be used with bank cards (Visa and MasterCard), travel-and-entertainment cards (such as Diners Club and American Express), and specialized cards (like those issued by the oil companies or large retailers). Originally, bank cards were preferred for consumer offers, while travel-and-entertainment cards were preferred for selling to business and professional people. Today, bank cards are so popular that they are used for both consumer and business offers.

C.O.D. This is the U.S. Postal Service acronym for cash on delivery. The postal worker collects on delivery of the package. It's not widely used today because of the added cost and effort required to handle C.O.D. orders.

Sometimes there is a good reason for offering the customer only one of these payment options. But, in most cases, it's best to provide a choice of two or more payment terms. Such as a choice of installment terms or cash. Or bill me, charge cards, and cash. Some customers traditionally buy on a cash basis, while others prefer some type of delayed payment or installment billing. Giving them a choice makes it easy for both types to take advantage of your offer.

Case Study of a Consumer Mailing Offer

In talking about the offer at direct marketing workshops and seminars, I've learned that it's much easier for someone to grasp the concept when they can see how it applies to an actual mailing sample.

The mailing package we'll analyze is one used some years ago by the firm of Haverhill's. It's selling a product known as the Townley Desk Central, a desk set with a number of built-in accessories. The complete mailing included a 6 × 9 outer envelope, a two-page letter, a two-color brochure illustrating the product actual size, and a combination order form and envelope.

In analyzing the offer, I'd like you to take a few minutes to read the letter and the order form (see Exhibits 4.2, 4.3, and 4.4). These two pieces contain all the details of the offer. It isn't necessary to see the brochure. There are six parts of the Haverhill's offer to look for.

Now that you've studied the letter and order form, jot down what you think are the six parts of this Haverhill's offer. To refresh your memory of our earlier definition, remember that the offer includes the product or service, the price and payment terms, and any incentives thrown in.

1. _____

2. _____

3. _____

4. _____

5. _____

6. _____

Compare your answers with those shown at the end of the case study. Those six parts comprise the exact proposition that Haverhill's is making to the customer, what it is offering the customer in return for an order.

Now let's do some brainstorming to see how this offer can be improved. Pretend for a moment that you're the advertising manager of Haverhill's. Your job is to improve this offer, and you have an unlimited budget. What else could you do or throw in to make the offer more attractive to the customer? You call in your ad agency people or direct marketing consultant and have a brainstorming session. Here are some of the ideas that might come out of such a meeting, along with appropriate comments:

1. Offer a quantity discount. (Could be a good way to encourage quantity orders as a business gift.)

♦

haverhill's

584 WASHINGTON STREET, SAN FRANCISCO, CALIFORNIA 94111

Dear Customer:

YOU HAVE ATTAINED SUCCESS IN YOUR BUSINESS OR PROFESSION AND HAVE
REACHED A POINT IN YOUR CAREER WHEN THE BEST "TOOLS" AND THE BEST
SETTING ARE NOT A LUXURY, BUT A NECESSITY.
That is why you may wish to add an extra measure of efficiency and
enjoyment to the spot where you spend most of your working hours, with:

Townley Desk Central

THIS EXTREMELY USEFUL UNIT IS "ALL BUSINESS" AND STURDILY HANDSOME.
You've probably seen many fanciful desk accesories — combination
intercoms, TV's, coffee-makers and phone loudspeakers! You need a
special course of instruction to operate some of them, and you might
have to be willing to give up a third of your desk space to accomodate them.

IF YOU TAKE A DIM VIEW OF SUCH BUSY CREATIONS, YOU WILL APPRECIATE THE
TOWNLEY AS MUCH AS WE DO. This black-and-walnut, chrome-trimmed beauty
has everything you look for in an executive working desk set:

● TWO FINELY CRAFTED SLIMLINE BALLPOINT PENS
One red, and one blue, in chrome swivel holders.

● AN EXCELLENT CLOCK
with luminous face and bell or radio/alarm.

● A REVOLVING PERPETUAL CALENDAR
with easy-to-read white-on-black numerals and letters.

● A GENEROUS SPACE FOR NOTE PAPER
with paper supplied.

● A POWERFUL 8-TRANSISTOR BATTERY AM RADIO
with 2 1/2" speaker and radio/alarm.

THE RADIO IS EXCEPTIONALLY SELECTIVE,
with clear, static-free tone, that can easily be heard even at low
volume (without disturbing others.) You may operate it (off/on) in the
usual manner, but you can also set it to be switched on by the alarm
clock . . . automatically.

I DON'T CALL THIS AN ALARM CLOCK/RADIO
because that would imply rousing a sleeper — certainly an unlikely
event at your desk! But, it can remind you of a favorite news program,
jog your memory about an important phone call, or call your attention
to those "must-not-forget" things in your business day.

THE TOWNLEY DELIVERS WHAT IT PROMISES!
It doesn't play tapes or records . . . won't answer phone calls when
you are away . . . and it contains no hidden safe to store your valuables!
IT IS A PRACTICAL DESK ACCESSORY THAT WILL PROMPTLY BECOME INDISPENSABLE
TO YOU. YOU WILL USE IT EVERY DAY, AND YOU WILL BE PROUD TO OWN IT.

EXHIBIT 4.2   Haverhill's letter (first page)

AND IT'S BEAUTIFUL!
JUST HAVE A LOOK AT THE ATTACHED COLOR PICTURE OF THE TOWNLEY - ACTUAL SIZE!
It's finished in black pebble crushed vinyl, with simulated walnut panels
on three sides and framing the speaker - and the entire unit discreetly
chrome trimmed.

GO AHEAD . . . CUT ALONG THE DOTTED LINE AND PLACE IT ON YOUR DESK!
Doesn't it look great? Doesn't it look as though it belongs on the desk
of a busy executive? And, although it's designed with the executive and
professional in mind, its clean good looks and usefulness make it a
perfect accessory at home too. Your wife will be flattered to have one
in her study or on her kitchen counter . . . for messages, weather reports, notes, time, etc. And it's great at bedside too!

But, it is primarily an executive unit and a real working aid. Therefore,
consider the Townley in two ways:

> 1. AS AN IDEAL GIFT TO YOURSELF
>   and a sensible addition to your work scene. Not
>   a gimmicky conversation piece, but a dignified
>   tool — useful and attractive.
>
> 2. AS A "BUSINESS GIFT" THAT SPEAKS ELOQUENTLY
>   OF YOUR TASTE AND THOUGHTFULNESS,
>   and of your regard for the fortunate recipient.
>   (We giftwrap and ship direct, if you wish, and
>   can also include your gift card.)

A BONUS FOR PROMPTNESS:
For your prompt order (see order/envelope) we will engrave YOUR NAME,
OR ANY NAME YOU PREFER, on a special BRUSHED CHROME PLAQUE which we'll
mount on the Townley. It makes the Townley a bit more personal, and may
even protect it from the acquisitive designs of others!

THE TOWNLEY IS MODESTLY PRICED.
As a gift to yourself, or a favorite friend or co-worker, the Townley
is priced at just $39.95. It's a lot of desk-top usefulness and good looks
for a reasonable sum.

HAVERHILL'S CLEAR-AS-A-BELL GUARANTEE GOES WITH IT.
You must be satisfied or you may return the Townley within two weeks for
full credit or refund — no questions asked. Even with the personalized
plaque we'll accept its return. That's how sure we are that you will
approve of the Townley.

Sounds good? It is! Order the Townley Desk Central today and see for
yourself. I know you will be pleased you did.

Sincerely yours,

Gerardo Joffe, President

PS: PLEASE REMEMBER: The personalized brushed
    chrome name plaque is A BONUS FOR PROMPTNESS.
    Take advantage of this and order right away.

EXHIBIT 4.3   Haverhill's letter (second page)

◆

EXHIBIT 4.4   Haverhill's envelope/order form

Please send the Townley Desk Central to:

NAME_____

ADDRESS_____

_____ ZIP_____

☐ I enclose $40.95 ($39.95 plus $1 postage and insurance).
Return in two weeks if not delighted. California residents add tax.
☐ Gift wrap.   ☐ Enclose my gift card.

YOUR NAME

Bonus for promptness:

☐ Check this box if you are placing
your order within 7 days of receipt
of this mailing. For your prompt
response we will engrave
YOUR NAME (or any recipients)
on a brushed chrome plaque and
mount this on the desk set—with
our compliments. Name to appear is :

2. Free year's supply of note paper. (This might make sense because many desk accessories take an odd-size paper which is difficult to obtain at an office supply store.)

3. Include an extra set of batteries. (This idea could be negative. It reminds the customer that batteries will wear out and must be replaced. Unlike the case of the note paper, standard sizes are readily available for replacement.)

♦

4. Offer a free trial instead of the money-back guarantee that requires cash with order. (That's a good one! Probably the best single way to improve response on this offer.)

5. Let the customer make two monthly payments of roughly $20.00 each instead of one payment of $40.95. (This could make sense, because low monthly terms are important when selling consumer products. Another way to accomplish the same thing would be to let the customer put the purchase on a bank card, which has built-in installment terms.)

6. Offer the Townley Desk Central in a choice of colors rather than just black with walnut trim. (The black and woodgrain combination is probably good for business offices, but other color choices might be important to sell the product for at-home use.)

7. Give a free Cadillac with every purchase. (Every brainstorming meeting comes up with at least one wild idea like this! There's no doubt a free Cadillac would improve response substantially, but. . . .)

8. Include personalized note paper with the customer's name imprinted. (This might add some appeal to the offer, although the name plaque already provides personalization.)

9. Offer a full-year guarantee on the product. (This makes sense, especially with a product whose brand name is unfamiliar. The customer may hesitate to order if he or she thinks it will be difficult to get the product serviced locally.)

10. Provide a discount to encourage the customer to send cash with the order. (If we add other ordering options like a free trial, monthly payment terms, or charge cards, this discount would be logical. Many mail order firms add a postage and handling charge on credit orders, but they pay postage and handling on cash orders.)

Answers for Haverhill's case study
Here are the six parts of the Haverhill's offer:
1. Product—Townley Desk Central.
2. Price—$39.95 plus $1.00 for postage and insurance.
3. Terms—customer must send cash with order.
4. Free gift for promptness—personalized name plaque.
5. Two-week guarantee of satisfaction.
6. Gift service—free wrapping and shipping of gift orders.

Case Study of a Business Mailing Offer

As we did with the Haverhill's example in the consumer area, let's look at an actual business mailing. The letter shown in Exhibit 4.5 was used by Eastman Kodak's incentive marketing division. The letter was sent to advertising managers who can use Kodak cameras for their premium or incentive programs. Take a few minutes to read the letter and analyze the offer.

In this case I won't keep you guessing about what the offer is. It's a "nothing offer." I purposely use it as an example because it's typical of a lot of business direct mail I've seen. Someone decides to do a mailing without giving any thought to the offer.

If the objective of this particular mailing was just to send out some literature, that's fine. But if it was designed to produce an immediate response, no offer was made to help accomplish that objective. How could it be improved? What could you do or throw in to make it an interesting offer to the advertising managers who received this letter?

EXHIBIT 4.5   Kodak letter

> ### EASTMAN KODAK COMPANY
> 1901 WEST 22ND STREET
> OAK BROOK, ILLINOIS 60521
>
> HOME OFFICE
> ROCHESTER NEW YORK 14650
>
> TELEPHONE
> AREA CODE 312   654 5300
>
> The Kodak name is well known around the world. Over the years Kodak products have earned fame for quality and dependability. The brand name KODAK helps to sell your products faster, no matter what you plan to promote or how you plan to promote it.
>
> Kodak's national advertising, telling millions of consumers about the "world's most gifted cameras", helps to sell your promotion. When you choose a Kodak premium, Kodak printed and television advertising, direct mail, and displays promote the appeal of all products--movie and still--to your customers.
>
> I am enclosing our Kodak Premium Catalog to provide you with further information on the products and services available to our premium customers. Our complete line of still and movie cameras and projectors is available for sales incentive programs and dealer loaders, and our special "Kodak HAWKEYE" line is available for the previously mentioned functions as well as self-liquidators. Our new fulfillment program offers a complete service package--from factory to consumer--and allows you to concentrate on promoting your goods and services with no inventory investment or handling worries.
>
> May I have the opportunity to work with you in planning your next promotion.
>
> Yours very truly,
>
> *John Hackett*
>
> TFHackett:CP
> Enc.
>
> INCENTIVE MARKETING REPRESENTATIVE
>
> **Kodak**

Let's have another brainstorming session. Here are some ideas that might come out of such a session, along with appropriate comments:

> 1. Offer a camera as a free gift. (Because an incentive program usually produces a fairly

good-size order, we should be able to afford to give one camera away to the ad manager. It's an easy way to familiarize the manager with product features, quality, and so on.)

2. Provide free promotion planning service. (This is a logical offer. Most people are busy or lazy or both. So you offer to help them do their job and show them how to plan an effective promotion using Kodak cameras, it could spark their interest.)

3. Offer free advertising support literature. (Like the idea above, this could be helpful to a busy advertising manager who must come up with a complete premium program. If he or she buys a camera for a traffic-building program, we could offer to provide free store posters or window banners and let the manager request samples of them.)

4. Give the manager a quantity discount. (Chances are Kodak already has a quantity discount for premium buyers, so this offer would be easy to make.)

5. Offer a free Kodak premium catalog. (If the objective is to provide sales leads or qualify the ad manager's interest, this idea is a natural. Instead of enclosing the catalog with the letter, as Kodak did, ask the prospect to request it. That's exactly what camera competitor Polaroid did in a recent promotion.)

6. Provide drop shipping service to premium users. (Judging from the letter, this is apparently something Kodak will do, and it can be an appealing benefit to the prospect.)

7. Offer free film. (That's an idea with a lot of possibilities. We could offer the ad manager a roll of film to give away with every premium camera purchased. Or, provide free film for the salespeople to demonstrate the camera to retailers and help get good display space for their promotion. Or, just give the ad manager a year's supply of his or her favorite film to get an inquiry.)

8. Make it a "your choice" offer. The ad manager requests information on the type of premium program he or she is most interested in—a sales incentive program, dealer loader, self-liquidator, and so on. (These are all common types of incentive programs. By offering information on each type, we show that we have one or more Kodak cameras suitable for each objective.)

9. Offer a free price list. (This is not a very exciting offer in itself. Maybe it could be combined with one of the other offers, such as a free catalog and price list.)

10. Offer to send case histories of actual promotions using Kodak cameras as premiums. (Sounds good! If you were an ad manager considering the use of Kodak cameras, you would probably like to know what other marketers have done with them and how their promotions worked out.)

◆

Most Popular Consumer and Business Offers

WHEN YOU SIT DOWN TO MAKE a list of direct response offers and their variations, it's amazing how many you can come up with. I know, because I did it many years ago. And my list of 99 proven direct response offers has been widely reprinted. A complete description of all these tested and successful propositions is in the appendix, and a handy checklist is provided at the end of this chapter.

With the exception of the basic offers and payment options we've already covered, the 99 offers fit rather nicely into 11 categories. In reviewing them, keep in mind that most of these offers are used to get an order rather than an inquiry. Not all of them are suitable for all types of products. Some can best be used on their own, while others can be readily combined into one master offer.

1. Free Gift Offers

The number of ways you can offer a free gift is only limited by your own imagination. Some of the most popular offers include a gift just for inquiring or requesting more information, a gift for agreeing to *try* the product (which the customer is usually allowed to keep even if he or she sends the merchandise back), a gift for *buying* your product or service, or a gift related to the amount of the customer's order.

With a catalog operation, for example, you can use a free-gift offer to help upgrade your average order. Let's say your average order has been $16.00. You might offer a free gift for any order of $20.00 or more. Or you might offer gifts of varying value: an inexpensive gift for orders under $25.00; a better gift for orders running between $25.00 and $50.00; and a deluxe gift for orders over $50.00.

Others in this category include multiple free gifts, mystery gifts, and "your choice" of free gifts. Be careful with the "your choice" offer. It sounds logical. But every time I've tested it, a single gift comes out better than giving people a choice of two or three different gifts.

Care should also be taken in selecting the right gift. I've seen some gift offers that have pulled two or three times better than others! There's no absolute rule of thumb for what percentage of the merchandise selling price you should spend on a free gift. An inexpensive gift will sometimes produce a better net profit than an expensive one. Or vice versa.

Beware of gifts so appealing that they overshadow the merchandise or attract bad credit risks. Likewise, if gifts are used to get inquiries, a gift that's too appealing can have a negative effect on closures. If possible, make a test and find out which gift does best for your market and your product or service.

When you are planning a gift offer for the business market, the only real difference to consider is how it affects the business purchase. Some advertisers believe that a free gift or premium should be related to the business product they are selling. On the other hand, one large business mailer I know has literally built his business on premium offers. The firm tries to select premiums that can be used either at the office or at home. Such as a calculator or desk lamp. This appeals to the larceny of some prospects. They know they can take the premium home if they wish, and still justify the purchase as a sound business decision.

Perhaps the best example of how successful gift offers can be is Fingerhut Corporation's marketing efforts. The company tested one gift and found it improved results. So a second gift offer was added to the same mailing and the firm did even better. Fingerhut now routinely offers three or more free gifts for a single order!

2. OTHER FREE OFFERS

The word "free" has a lot of magic to it. And it's been used to develop a variety of proven offers. Most of them in this category are designed for lead-getting situations, especially in the business market where the usual objective is to get an inquiry for a salesperson to follow up. It's important to realize that your offer can control both the quantity and quality of inquiries you receive.

If you want a good *quantity* of leads, make your offer as generous as possible. The more you promise to send or give away, the more leads you will get. But this tends to lower the *quality* of leads. On the other hand, if you want a smaller number of better-qualified inquiries, make your offer less generous. And you'll get fewer leads. Inquiries themselves are easy to get. You have to know what kind of inquiries you want before you finalize your offer.

The more generous types of lead-getting offers include free gifts, free information, a free catalog, or a free booklet. Catalog offers can be very appealing. Especially in the business market. Many business or industrial catalogs are used as buying guides. They are reviewed, studied, and often filed for future reference.

♦

A free booklet is one of the best ways to establish your company's expertise and know-how about the specific problems of the industry you serve. Such a booklet need not be elaborate in terms of size or illustrations. The key factor is the information it contains. That information should include some down-to-earth helpful material, not just a straight commercial for your product or service. Sometimes, it helps to have the booklet written by an outside authority whose name is known and respected. And the booklet should be played up prominently in your ad or mailing package, so the reader quickly sees he or she can send for it without obligation.

The real value of a booklet like this is to provide a "door opener" for the salesperson. It gives the salesperson an excuse or reason for a sales call—the chance to deliver the booklet, get acquainted with the prospect, and see how to help solve the prospect's problem. In many cases it will get the salesperson in to see a key person or decision maker, where ordinarily he or she would be asked to see the purchasing agent. The prospect gets the booklet he or she wants, and the salesperson gets a few minutes of valuable time which might otherwise be very hard to get.

Today some advertisers offer a fact kit or video in lieu of a booklet. A video brochure can be an effective way to show the product in action.

Other free offers that tend to produce more-qualified inquiries include a free survey, free estimate, or free demonstration. The latter is valuable for business equipment that has to be demonstrated to be fully appreciated. The offer's appeal depends largely on the equipment itself. The demonstration of a revolutionary new product obviously is going to be more appealing than one that's been around for years.

Perhaps the most qualified free offer of all is one I call "send me a salesperson." Anyone who responds is probably a highly qualified prospect, who is either ready to order or seriously considering it.

The actual wording of your offer will probably be a little more discreet than "send me a salesperson." You might ask the prospect to fill out a reply card that says, "Have your sales representative phone me for an appointment." Or you might provide space for the prospect to suggest the best time for the salesperson to call. On the other hand, if you are offering free literature or additional information that will *not* be delivered by a salesperson, this can add appeal to your offer. Many businesspeople may want to learn more about your product or service without getting buttonholed by a salesperson. So by all means play up the fact that "no salesperson will call" or "we'll send free literature by mail."

3. DISCOUNT OFFERS

Everyone loves a bargain. And that's what makes discount offers work. Some of the most popular types include a cash discount, a quantity or volume discount, and an early-bird discount.

One form widely used for direct response is the short-term introductory offer. An example of this technique is "Try 13 weeks of the *Wall Street Journal* for only $34.00." One insurance company I know boosted response by 55 percent by offering new policyholders 30 days of accident protection for $1.00. These offers work because they break down human inertia by making the introductory offer easy to accept. This substantially increases the initial response.

To be truly successful, however, you must be able to convert such respondents to a long-term sale. You need to sell a year's subscription or get that policyholder to pay the regular premium to continue his or her coverage after the 30 days are up. If your proposition is a good value and you have a strong follow-up mailing series, it's not unusual to get conversions of 30 to 40 percent.

Another type of discount is the refund certificate. Technically, it's a delayed discount. You might ask a prospect to send $2.00—or even $5.00—for your catalog and tell him or her you'll include a refund coupon good for the same amount on the first order. I've seen this offer work very effectively because it can not only increase your front-end response, it can also improve your back-end results—the number who order once they get the catalog. A refund certificate is like an uncashed check. It's difficult to resist the urge to cash it in.

In general, discount offers are most effective when your product or service has a well-established value. But they should be tested carefully. In most cases, a discount offer will *not* do as well as an attractive free gift with the same value. When it tested the two ads shown in Exhibit 4.6, MCI discovered that because customers perceived 30 free minutes of long distance calls as a greater value than $5.00 off, "30 minutes free" pulled roughly twice as well as the discount offer.

4. Sale Offers

This is the "first cousin" to a discount offer. A sale is really like a discount for a specified period of time. There are umpteen different names used for sales but most of them fall into the category of a seasonal sale or a reason-why sale.

As the late Paul Bringe, a leading direct mail consultant, pointed out in *Direct Marketing* magazine, "A sale of known value goods can stand on its own feet. It needs no justification to be believable. But a sale on merchandise of unknown quality must have a 'reason why' if it is to be accepted. It must be an Inventory Reduction, Post-Holiday, Going-Out-of-Business or similar sale. All these explanatory terms have one purpose, to make the sale believable to the prospect."

EXHIBIT 4.6   Which ad pulled best? See text for details.

5. Sample Offers

A sample offer is designed to do just one thing: get your product into the prospect's hands. This is because a sample of a good product will sell itself better than all the fancy words and pictures we can use to describe it.

When a sample offer is mentioned, many advertisers automatically think of a *free* sample. Yet I've seen test results that show it's better to make a nominal charge for the sample. Apparently people are somewhat suspicious of free offers and don't really expect to get something valuable for nothing. A nominal charge also helps screen out some of the curiosity seekers.

Another approach to the sample offer is to tie it to a tentative commitment. A number of magazines use this technique. The offer usually reads something like this: "Yes, please send me a free sample issue of (magazine) and enter my name as a trial subscriber for one year." The subscriber is told that if he or she is not satisfied with the sample copy, to just write "cancel" on the bill and send it back. Once again, it's hoped that the sample product will sell itself.

6. Time Limit Offers

If you want somebody to take a specific action, it often helps to give him or her a time limit to do so. And if your offer is really a special one, this approach makes it seem even more so. It implies the offer is so generous that you cannot afford to continue it indefinitely.

Limited-time offers work because consumers know they must make up their minds if they want to get in on the deal you're offering. This tends to force a quick decision and avoids procrastination. It's usually best to mention a specific date rather than a time period. For example: "This free gift offer expires June 27," rather than "This offer expires in 10 days."

A number of time limit offers have become favorites for specific types of products or services:

♦ An enrollment period, widely used in selling mail order insurance.

◆ Prepublication offer, used by publishers to offer a savings before the official publication date of a new book.

◆ Charter offer, ideal for introducing new clubs, publications, and other subscription services.

◆ Limited edition offer, proven effective for selling coins, art prints, and other collectible items.

7. Guarantee Offers

Earlier we reviewed the basic money-back guarantee which helps overcome the customer's reluctance to order an unseen product by mail. You can often use an extended guarantee, and, if the product is sound, have little or no increase in returned goods. For example:

◆ If you have a spring promotion on a fishing lure, you can offer a six-month guarantee and tell the customer to use it for the entire summer fishing season.

◆ If you are selling an annual investment service, tell the customer that he or she can get a full refund any time within twelve months.

◆ If you are selling a magazine subscription, offer to refund the unexpired portion of the subscription any time before it runs out.

8. Build-Up-the-Sale Offers

Most direct marketers are interested in increasing the size of their average order. A number of special offers are designed to accomplish just that. They're structured so the customer can easily order more than one item or add something to the basic-purchase.

♦

A good example is the deluxe offer. A book publisher might offer a certain volume for $19.95 in a standard binding. On the order form the publisher gives the customer the alternative of ordering the same volume in a deluxe edition with a nicer binding for only $5.00 extra. It's not unusual for 10 percent or more of those ordering to select the deluxe option.

Also in this category is the multi-product offer—two or more products featured in the same ad or mailing. This and other similar offers should be tested carefully. Giving the customer a choice can often depress results because indecision sets in and he or she doesn't order at all. But, used wisely, such offers can be effective in building up the sale. The best proof of this is the success of catalogs, which are really multi-product offers featuring as many as a hundred or more different products.

9. SWEEPSTAKES OFFERS

Today's sweepstakes must be a "guaranteed winner" contest in which all prizes are awarded and the prospect can enter whether or not an order is placed. Common types include pre-selected numbers, drawings, everybody wins, and involvement sweepstakes.

It's not unusual to see a sweepstakes improve results by 30 to 50 percent. That's because the dramatic excitement of big prizes attracts attention, which in turn focuses interest on the product or service being offered. But the psychology of how consumers react to sweepstakes is also interesting. Although it isn't so, a great many customers *think* they have a better chance to win if they place an order. So, if the prizes are really attractive to them, many will place an order who would not have done so otherwise.

Here are the four main ingredients I have found make a successful sweepstakes.

LARGE UNIVERSE Because sweepstakes need a fairly large mailing universe, they are used primarily by large catalog mailers and general-interest magazines. Unless you are mailing at least 500,000 to 1,000,000 pieces, it's hard to offer enough expensive prizes without overly increasing your promotion costs. A couple of specialized magazines have run effective low-budget sweeps, but they're the exception.

♦

For example, let's say you plan a sweepstakes with a total prize budget of $100,000 and mail one million pieces. The prizes add $100.00 per thousand to your promotion cost, which should be more than offset by improved results. But the same prize budget on a mailing of 250,000 pieces would add $400 per thousand to your promotion and make it difficult for the sweepstakes to recover its cost.

ATTRACTIVE PRIZE STRUCTURE A good sweepstakes should feature a valuable grand prize. But as direct marketing consultant Joan Throckmorton notes, "You sell a sweepstakes on fantasy and fulfill it with cash." Even if you feature a Rolls Royce or a trip around the world as the grand prize, it makes sense to offer cash as an alternative choice. Winners invariably choose the cash. And these days, the trend for mass mailers like Publishers Clearing House is to offer a grand prize of at least a million dollars.

In addition to the grand prize, there should be a good quantity of attractive runner-up prizes. Widescreen TVs, video cameras, and personal computers are always appealing. The idea is to offer enough prizes so the readers feel they have a fair chance of winning something. Most people are naturally attracted by the main prizes. But they probably figure, "I really don't have much of a chance to win that top prize, but there are enough other interesting prizes so maybe I'll win something."

PREQUALIFICATION Generally, your results are better if the reader goes through some prequalification process, so he or she feels that there is a better-than-average chance to win . . . or a better chance to win a bigger prize than other people. You can accomplish this by having each respondent match his or her lucky number against a list of potential winning numbers. Or letting the respondent find out how big a grand prize he or she will be eligible to win. This makes the reader more likely to enter and place an order.

One of the most successful sweepstakes concepts I ever developed included a seven-part grand prize: cash, car, trip, freezer, color TV, diamond ring, and sterling silver dinnerware. The prequalification device established whether the entrant would get four, five, six, or seven parts of that grand prize. But everyone qualified for the "big three" prizes—cash, car, and trip—plus one other.

So the prequalification device established a pleasant surprise that led to a high entry and order rate.

INVOLVEMENT My experience has shown that the involvement aspect is as important as the price structure or sweepstakes theme, sometimes even more important. Getting somebody to open a mystery gift envelope, rub off a spot to find a hidden number, play a game, or just compare his or her number against a lucky number list all tend to increase content entries and sales results. Of course, you don't want to make the contest so complex it's hard to figure out. The instructions should be clear and should be repeated in two or three different places so the reader knows exactly what he or she has to do.

If you have a large universe and do put together a sweepstakes with an attractive prize structure, prequalification, and involvement, your effort can add up to a very successful promotion. But, before you contemplate undertaking one, be sure to consult with a lawyer or judging firm. Sweepstakes law is tricky, and expert advice can save you money and problems.

10. CLUB AND CONTINUITY OFFERS

These offers are favorites with the music clubs, book clubs, and other publishers. Some of them have also been successfully used for other special-interest clubs. While there are many variations, as the 99 Offers checklist demonstrates, let's look at the three most popular ones as they might be viewed by a consumer:

POSITIVE OPTION You join a club and are notified monthly of new selections. To order a particular selection, you must take some positive action, e.g., send back an order card, before the club will ship.

NEGATIVE OPTION As with the positive option, you join a club and are notified monthly of new selections. However, unless the rejection card is returned by a specific date, the publisher has the right to ship. Under the terms of membership to which you agreed when joining, non-action on your part is considered a "yes" vote for that month's selection.

♦

Automatic shipments This variation eliminates the advance notice of each new selection. When you sign up for the book club offer, you give the publisher permission to ship each new selection automatically, usually every month or two, until you notify the publisher to stop. It's commonly called a "till forbid" offer.

These offers and their variations might seem similar but their results can be substantially different. A positive-option book club, for example, might only get five to ten percent of its members to accept each monthly selection. On the other hand, a negative-option club can get 20 to 40 percent of the members to accept a monthly selection. So the negative option results can be four to eight times better!

All the club and continuity offers get somewhat complicated and must be spelled out clearly. It's best to make sure the consumer understands how the offer works and what he or she is agreeing to in advance.

A final point to remember when designing a club or continuity offer is this: a customer responding to your offer is making a commitment. And the terms of your offer can determine the quality of that commitment. Generally speaking, a customer who buys four books for $1.00 and agrees to buy four more books at the regular price will be a better customer than one who only buys four books for $1.00. That's because the greater the commitment a prospect makes at the start of your relationship, the better a customer he or she will be in the long run. Make sure your offer attracts customers with the level of commitment you need to encourage repeat orders. Some sophisticated advertisers will use a mix of commitment and no-commitment offers, depending on the media and audience.

11. Specialized Offers

This group frankly includes all the leftovers that don't fit neatly into one of the other categories. Many of them are rather specialized and only fit a certain type of direct marketing operation.

A good example is what I call the "philanthropic privilege." This is the basis of almost all fund-raising offers. When you give a contribution, you get nothing tangible in return. But your contribution, coupled with thousands of others brought in by an extensive direct marketing program, helps make the world a better place in which to live.

Another example that dramatizes what was said earlier about being able to combine two or more offers is the self-qualification. With this offer, you provide a choice of options to get the consumer to indicate his or her degree of interest in your product or service, such as different check boxes on your order form for a free booklet and a free demonstration. Those who request the latter qualify themselves as more-serious prospects and should get more-immediate attention.

PRESENTING YOUR OFFER MOST EFFECTIVELY

ONCE YOU'VE ZEROED IN on the offer or offers you are going to use, give some thought to the best way to present your proposition. What part of the offer should be emphasized? How should it be worded? Will more people respond to a half-price offer or to 50 percent off?

A good example of how you can take the same basic offer and present it in different ways comes from one of the leading book clubs. The club tested the following three offers. To help you compare them, I've added alongside of each what the customer gets and what the customer pays.

	CUSTOMER GETS	CUSTOMER PAYS
1. *Two books free* (if you agree to join and buy four more books at $10.00 each)	6 books	$40.00
2. *Two books free if you buy one now* (and agree to buy three more at $10.00 each)	6 books	$40.00
3. *Three books for only* $10.00 (if you agree to buy three more at $10.00 each)	6 books	$40.00

Note that in each case the customer winds up with the same number of books and pays exactly the same amount. Yet, at first glance, the offers seem quite different. And when they were tested, offer number 3 produced a much better response than the other two!

♦

The Last Word on Offers

If you have a limited mailing list universe, it might make sense to vary your offer from one mailing to the next. Different things appeal to different people. Some consumers will never respond to one type of offer, even if they receive it a dozen times or more. By using a change of pace, you can pull in some people with one offer and then come back next time with another offer that pulls in others.

Make sure the offer is featured prominently in your ad or mailing package. If you have a free gift offer, it's usually more effective to enclose a separate gift slip rather than put the gift offer in the circular. If you have a guarantee, put an official-looking certificate border around it. If you have a free trial offer, make sure it's played up strongly in a heading or subhead and not buried in the body copy.

Checklist of 99 Proven Direct Response Offers

BASIC OFFERS

1. Right price

2. Free trial

3. Money-back guarantee

4. Cash with order

5. Bill me later

6. Installment terms

7. Charge card privileges

8. C.O.D.

FREE GIFT OFFERS

9. Free gift for an inquiry

10. Free gift for a trial order

11. Free gift for buying

12. Multiple free gifts with a single order

13. Your choice of free gifts

14. Free gifts based on size of order

15. Two-step gift offer

16. Continuing incentive gifts

17. Mystery gift offer

OTHER FREE OFFERS

18. Free information

19. Free catalog

20. Free booklet or video

21. Free fact kit

22. Send me a salesperson

23. Free demonstration

24. Free "survey of your needs"

25. Free cost estimate

26. Free film offer

27. Free house organ subscription

28. Free talent test

29. Gift shipment service

DISCOUNT OFFERS

30. Cash discount

31. Short-term introductory offer

32. Refunds and rebates

33. Introductory order discount

34. Trade discount

35. Early-bird discount

36. Quantity discount

37. Sliding-scale discount

38. Mystery discounts

SALE OFFERS

39. Seasonal sales

40. Reason-why sales

41. Price increase notice

SAMPLE OFFERS

42. Free sample

43. Nominal charge samples

44. Sample offer with tentative commitment

45. Quantity sample offer

TIME LIMIT OFFERS

46. Limited-time offers

47. Enrollment periods

48. Pre-publication offer

49. Charter membership (or subscription) offer

50. Limited edition offer

GUARANTEE OFFERS

51. Extended guarantee or warranty

52. Double-your-money-back guarantee

53. Guaranteed buy-back agreement

54. Guaranteed acceptance offer

BUILD-UP-THE-SALE OFFERS

55. Multi-product offers

56. Piggyback offers

57. The deluxe offer

58. Good-better-best offer

59. Add-on offer

60. Write-your-own-ticket offer

61. Bounce-back offer

62. Increase and extension offers

SWEEPSTAKES OFFERS

63. Drawing-type sweepstakes

64. Lucky number sweepstakes

65. "Everybody wins" sweepstakes

66. Involvement sweepstakes

67. Talent contests

CLUB AND CONTINUITY OFFERS

68. Positive option

69. Negative option

70. Automatic shipments

71. Continuity load-up offer

72. Front-end load-ups

73. Open-ended commitment

74. "No strings attached" commitment

75. Lifetime membership fee

76. Annual membership fee

SPECIALIZED OFFERS

77. The philanthropic privilege

78. Blank check offer

79. Matching check

80. Executive preview charge

81. Yes/no/maybe offers

82. Self-qualification offer

83. Exclusive rights for your trading area

84. The super-dramatic offer

85. Trade-in offer

86. Third-party referral offer

87. Member-get-a-member offer

88. Name-getter offers

89. Self-liquidating premiums

90. Purchase-with-purchase

91. Delayed billing offer

92. Post-dated checks

93. Reduced down payment

94. Stripped-down products

95. Sweeten-the-pot offers

96. Rush shipping service

97. The competitive offer

98. The nominal reimbursement offer

99. Establish-the-value offer

5

MARKETING STRATEGIES

♦

STRATEGIC PLANNING IS A CONCEPT that has transformed the way business operates today. But until recently it had almost no impact on direct marketing. Historically, direct marketers have tended to emphasize the *tactics* of creative execution that can be readily tested, like copy, graphics, and offer. In focusing on tactics, we have often neglected to consider the basic strategy beneath our execution.

And to our sorrow, we've learned that even great creative tactics won't save a weak strategy. Some years ago General Electric tested a Customer Club for major appliance buyers. Its creative package, singled out for praise by some experts, looked great. But because it didn't offer consumers any meaningful benefits, the Customer Club failed. Ultimately, it was strategically weak.

Strategy doesn't just determine the success of an offer. Strategic planning can make or break a company. That's why I've always liked what Harvard professor Michael Porter says on the subject: "It is the unity, coherence, and internal consistency of a company's *strategic decisions* that position the company in its environment and give the firm its identity, its power to mobilize its strengths, and its likelihood of success in the marketplace."

This chapter will help you learn to assess your own situation and develop appropriate, effective direct marketing strategies that can help your company flourish.

UNDERSTANDING WHO AND WHERE YOU ARE

THE CLASSIC APPROACH TO STRATEGIC planning starts out by developing a *situation analysis*. It's merely a fancy way of saying, "Where are we now?" But a summary like this is a good way to make sure that everyone on your management team holds the same basic assumptions about your business. If you do your homework properly, your situation analysis should provide a comprehensive snapshot of what your firm is today and where your business is going.

A well-thought-out situation analysis should address six areas.

1. *Who your customers and prospects are.* What kind of people or companies are they? What are their interests? What are their demographics and psychographics? What about the people or companies who haven't responded yet? How do their characteristics compare with those of your active buyers?

2. *Current sales trends and what they suggest.* Is your market growing? Declining? What is your market share? Where are your sales strong? Where are they weak?

3. *Present strengths and weaknesses.* How do your strengths and weaknesses measure up to current and future competition? Are you stronger in merchandising or new product development? Do you have a large database? What consumer trends are likely to affect your business?

4. *Key factors in the marketing environment.* What political, social, regulatory, and governmental factors influence your industry and your company? What about economic, environmental, and technological factors? How do they affect your customers? What major threats and opportunities may challenge your industry?

5. *Competitor activities.* Where are your competitors positioned in the marketplace? What are their strengths and weaknesses? What are their

◆

goals? And what is their current and probable future strategy?

6. *Results you expect from your present way of doing things.* What's likely to happen if you just keep doing what you're doing? How will your current plans be impacted by trends in the marketplace? By competitive activity?

THE MISSION STATEMENT

Most first-time strategic plans contain a mission statement that carefully defines the business the company is in, the logical growth areas that can be pursued, the specific market to which the company is targeted, and its position in that market.

Defining the business you are in is especially important. Some companies define the scope of their business too narrowly, others too broadly. Day-Timers, for example, sells executive planners and diaries. But instead of confining its business to diary sales, it considers itself to be in the business of time management. On the other hand, Kentucky Fried Chicken floundered during the years its management viewed the company as a food service conglomerate. Changing its mission to become the preeminent fast food chicken restaurant helped management focus on strategies that have fostered enormous growth.

An effective mission statement generally grows out of your situation analysis, and, once established, can help you develop reasonable goals to shoot for and concrete objectives to plan and achieve.

OBJECTIVES, STRATEGIES, AND TACTICS

The strategic planning process really begins when you answer the question, "Given what we know about our past and our present, where do we want to be a few years down the road?" Some planners use a five-year period. I think three years is a more realistic timeframe to deal with. Making your answer a reality means establishing specific objectives and determining the strategies and tactics you will use to reach them.

First, let's review the difference between marketing objectives, strategies, and tactics.

Objectives are specific, measurable goals that are to be achieved in a certain period of time. Simply saying that you want to boost sales from your house list by 25 percent is not a solid objective. A bona fide objective has to be quantifiable. In this case, I would quantify both the time period and the amount, and say something like "boost sales from the house list by 25 percent in the current fiscal year."

Strategies are the planned actions to reach those objectives. One strategy to boost sales from the house list might be to mail the house list more frequently. Another strategy might be to increase the average order from the house list mailings.

Tactics detail how you will execute the strategies. Tactics for the strategy of mailing the house list more often might include mailing three times during the Christmas season instead of two or sending a re-mail catalog to your best names. Tactics for increasing the average order could include offering higher-priced merchandise or pushing credit rather than cash purchases, a tactic that can tempt customers to place higher-value orders.

Objectives, strategies, and tactics should come from the problems and opportunities uncovered in your situation analysis. It's hard to say exactly how many objectives, strategies, and tactics you will need to meet your overall goal. The important thing is to develop the number of strategies required to accomplish your objectives and the number of tactics needed to accomplish your strategies.

Basic Direct Marketing Objectives

Direct marketing objectives fall into two broad categories. They are intended either to acquire new customers and prospects at the lowest possible cost or to maximize the value of customers and prospects through conversion, retention, and repeat sales.

The first of these objectives is crucial. New customers and prospects are the lifeblood of any business. I like to refer to this as "front-end" marketing. It's where most firms spend the lion's share of their time and budget. The second objective is also critical. Because making a sale or generating an inquiry often costs you money, what you do in this area of "back-end" marketing determines whether you get a profitable return on your advertising investment. To put it another way, you usually spend money on the front-end to make money on the back-end.

In my opinion, most firms don't spend enough time or attention on the back-end. A small boost in your inquiry conversion percentage, for example, can make a big difference in your sales and profits.

Your marketing plan should address both of these objectives. You might have three, four, or more objectives for the front-end and, likewise, two or more objectives for the back-end. But how do you decide *which* objectives or strategies to include in your marketing plan?

KEY STRATEGIC GROWTH ISSUES

IN MY EXPERIENCE WITH CLIENTS over the years, I've found that seven key strategic planning questions come up over and over again. While all seven relate to growth strategies, these are not just strategies to reach an objective. They are "strategic" questions with broad ramifications—the kinds of questions you should be asking before you even begin to develop your company's objectives.

1. IS IT MORE IMPORTANT THIS YEAR TO BUILD SALES OR PROFITS?

The answer to this crucial question usually depends on how your company is doing. In general, in a lean year most businesses try to maintain as high a level of profit as possible. That typically means cutting expenses and eliminating marginal advertising. In a good year, the concern is usually to increase sales while maintaining an acceptable profit level. The right answer to this question is also dependent on the economy, on your position in the marketplace, and on your internal resources, including the budget available to you.

When a company wants to build *sales,* it will promote its products heavily, use lists or media that produce marginal results, and spend a large share of its advertising or direct marketing budget on prospecting. It may also undertake some riskier projects and launch new products or even new businesses.

When the focus shifts to building *profits,* a company cuts back on advertising and promotion expenses. It eliminates marginal advertising, concentrating on proven lists and media that produce good results. A large share of the budget will be spent on promoting to current customers, while the amount spent on developing new products and businesses will be reduced or eliminated. It's easy to "milk" a mail order business this way and maximize short-term profits. But beware: By paring down your new customer acquisition efforts, this kind of strategy can hurt you in the long run.

Western Publishing is a good example of a company that has pursued both strategies. Some years ago, when parent company Mattel was going through a lean period, Western was told to maximize profits. It concentrated on proven, successful products—like the Sesame Street Book Club and an adult knitting continuity program—that produced solid, predictable results. A more recent change in ownership signaled a return to a sales orientation. While it continued to promote old standbys, Western's major effort shifted to establishing new products. The company developed a book series on ancient history, the Betty Crocker Recipe Collection (See Exhibit 5.1) and other continuity programs for parents and children.

A company can choose to build sales *or* build profits. Either may be a valid goal. But bear in mind that strategies intended to achieve one will probably be wrong for the other.

2. How Heavily Should You Invest in New Customer Acquisition?

This is a deceptively simple question, but I'm constantly surprised at how often supposedly sophisticated marketers fail to grasp what a new customer is worth. If you don't know what a new customer is worth, you don't know how much you can profitably invest to get one. You may be spending too much which will eventually hurt your bottom line. Or, by spending too little—you may be losing sales to more aggressive competitors.

To determine how much you can afford to spend on new customers, you need to know two things: What your *repeat business potential* is and what *payback period* you want from new customers.

If you're selling a $3,000 copier to small businesses, the odds are it will be a number of years before your new customers are ready to reorder. Other than a rather small aftermarket in copier supplies, you have no repeat business to

EXHIBIT 5.1   New products like this one help a company build sales.

look forward to. You can't afford to invest in new customers; you have to acquire them at breakeven or better. But if you're in the yearbook publishing business, you can take advantage of excellent repeat order rates. Your investment in new customers will pay back handsomely in future sales.

The mail order photofinishing business seems to offer good repeat business, since people are always snapping pictures. But in reality, it's a deal-oriented business whose customers have very little loyalty. They typically send their next roll of film to the company offering the best processing price. Like the copier example above, mail order photofinishers can't afford to invest in getting new customers.

Investing in new customer acquisition is *the* most popular strategy for building direct marketing sales. But too often firms shortchange themselves by limiting new customer acquisition to the lists or media they can use on a break-even-or-better basis. At the same time, they limit their growth, because they are overlooking a simple but critical truth: *The higher the lifetime value of a customer, the more you can afford to spend to acquire one.*

3. Can You Profitably Contact Present Customers More Often with Existing Products or Services?

Chances are, you can, whether it's more of the same product or related products.

Too many companies overlook this growth path because they neglect to develop a formal contact strategy. Consultant Robert Kestnbaum defines contact strategy as the specific decision of how many times each customer *segment* will be contacted each year. Segmentation specifies who will be reached. Media selection specifies how offers will be delivered. But contact strategy, Kestnbaum says, refers to a positive commitment to reach designated buyers and/or inquiries a specific number of times each year.

Some sophisticated direct marketers like Fingerhut mail their best house list segments as often as once a week. Consumers who make a purchase from a Spiegel prospect catalog will get ten or more customer catalogs (some of them "remails" with a new cover or outside signature only) in the following year. Buy some clothes from Haband, and you'll get up to six mailings a month. Business mailers also promote heavily to their customer lists. According to a recent study, they send 14.5 mailings annually to their average customer.

You can usually start the "who gets what" part of a contact strategy by analyzing customer purchases. Then develop a recency/frequency/monetary formula to identify and target your database segments. For an example of how this is done, see Chapter 19.

To be able to mail your customer list heavily, you usually need a variety of different products or services. Starcrest, which sells gifts and gadgets, offers similar merchandise under three different names: Starcrest, Signature, and Handsome Rewards. This strategy, which I call "competing with yourself," is an interesting and successful way to contact customers more often. It will be discussed further in Chapter 18.

4. SHOULD YOU BE TRYING TO GROW THE PRODUCT CATEGORY OR PENETRATE IT?

You can't determine which strategy is best for you without first understanding both the life cycle of your product or service *category* and your *product's* own life cycle. In most cases, the life cycle of the product *category* is the most important. An insurance company, for example, doesn't have to sell someone on the *need* for hospital insurance as much as it has to sell a particular policy. That's because medical insurance is an established category. But if you're promoting a product or service in a new category, such as a health maintenance organization (HMO), you need to educate your customers on what HMOs are all about. In essence, if the category is *not* established, you must first sell the category before you can sell your service.

Exhibit 5.2 illustrates the life cycle concept. A typical product has relatively low sales during the testing/introduction stage, good sales during the growth stage, and its strongest sales during maturity. But during the saturation stage sales begin to drop and then fall off rapidly as the product enters the declining stage. The challenge facing marketers is to thwart this natural cycle, keeping sales as high as possible for as long as possible.

Another challenge is to maintain a mix of products in various stages of the product life cycle. When many of a company's products are in the maturity stage, the present sales picture might look fine. But sales could drop off sharply if all the products begin to decline at the same time.

The market share your product has often dictates the strategy to follow. If your category is expanding and you just maintain your position, your sales should increase. But if your category is a mature one offering only nominal growth, you will have to get a bigger share of sales—probably by stealing someone else's share—to see significant growth. A good example is the battle now raging among credit cards and affinity cards for new customers. Because saturation levels are so high, it's a share fight, pure and simple.

Sometimes, as a category moves into a new stage of its life cycle, a company must shift strategies from growth to penetration. When the cable business was booming, Home Box Office (HBO) achieved a high level of sales by maintaining a growth strategy. Promotions sold the concept of cable TV, knowing that, as the category leader, HBO would accrue a large share of the added sales.

◆

EXHIBIT 5.2 Dotted line at right represents a marketers's job—to maintain high product sales as long as possible.

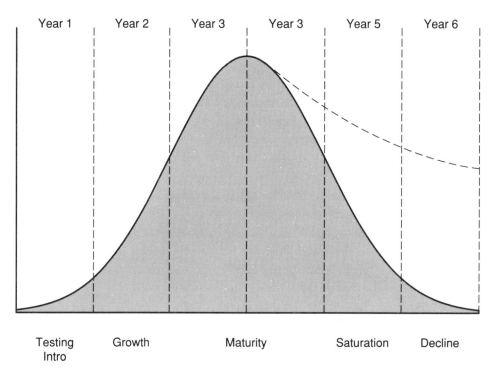

| | Year 1 | Year 2 | Year 3 | Year 3 | Year 5 | Year 6 |

Testing   Growth   Maturity   Saturation   Decline
Intro

But as the U.S. cable market began reaching maturity, HBO shifted from a growth to a penetration strategy. The company's mailings changed with its strategy. Instead of playing up the variety of cable TV programming, they focused on what HBO's premium channel had to offer. This penetration strategy paid off handsomely in continued subscriber growth.

5. HOW DO YOU POSITION AND PRICE YOUR PRODUCT OR SERVICE?

Positioning is another concept, like market share, that is more familiar to package goods firms and general advertisers than to direct marketers. But to develop a successful direct marketing strategy, you must have a clear idea of how your product or service should be positioned and priced.

Positioning helps you segment the market. For example, you may identify market niches or segments that can be better served with a flanker product or line extension than by the existing product. This may lead you to develop a deluxe version of the product or a lower price, stripped-down version, specifically for the newly-identified niche.

Bally, which initially marketed exercise equipment only to health clubs and fitness centers, cracked the consumer market by developing a lightweight model of its Lifecycle bike specially designed for use at home. The new product was priced lower and positioned quite differently from Bally's traditional product line.

The strategy you develop doesn't have to apply to a single product. It can cover your entire product line. For example, Quill became the leader in mail order sales of office products by promising low prices and big savings on all products. The company sticks with that positioning year in and year out, in mailing after mailing.

Positioning applies to the service category, too. Stockbrokers used to offer nearly identical services at nearly identical prices. But since Charles Schwab introduced discount brokerage, consumers have been able to choose among regular brokers, discount brokers, and now even deep discount brokers. Other service sectors have been similarly segmented.

Pricing strategy goes hand in hand with positioning. If you look at your full product line, there are three kinds of pricing strategies you can pursue. Like Quill, you can try for overall cost leadership. You can also price higher, as upscale products do. Or, like most direct marketers, you can offer average values coupled with good service.

Pricing strategies should be considered with care. The traditional cost-plus method of determining prices never reveals what customers might be willing to pay. It also neglects to consider questions of competition and demand. Newer pricing methods even consider the timing of price cuts as a means to discourage competition.

Exhibit 5.3 provides some general guidelines for pricing strategies.

6. CAN YOU EXPAND THE MEDIA OR DISTRIBUTION CHANNELS USED?

For a mail order firm, media play the role that stores play for other marketers who sell products through the retail channel. The latter companies know that

♦

EXHIBIT 5.3   Important factors in setting prices

PRODUCT FACTOR	HIGH PRICE WHEN:	LOW PRICE WHEN:
Type of product	Proprietary	Commodity
Production method	Labor intensive	Capital intensive
Product life	Short	Long
Product turnover	Slow	Fast
Promotion effort	Heavy	Light
Relation to other products	Little	Much
Requires support services	Many	Few
Market share	Small	Large

Source: Business Lines, June 1988.

they can't expect maximum sales if their products are only available in one to two types of stores. Yet many direct marketers arbitrarily limit their sales by restricting the media options they use.

Cincinnati Microwave has been selling radar detectors almost entirely through mail order space advertising since 1981. Even when it introduced its first new product in years, it continued to rely on space ads. By contrast, Haband has shifted a major portion of its prospecting budget from its traditional direct mail packages to space ads like the one in Exhibit 5.4.

In addition to expanding their media options, many direct marketers have added retail distribution to their marketing efforts in the last ten years. Overall, retail accounts for roughly 20 times the sales volume of mail order. For mature catalogers like Sharper Image, Talbots, and Eddie Bauer, retail sales now surpass mail order sales. These catalogers have recognized the fact that large numbers of consumers will never be converted to buying by mail. Retail distribution also allows them to test and sell many more items. A typical Sharper Image store carries about 450 products—almost three times the 160 items offered in its catalog.

Some traditional retailers have also built strong catalog businesses, most notably Neiman-Marcus, Bloomingdale's by Mail, and Saks Fifth Avenue. And experience is proving that dual distribution of retail and mail order is the best way to maximize sales from the customer base.

EXHIBIT 5.4   Haband prospecting ad

An even newer trend is "channel integration." Traditional retailers are adding direct marketing methods to better serve their customers. Florsheim Shoes, for example, has installed interactive video terminals in its stores (see Exhibit 5.5). If the store inventory doesn't have the exact style, size, and color shoes a customer wants, they can be home-delivered in a couple of days from a central distribution center. Other major retailers are testing self-contained video kiosks and projecting major growth for them.

7. SHOULD YOU TRY TO ADD NEW PRODUCTS, DEVELOP NEW MARKETS, OR LAUNCH NEW BUSINESSES?

All three of these options are somewhat risky, but most firms have to explore one or more to maximize long-term growth. So it's largely a question of *which* makes most sense for your company.

Obviously, it's easier for a cataloger or retailer to add new *products* than it is for a manufacturer. Start-up manufacturing costs are expensive, especially when you consider that the majority of new products are not successful. Even so, developing a new product is usually less risky, less time-consuming, and requires less of an investment than launching a new business.

Ace Pecan is a medium-size firm in the nut business that competes at retail with firms like Planters and Fisher Nuts. It built its mail order business by selling gourmet nuts through solo mailings. When Ace Pecan expanded from solo mailings to a catalog, it successfully added other snack products, ranging from candy to cheese. It was a lot easier to make a few cheese pages pay out than launching a cheese-by-mail business.

When you're contemplating adding new products or services, a key consideration is whether or not they work off your existing database. This and other new product issues are discussed in Chapter 18.

But what about new *markets*? They can usually be tested less expensively than by launching new products or businesses. Often you can do the test with an existing product and control mailing.

But sometimes a new product model may be required to really tap the potential of a different market segment. As pointed out earlier, Bally developed a completely new model of its Lifecycle exercise bike to penetrate the consumer market. Other times you can use an existing product to explore new markets,

EXHIBIT 5.5 Florsheim's interactive video terminals let customers order shoes in their exact style, size, and color—even if the store is out of them.

but need a new ad or mailing. Let's say you have a health newsletter that's being sold to consumers and you want to try offering group subscriptions to businesses. You will probably have to develop a new mailing package that emphasizes the benefits of healthier employees, otherwise you're not giving this large market a fair chance to pay out.

Catalogers can explore new markets with spin-off catalogs featuring merchandise that is somewhat different from products carried in their core catalog. A database detailing information about customers and their purchase history can help you identify product categories for a specialty catalog.

By adding a few casual clothing items to its catalog of gardening tools, Smith & Hawken was able to test the waters for an apparel business before committing itself to a separate catalog. The carefully selected and designed clothing turned out to be highly appealing to Smith & Hawken's customers. So the company started a new clothing catalog, which turned profits soon after it was launched.

Adding new *businesses* is the final and most expensive means of growth available to direct marketers. Start-ups, joint ventures, and acquisitions are all costly. But if you can afford the risk, the rewards can be great. Naturally, any expansion in this area should fit the firm's mission statement and strategic plan. And you can reduce your risk with careful planning, adequate lead time, and research.

IS YOUR ADVERTISING EXECUTION CONSISTENT WITH YOUR MARKETING STRATEGY?

This is not as much a strategic planning issue as it is a "checkpoint" question. It's one that almost every direct marketer I know would like to respond "yes" to—but I've found it's dangerously easy to let creative executions lead you in different, wasteful directions that depart from your strategy.

A photofinisher, for example, may want to promote a quality image. But that would be inconsistent with a deal-oriented business. It sends confusing signals to the consumer. That's why virtually all mail order photofinishers provide such promotion-oriented envelopes to send in your film.

WHAT IS THE RIGHT STRATEGY FOR YOU?

ALL SEVEN OF THE STRATEGIC alternatives we reviewed require an investment of time and resources. How you allocate your time and resources among them will determine how well you can optimize your growth.

The strategies you adopt should be fluid enough to shift with competitive changes in your marketplace. And that brings us back to strategic planning basics. There's no substitute for a comprehensive situation analysis and a focused mission statement. Solid, thorough assessment of your company's strengths, weaknesses, position, and plans will help you determine which strategies will pay off best for you.

THE LAST WORD ON MARKETING STRATEGY

STRATEGIC PLANNING IS A MARVELOUS tool, but keep in mind that the purpose of planning is to create success in the marketplace, not thick planning books. A strategic plan is not just a projection of *where* your company expects to be at the end of a given period of time; it should be an action plan that tells *how* you intend to get there. As Kentucky Fried Chicken chairman, Richard Mayer, has pointed out, a strategic plan that doesn't include action steps isn't a plan at all. It's only a wish book.

6

DIRECT MARKETING'S TESTING LABORATORY

♦

IT'S ESTIMATED THAT GENERAL advertisers spend over $1 billion a year for research and copy testing to find out which ad or TV commercial *might* move the most merchandise. But they are forced to rely largely on assumptions such as: The TV spot that gets the highest test score will sell the most goods; or most of the people who *say* they'll buy a product will actually do so. Assumptions like these often don't hold up in the marketplace.

Perhaps the one unique thing about direct marketing is its ability to scientifically test different ideas and approaches to find out what works best. Not by measuring opinions. Or readership. Or promises. But by counting the actual orders received.

Even direct marketing professionals with years of experience have difficulty predicting exactly what will strike the consumer's fancy. This point was really driven home to me early in my agency career when I put together a panel session on testing for a Direct Marketing Association conference. My fellow panelists and I presented eight testing case histories, using slides to show the mailing packages or ads that were split-tested. Each member of the audience had a scoresheet so he or she could pick his or her favorite before the results were revealed.

When we finished not a single one of the 400 direct marketing pros in the audience had picked more than six of the eight test winners! But somebody had correctly picked all eight winners, namely, the consumers who had voted by sending in their respective reply cards and coupons.

That, of course, is why advertisers invest money in testing. Nobody can consistently predict how the consumer will react to specific products, selling methods, and creative approaches. Some tests turn out as you hope and expect they will. Others may be disappointing, but you still learn something. Before looking at the major areas to test, let's consider the basics for a solid testing program.

♦

EIGHT TESTING GROUND RULES

1. TEST A SINGLE ELEMENT OR A COMPLETELY DIFFERENT APPROACH   These are the two main ways to get meaningful test results. First, you can test a single element or variable in your ad or mailing package. One letter against another, for example. Or one ad headline against another. If all the other elements of your ad or mailing remain the same, you know any difference in results can be attributed to the one element you changed, such as the letter or the ad headline.

On the other hand, you can test two completely different ads or mailing packages against each other. In this case, you won't know exactly which element accounted for the difference in results. But you do know which ad or mailing package did best. By testing two completely different approaches, you stand a greater chance for a substantial difference in results.

So, when you're launching a new program or looking for breakthroughs, it's usually best to concentrate your testing on completely different approaches. Once you have a winning ad or mailing package, it often pays to test its individual components. In so doing, you isolate what's making the difference and find ways to further improve results or reduce costs.

2. BE PREPARED TO RECORD TEST RESULTS   By assigning each ad or mailing package a separate key number, you have the mechanism to record responses and measure test results. In direct mail, the key number can appear anywhere on your reply card or order form. For space advertising, the number is often buried in a corner of the coupon. You can also work it into your return address, such as assigning a different department number or phone number for each effort.

A key number can be strictly numerical, such as Dept. 204. Or it can be a functional abbreviation, such as WSJ827 to stand for a *Wall Street Journal* insertion of August 27. How you do it isn't important. But keeping a master record is.

3. WORK ON THE "BEAT THE CHAMP" PRINCIPLE   In sports activities, a new champion is never crowned until the old one is counted out. Smart direct marketers operate the same way. Their most successful current mailing package or ad is considered the champ. This is the "control" mailing or ad against which all

new approaches are tested. They continue to use the control, without making any significant changes, so long as it keeps working.

In general advertising, an ad or campaign is often changed when the agency or client gets tired of it. In direct response advertising, a successful control is often continued for years, until it wears out or you find a new approach that beats it.

4. MAKE SURE YOUR TESTS ARE STATISTICALLY VALID Each portion of the test should be large enough to be meaningful. You can use probability tables to determine accurately the mailing quantity or ad circulation required. In addition, the list for each part of the test must be selected on the same random basis. Thanks to the fact that all large lists are maintained on computers, this is relatively simple. Moreover, all test mailing pieces should be mailed at the same time, and all test ads should appear in the same issue. To put it another way, all test cells should reach the target audience at the same time. Otherwise, you introduce another variable—timing—that can affect test results.

5. ANALYZE YOUR RESULTS CAREFULLY If you sell by mail, it's important to measure results based on the "net" dollar return. With a mailing, for example, you should take into account such cost factors and variables as the quantity mailed, production cost of each mailing package, products and premiums, fulfillment expense, and collections. Likewise, if you use lead-getting advertising, look beyond the number of inquiries produced. Your analysis should include the conversions or actual sales that result from each lead-getting effort. Experience has shown that it's a good idea to track all future transactions with a customer by the original key number or source code. This way you can measure the long-range value of a customer and see if one approach attracts better repeat buyers than another. It's also valuable to do a written report after each test to summarize the objective, test plan, results, and action taken (see Exhibit 6.1). As time goes by, these can become extremely valuable reference tools.

6. TEST FOR YOURSELF It's nice to learn what you can from the testing experience of others. But don't assume someone else's results will turn out the same way for your market, your product, and your offer. It's better to test for yourself—and find out. I've seen numerous examples where direct marketers have

◆

EXHIBIT 6.1 Written test report

```
                                                              TEST REPORT
                                                                 NO.
                                                                  27

October 1, 1991

GENERAL DESCRIPTION

A continuation test of the Standard Life Inquiry offer vs. a Life Inquiry mailing offering
a magnifying glass as a premium gift to inquirers.

PURPOSE

To confirm with more statistically valid quantities the fact that the premium offer
results in a lower cost per conversion -- at the same time supplying additional quantities
of inquiry names for later solicitation on other offers.

COMPONENTS

Standard:  E747, DP L853, DP:  1N40

Magnifying Glass Premium Offer:  E747, DP:  L853, DP:  1N100

MAILING PLAN

Released from Albany in September and October of 1992 to OA-1 Remails in states as they
are available.

STATISTICAL DATA

This is a $2,000 Golden Eagle Life Inquiry with the same test costs as the standard except
there is an 80¢ additional charge per inquiry.

RESULTS

Description    #Mailed    #Inq    P/M    #App    P/M    #Conv.    C/M    Conv/Sale

Standard Inq.   888.                                                        88.8

Mag. Glass Inq. 888.                                                        88.8

ANALYSIS

The magnifying glass premium produced almost 5 times as many inquiries as the standard
inquiry offer without a premium.  However, that's all it did was produce lots of
inquiries -- very few applications  The relative response rate of the results was so poor
as not to justify the cost of the premium.

ACTION

No further action is warranted.
```

tried to knock off or copy a competitor's successful mailing, and for some reason, it doesn't work for them.

7. Don't Think Test Results Are Forever Just because something worked best for you five years ago or even two years ago doesn't mean it's best today. Your market changes from year to year even if your product or service doesn't. Important elements of your ads or mailings should be retested regularly. Especially those that are being used in volume and can represent substantial result improvements or cost reductions.

8. Finally, avoid the disease of overtesting   Some direct response advertisers get carried away with what's known as "trivia testing." They test one envelope color versus another. Or they test whether underscoring certain words in a headline improves response. What's wrong with testing these things? They generally make a very minor difference in results. So, unless you mail millions of pieces or run space with very large circulation, the minor difference won't amount to much. There are so many bigger or more important factors that should be tested instead.

Major Areas to Test

If you want to learn some meaningful things by testing, you have to concentrate on testing meaningful points. Things like pricing and payment options, offers and premiums, formats and copy. Let's consider each of these areas individually and look at a few actual testing examples to show how significant they can be in affecting results.

Pricing and Payment Option Tests

When you are launching any new product or service being sold by mail, it's important to test a variety of prices. It's not uncommon to find one of the higher prices pays out best.

Example: A 293-page business manual was launched with a three-way price test—$59.95, $79.95, and $99.95. The $59.95 price pulled the most responses. However, the second highest price—$79.95—was the most profitable in terms of the net dollar payout.

Pricing is also important on sample offers, and the results can be completely different depending on the product and market involved.

Example: On a product sample offer to fund-raising groups, a $1.00 offer pulled 58 percent better than asking $5.00 for the sample. On a product sample offer to business firms, however, a $2.00 offer helped establish the value of the product and actually produced more responses than a free offer.

Also important are the payment options under which a product or service is offered—cash, bill me, or charge card privileges. For instance, you would naturally expect a bill-me offer to produce more response than a cash offer. But exactly how much better do you think it might do?

Example: A bill-me offer will usually do about twice as well as the same item offered only on a cash basis. Even on an inexpensive $19.95 item, I've seen a bill-me offer do 77 percent better than a cash offer. (After taking bad debts and collection costs into account, it was still much more profitable.)

Offer and Premium Tests

The product and pricing you establish are often considered to be your main offer. But there's a lot you can do to sweeten that offer by the use of premiums, sweepstakes, or other incentives. Premiums alone provide plenty of testing opportunities. And a good premium need not be expensive.

Example: A 50¢ package of flower seeds, offered as a bonus with the first volume in a set of gardening books, boosted response by 42 percent. On a $50.00 item being offered to business firms, a premium costing less than $1.00 caused a 20 percent improvement in results.

While a premium offer will almost always do better than no premium, it's important to realize that a good premium will work a lot better than a poor one. This is an area that's often overlooked in testing but one that certainly bears exploration.

Example: On a mailing to PTA groups, three different premiums were split-tested. All had been carefully chosen to tie in with the known interests of the audience. Yet results showed that the most attractive premium offer did 51 percent better than the least attractive item. And the winning premium in this case happened to be the least expensive one!

Formats

Next to the offer, the physical format of your ad or mailing is one of the most important areas for testing. Do you use a No. 10 envelope, a 6 × 9, or a 9 × 12 size? Should you use two-color printing or four-color? Do you run a full-page ad with coupon or use a bind-in reply card? For example, take a personalized letter. The same basic copy approach with the addition of laser personalization can often boost your response by 25 percent or more. Likewise for adding a bind-in card to a full-page ad. Even though your costs can be two to three times higher, your results can be more than four times greater.

COPY TESTING

We've talked about testing pricing, offers, and formats. What about *copy,* which many think of as the heart of an ad or mailing package? Copy, too, is certainly worth testing, especially headlines and letter copy. One of my favorite examples concerns two letters that were tested in selling a home organ by mail. The first letter presented the product story and features in a good, professional way. It was well written and covered all the bases. The second letter differed in only one respect. About a third of the copy was devoted to explaining how much each member of the family would benefit from having this musical instrument in the home—the father, mother, and children. The writer felt it would be easier to sell this expensive product if the prospect could visualize the whole family enjoying it. As you may have guessed, the second letter did better—34 percent better, in fact.

There's an important message hidden here about copy testing. The second letter wasn't written any better than the first one. But there was a "big idea" behind the copy that made it more successful. So, when you get involved in copy testing, be sure to test copy that's based on completely different ideas or approaches.

If your budget permits you to test a number of copy approaches, it's not a bad idea to include one that might be considered "way out." An unusual or offbeat copy approach sometimes produces a real breakthrough.

PUTTING IT ALL TOGETHER

If you believe you're ready to go into business and open up your own testing laboratory, wait a moment! One other important principle is needed to maximize your testing success. The best way to realize how important it can be is to look back at the examples we've just covered. We've seen price and payment options that have improved results by 77 percent, premium offers that boosted results by 51 percent, format and copy tests that boosted results by 34 percent. The important thing is to do some testing in as many of these areas as you can, and then put the pieces together to really parlay your success.

Example: A mailing program for an association soliciting membership called for a variety of testing. An invitation format did 26 percent better than a standard 6 × 9 mailing package. An inexpensive premium boosted response by 49 percent over a non-premium offer. And the best letter copy accounted for a 32 percent increase. When the best format, offer, and copy were combined, the new mailing package substantially boosted response! The result was a very profitable mailing.

HOW TO TEST A NEW VENTURE

IN MAKING THE FIRST TEST OF A new venture, some direct marketers make the mistake of trying to test as inexpensively as possible. More often than not, the result is a small test that produces poor results. Little if anything is learned from such a test, for you don't know if the same product or service might have been a winner with the right test approach. So your first goal in testing a new venture is to have a soundly constructed test program that will get you some definite answers on whether your proposition has potential drawing power.

If you launch a new venture with a direct mail test, your testing should be concentrated on the two factors that have the most significant impact on results—lists and offers. With a sound test plan, I've found you can usually get the answers you want with a mailing program of 50,000 to 100,000 pieces.

Let's suppose you're a manufacturer of microscopes. You have a microscope starter kit for the educational market. And you want to see if you can use direct marketing to sell to grammar schools. You know that microscopes are not widely used in grammar schools. You believe, however, that the key buying influences are principals and fourth through sixth grade teachers.

The basic offers you believe to be most important are the sale of a single kit at $79.95, a classroom kit with enough microscopes and lesson material for an average size class, a free gift offer, and a ten percent educational discount.

THE TEST MATRIX

The test matrix you develop (see Exhibit 6.2) allows you to test all these variables with a single mailing of 50,000 pieces. This is what I call an *unbalanced* test matrix. It isn't necessary to test every offer to every list segment, as you would do with a balanced test matrix.

EXHIBIT 6.2   Microscope test matrix

LIST	Offer A	Offer B	Offer C	Offer D	TOTAL
4th Grade Teachers	5,000 Key 101A				5,000
5th Grade Teachers	5,000 Key 102A	5,000 Key 102B	5,000 Key 102C	5,000 Key 102D	20,000
6th Grade Teachers	5,000 Key 103A				5,000
Principals	5,000 Key 104A	5,000 Key 104B	5,000 Key 104C	5,000 Key 104D	20,000
TOTALS	20,000	10,000	10,000	10,000	50,000

Offer A - Single Kit
Offer B - Classroom Kit

Offer C - Free Gift
Offer D - 10% Discount

If you study the matrix, you will see it includes four list segments and four offers with ten test cells, each assigned a separate key number. Instead of mailing all four offers to every list segment—which would require mailing an additional 30,000 pieces—you have concentrated the test quantities in the areas you think are most likely to work. And you can extrapolate the results for the other areas.

Let's say, for example, that fourth grade teachers prove to be the best list segment and the free gift is the strongest offer. You didn't test the free gift to fourth grade teachers. But when mailed to the fifth grade teachers, the free gift offer did 18 percent better than the non-gift offer; to principals, it did 23 percent better. You can safely assume that the free gift will work about 20 percent better when mailed to fourth grade teachers.

Naturally, it would be great if every test cell produced results at break-even or better and it was simply a question of which area was most profitable.

But it's much more likely for a test matrix like this to produce some profitable cells and some unprofitable ones. And that's why you want the test to be big enough to uncover the areas that can prove profitable.

THE TEST STRATEGY STATEMENT

Tests can become quite complicated. And, because they often entail minor changes in ads or mailing packages, there is plenty of opportunity for errors in test execution.

It's a good idea to write up your test strategy showing the objective of each test and explaining how it will be executed. Then make sure every one concerned gets a copy of your test plan. The chart in Exhibit 6.3 shows how the microscope kit mailing could be summarized.

CONFIRMATION TESTING

Once testing shows your new venture can succeed, it's time to do confirmation testing. This stage can confirm the results of the initial areas that showed promise, with larger quantities, and test important options not included the first time around. For example, the microscope kit company might try to expand its audience potential by testing lists that reach curriculum coordinators or PTA groups who might like to buy the kits for their schools. Or it might test other free gift offers.

When you retest, you naturally expand the test to a bigger universe. As a rule of thumb, most marketers believe you shouldn't expand a test more than five to ten times the quantity you originally tested. If your universe is bigger than that, you use it up in chunks or stages. I call this the *safety expansion factor*—and adhering to it can spare you some expensive mistakes.

WHAT TO TEST ON A PROVEN VENTURE

WHILE EARLY MARKET TESTS SHOULD concentrate on the "best shot" options that can make or break a new venture, there are still plenty of things to test on an established product or program. This stage includes continual refinement testing to improve response or reduce costs. You are always trying to learn better ways

EXHIBIT 6.3   Test strategy statement

KG&P

KOBS, GREGORY & PASSAVANT, INC.
225 N. Michigan Avenue, Chicago, Illinois 60601
(312) 819-2300

Test Strategy Statement

client: ABC COMPANY

project: Microscope Mailing

TEST	OBJECTIVES	METHOD
Single Kit	To test the potential of the grammar school market, and provide a benchmark against which other offers can be measured.	Develop basic mailing package ... including 6 x 9 outer envelope, 2-page letter, brochure, and order card.
Classroom Kit	To increase the average order and profitability by offering a larger kit with enough micro-scopes and lesson material for an average size class.	Change main brochure illustration to show classroom kit. Describe kit fully in letter, and change order card to include price and details of classroom kit.
Free Gift Offer	To improve response by offering a free gift. Gift will be an attractive poster showing magnified illustrations as if seen through a microscope.	Add 5 1/2 x 8 1/2 gift slip to the package. Mention free gift in P.S. on the letter, and add to order card description of the offer.
10% Educational Discount	To determine whether a discount will be more effective than the single kit at full price or the free gift offer.	Play up discount in the price area of brochure and letter. Also emphasize the discount on the order card.

to market your product. Again, the manufacturer of microscope kits can experiment with a number of factors, including:

◆ Testing private schools versus public schools.

◆ Testing different payment options.

◆ Testing "looser" offers to marginal list segments.

◆ Testing new copy approaches.

◆ Testing a more elaborate mailing package that includes a sample lesson.

◆ Testing a lower cost or "stripped-down" package with a smaller outer envelope and/or a less expensive brochure.

◆ Testing a four-color brochure vs. a two-color one.

◆ Testing a personalized letter vs. "Dear Professional."

◆ Back-end tests to stimulate reorders after the initial shipment.

How to Test Lists

NATURALLY, YOUR OBJECTIVE IS TO come up with enough profitable lists to reach the maximum universe that can be successfully mailed for your product or service. It's usually best to test a variety of logical list types or categories. And, when you find a successful list, test as many similar ones as you can find.

Many direct marketers have their own pet theories for list testing. But let's look at the guidelines used by a leading list user and a leading list broker.

The list user is Old American Insurance Company. The firm's written guidelines for list testing and continuation include:

> 1. Always test the "presumed" best segment of the list first, such as hot line buyers or buyers rather than inquiries.
>
> 2. Use selectivity factors that have proven successful on other mailings for this same policy, such as sex and state selection.
>
> 3. If the initial test of 10,000 pieces projects acceptable results, reorder 50,000 pieces. If still acceptable, order the entire list.
>
> 4. Reorder additional names on a successful list as they become available, and try to remail a successful list every six months.
>
> 5. Test other segments of a successful list. If appealing to buyers works, try the inquiries. If soliciting one-year-old buyers works, try two-year-old names.
>
> 6. Test a successful list for other suitable policies.

The broker is Dependable Lists, Inc. In a booklet, *How to Test a Mailing List,* the firm suggests that you always mail one or more proven lists at the same time you do list testing to get comparative results.

Knowing what to do about a list that's a real winner or a real loser is no problem. But when your results are marginal, at or near breakeven, list evaluation can be a problem. Dependable Lists wisely points out that a marginal list probably includes some profitable and some unprofitable segments. Before discarding the list, you should see if there is some way to increase response by changing the selectivity you used. You may end up with a smaller list but one that is well worth mailing.

◆

How to Test Space and Broadcast

While the media are different, you can apply some of the same principles used for testing lists. Start with areas most likely to work and then expand the areas that are successful, as the pyramid testing structure in Exhibit 6.4 illustrates.

Magazines Pick the magazine categories that are most likely to work for your product or service, such as sports, women's service, shelter magazines, etc. Certain magazines seem to have a special mail order or direct response character. So it usually makes sense to start off with the strongest direct response publication in each category, the one that carries the most direct response advertising. In some cases, you can keep your test costs down by buying only a regional edition. Or you can run an A/B split test, where two ads are alternated in every other copy of the same issue.

Newspapers Select at least three to five markets for a good test and use the leading paper in each market. A/B split tests are rarely available except in the case of free standing inserts. If you want to test two or more inserts that are the same size and format, you can have the printer "shuffle" them so they will arrive at the paper pre-mixed. Experience has shown that this is much more reliable than sending the paper two different inserts and leaving it to them to give you an accurate split test.

Radio and television Here, too, it's usually best to select three to five proven markets for a good test. You normally try to mix different market sizes and geographic areas. Care should be used to select the right stations and time buys for your direct response offer. It is virtually impossible to test different spots in the same market and get meaningful results, which is one of the limitations of broadcast testing you have to live with.

Dry Testing and the FTC

On a new venture, direct marketing firms must choose between *wet testing,* in which the product is produced and fulfilled, and *dry testing,* where a product is advertised before going into production, and in fact, is only produced if the test results warrant it.

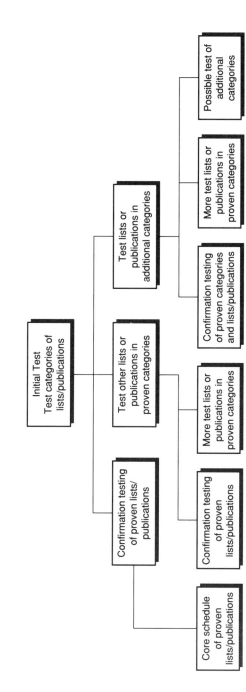

EXHIBIT 6.4 Pyramid testing structure has *Test Stage* at top, *Confirmation Stage* at second level, and *Roll-Out Phase* at bottom.

♦

Naturally, dry testing can offer attractive financial savings. And over the years this technique has been widely used in the publishing field. Before there were FTC guidelines, a publisher could avoid making a heavy investment in editorial and book production by simply spending the amount necessary to run an ad or mailing. The order form was designed to seek actual orders, not opinions of whether somebody might buy. To avoid "biasing the test," the copy never mentioned that the books weren't yet available or might never be produced.

But back in the seventies, the Federal Trade Commission issued an advisory opinion on dry testing. The FTC does not object to this method of testing, provided that:

> ♦ No representations are made to mislead the public that the books have been or definitely will be published.
>
> ♦ Adequate notice of the conditional nature of the publication is made.
>
> ♦ If the books aren't published, notice should be given to those who subscribed within four months.
>
> ♦ There is no substitute of other books for those ordered.

These disclosures naturally depress results somewhat, but still provide the opportunity to test new products and services inexpensively.

The Testing of Seasonal Propositions

If your results vary from month to month throughout the year, as they do for most direct marketers, it's naturally best to concentrate your testing in your strongest season. This is when you can expect the best test results. And, because you are probably promoting heavily at that time of the year, you can easily measure new mailing packages or lists against your control package and your proven lists.

However, you can also test safely at other times of the year. *Provided* you know what differences in results to expect. For example, let's say January is your best month, as it is for most direct marketing offers. For various reasons you want to make some tests in June.

You do your mailing and it pulls an even two percent, but your breakeven is two and a half percent. Using your historic figures, you know that if January results are rated at 100 percent, your June results are usually 67 percent. So January is normally half again better. You can confidently expect to mail in January and do about 50 percent better, which would mean a profitable response of three percent.

PROBABILITIES AND REALISTIC TEST SIZES

ONE OF THE AGE-OLD QUESTIONS IN direct response advertising is, "How large should a test be?" If you test too large a quantity, you spend more than is necessary to obtain reliable test results. And too small a quantity wastes money because you can't have much confidence in the numbers.

Probability tables can provide a scientific approach to minimizing your testing risk. One of the best explanations I've seen on the subject appears in a booklet called *Computing Probabilities,* published by Alan Drey Company, a leading list broker. The booklet likens direct marketing probabilities to tossing a coin. Just as there are only two ways a coin can land—heads or tails—only two things can happen to your reply card. It either comes back or it doesn't.

Probability tables are based on statistical formulas that take into account the relationship of *confidence* (how sure you can be that your test results are valid), *the limit of error* (how close your next results should be to the test results), *the sample size* (number of coins tossed or mailing pieces observed), and *the expected response* (the number of orders or inquiries).

Most direct marketers work with a probability table that has a 95 percent confidence level. In other words, 95 percent of the time, the results from a follow-up mailing or ad should fall within a prescribed range of the test results, for example, plus or minus two-tenths of a percent.

But experienced direct marketers also know there are times when the quantities called for by probability tables simply aren't realistic. You may find, for instance, that the tables call for mailing eighty thousand pieces on each side of a test. With many budgets, that just isn't realistic.

But even if it isn't practical to follow probability tables for all your testing, I strongly recommend you become familiar with them. Then work out test sizes you can live with. As an example, here are the guidelines one large publisher uses for testing: mailing package tests—10,000 to 25,000 pieces; price tests—50,000 to 100,000 pieces; and list tests—5000 pieces.

When Is a Test Really Over?

THE SOONER YOU KNOW WHETHER your test has worked or failed, the sooner you can decide whether to roll-out or abandon further testing. Instead of waiting for every order to trickle in, direct marketers have developed response curves that can predict future replies long before they arrive. For example, direct mail responses are usually heaviest on Mondays, and that day normally brings about half of the total weekly orders.

One formula that usually works for me says that 50 percent of all mail responses will be received in the two week period starting with your first order (not two weeks after your mail drop). By doubling the first two weeks' response, you should have a pretty good idea of what the final results will be, and can act accordingly. This "half-life" formula (shown in Exhibit 6.5) applies to solo mailings more than catalogs, which have a longer or slower response rate. In any case, you should still track orders on a daily basis and analyze them when they're complete to develop your own company's response curve.

Improving Your Testing Program

I'VE ALWAYS BELIEVED THAT MOST direct marketing firms don't do as much testing as they should. And they don't spend enough time studying and analyzing test results. Let's see how these two areas can be improved.

First of all, testing can be expensive, and this no doubt discourages many advertisers from doing more of it. As was mentioned earlier, a direct marketing firm should regard testing the same way a manufacturing firm views research and development. You invest money in testing or R&D to learn something for the future.

EXHIBIT 6.5   The "half-life" formula applied to a ten-week lead-generation mailing

WEEK #	% TOTAL LEADS	CUMULATIVE %
1	5%	
2	42%	47
3	28%	75
4	11%	86
5	5%	91
6	3%	94
7	2%	96
8	2%	98
9	1%	99
10	1%	100
TOTAL	100%	

A manufacturing firm I worked with spends almost ten percent of its sales dollars on R&D. The firm has achieved sales leadership in its field by introducing innovative products with unique features and benefits.

One way for direct marketing firms to put more emphasis on testing is to allocate a definite percentage of their budget for this purpose. Stan Rapp, cofounder of Rapp Collins Marcoa calls this a self-renewing testing budget. He knows that a sound testing program will usually improve results, and that the increased profits can offset what was spent on the test. So the testing budget continues to renew itself.

When it comes to analyzing test results, it's easy to look at the bottom line and make a quick judgment on what worked best. You can get a lot more out of your testing budget, however, if you creatively analyze the results. For example, one large client I know has an eight-member creative group that meets monthly to discuss all current test results. The actual mailing samples or ads are reviewed, along with the figures. Each test is individually discussed. From those discussions come many ideas for new creative approaches, marketing strategies, and additional testing.

Obviously, you can't expect all your tests to wind up as big winners. If you test wisely, however, you build up a tremendous amount of knowledge that's bound to increase your sales and profits.

♦

THE LAST WORD ON TESTING

THE GOAL OF ANY TEST IS TO ROLL out a direct marketing campaign that will achieve desired profit objectives. But keep in mind that with direct mail, list results are often off about five percent in a continuation or roll-out mailing. Sometimes internal duplication that can't be detected by a service bureau—such as the use of a married name one time, a maiden name another—throws off response. Another main reason is that conditions will have changed since the test was made. Economic conditions may have improved or worsened; the mailing date may be in a different season; or there may have been some competitive promotion in the interim.

But even assuming some drop-off in response, roll-outs have a lot going for them. By now, most of your development costs have been paid. You're concentrating on proven media and winning creative. And in the case of direct mail, you're buying printing and mailing services at volume prices, so naturally you can expect your roll-out campaigns to perform much better than any test program.

7

Effective Use of Research

♦

RESEARCH IS A VALUABLE TOOL. But direct marketers were not quick to adopt it.

They grew up with testing as a built-in research mechanism. Their tests showed them whether people actually responded to a given offer or copy approach . . . not how they *said* they would respond.

While traditional testing is a form of behavioral research, it also has its limitations. When we test package A versus package B, sure, we find out which works better. But we don't find out *why*. And we really don't learn much about the non-responders to help us sell them the next time around.

I'm happy to report that the old attitudes about research have changed. Because today's sophisticated direct marketers understand that research techniques used by consumer marketers for years are relevant to direct marketing, and they use research regularly.

Quantitative or Qualitative?

IN ITS SIMPLEST TERMS, research is a tool for learning and decision-making. It's used for learning facts and opinions about your company, your customers and prospects, your products, and your advertising. Different types of research can help uncover those facts and opinions.

Qualitative research uses open-ended probing to generate consumer viewpoints and opinions. The results are not considered statistically valid, because the audience sample is so small. But you can get valuable indications of customers' needs and attitudes, as well as product strengths, weaknesses, and problems. Their reactions can help you weed out weak ideas, and fine-tune good ones.

The most popular qualitative method is the focus group, which offers group discussion of a topic. Participants are carefully screened and paid a nominal fee for attending. The discussion is led by a trained researcher. By comparison, in-depth interviews work well when group interaction is not necessary or detailed individual reactions are required.

Quantitative research involves enough people or interviews to ensure that results are statistically valid. Techniques like phone calls, door-to-door surveys, mail questionnaires and street or shopping mall "intercepts" are useful for confirming that a concept or approach is good or bad. By using a larger and randomly-selected sample size, you can rely on the results.

Just about every research technique falls into one of these two categories. You'll probably find yourself using both. For example, in researching a new product, you can use focus groups to uncover important issues and theories. Then you can follow up with quantitative research to put meaningful numbers behind your theories.

SIMULATOR RESEARCH

This quantitative technique, which is often used by insurance direct marketers, is somewhat like dry testing. Let's say you have an idea for a new insurance product. Instead of finalizing the product and getting it approved by various state insurance commissioners, you create a test mailing to sell it. It's just like a normal mailing except a questionnaire takes the place of the application or order form, and asks consumers to rate their likelihood of purchase.

With experience, you'll be able to predict response. But interpret your test results carefully—the "would buy" answers can run as much as ten times the response rate you'll get when the policy is actually offered for sale.

IMPROVING THE SUCCESS RATE OF NEW AND OLD PRODUCTS

RESEARCH IS OFTEN CONDUCTED to discover whether a contemplated new product will succeed in the marketplace. It can help you understand the "big picture"— the market, consumer attitude trends, and product opportunities. Published secondary research is an inexpensive, preliminary way to monitor competitive products. Questionnaires and focus groups with your own customers can help you discover what consumers think about proposed product features, and how those features influence their buying decisions.

Product concept testing, long used by *Reader's Digest,* is a good example. A survey sent to a couple of thousand present customers describes several possible products—some established, most new—and asks readers to evaluate their likelihood to buy using a simple scoring system. The consumers' ratings of the new products can then be evaluated, using their scores on the established products as benchmarks. This can not only indicate a product's likelihood for success, but suggest modifications that could improve its chances in the marketplace.

Research can also improve results of existing products. One direct marketing firm I know enjoyed a consistent 15 percent sales increase for about 10 straight years. Then some new competition came on the scene, and sales dropped 30 percent. Product research was undertaken to compare the firm's product with the competitor's. The study showed clearly that the competitor had three unique features which were highly favored by consumers. These features, plus two others that consumers had rated highly, were adopted. As a result, sales shot up 40 percent the following year.

LEARNING MORE ABOUT YOUR MARKET

MARKET SEGMENTATION RESEARCH can help you determine who makes up your market and how you can best appeal to them. This type of research gathers demographic and psychographic information about your customers and prospects. How old are your customers, and how much do they make? Are they trend-setters, or are they conservative? Are they single, married, or parents? Valuable insights can also be revealed by responder/nonresponder research, which compares people from the same mailing list or publication to see how they differ. As Peter Drucker notes, "Only by asking the customer, by watching him, by trying to understand his behavior, can one find out who he is, what he does, how he buys, how he uses what he buys, and what he expects."

I'm often amazed to discover established direct marketing firms that don't have any profile information on their customers. They think they know who their buyers are, but have no hard data to back up their beliefs. Yet this is one of the most inexpensive types of research because it can usually be done with a mailed survey to a small, random sample of the customer file. More extensive surveys can compare active and moderately active customers to passive or former

♦

customers to determine their demographic and attitudinal differences. The results can be used to target special offers or promotional material to the most receptive portions of a house list.

Improving Your Advertising Message

Promotional materials research can indicate which copy or design elements of envelopes, brochures, or ads consumers respond to most favorably. It can tell how they rate your pieces compared to those of competitors. And it can help determine whether the message that seemed perfectly clear when it came out of your creative department makes any sense at all to your prospective customers.

All of these elements can be researched through qualitative techniques that let you test advertising concepts long before you commit to a creative execution, or quantitative techniques that let you evaluate creative alternatives.

Benefit ranking lets you determine which product or service benefit to emphasize in your creative execution. One example is the "Promise Laboratory" developed by direct marketing research specialists at Goldring and Company. Goldring uses focus groups to develop up to 30 promises or benefits for a product or service. In subsequent mail interviews, target market consumers evaluate the strength, appeal, and believability of each promise.

Kinder-Care Learning Centers has used benefit ranking to improve an already successful control mailing piece. After research on the day-care category showed what parents are most concerned about, Kinder-Care developed a new package that incorporated the five top-rated benefits into its creative (see Exhibit 7.1). By playing up what was most important to parents, the new mailing pulled twice as well as the control.

When it's time to interpret your results, trained researchers can help you distinguish between *real* and *pretender* benefits. Miller Brewing Company centered its first Lite Beer campaign around Lite's low calorie content, which in preliminary research men had said was an important benefit. But the campaign turned off the "macho" guys who traditionally are the heaviest beer consumers. More research convinced Miller to switch to "less-filling"—a benefit that suggests heavy beer drinkers can consume even more. Sales immediately took off and it became one of the longest-running ad campaigns in history.

EXHIBIT 7.1   Kinder-Care mailing package based on benefit ranking

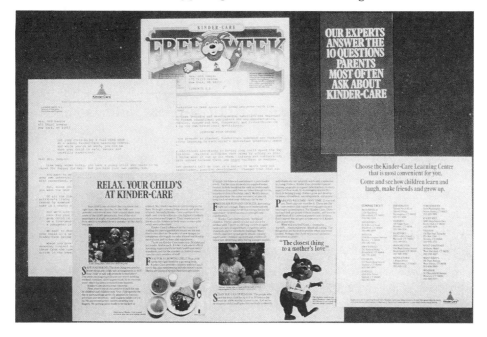

There are also research methods that let you test respondents' uncontrolled reactions to your advertising. These include readership studies that track eye movement, or galvanic skin response, where a prospect's hands are wired to measure "sweaty palms." While this might seem a little far-fetched, I've seen it used successfully. Especially for things which produce a quick emotional response . . . like envelope designs and catalog covers.

A well-done research study will not only help you sharpen and fine tune your promotional materials, it will usually suggest new ideas for future creative efforts.

APPRAISING THE VALUE OF YOUR CUSTOMER

A SIMPLE RESEARCH APPLICATION that direct marketers often overlook is *establishing the lifetime value of your customers*. And it doesn't require focus groups or interviews, just internal analysis. By understanding exactly how much a customer is worth, you'll have a better sense of how much you can afford to spend to acquire a new one. Chapter 18 discusses how to calculate a customer's lifetime value.

EVOLUTIONARY FOCUS GROUPS: MORE KNOWLEDGE FOR THE SAME PRICE

FOCUS GROUPS HAVE BEEN AN IMPORTANT research technique since 1955, when Sidney Furst and his colleagues first placed a see-through mirror and speakers in a BBDO conference room. Years later, some people from my agency and I were reflecting on how that evening's focus group had compared to the previous night's. Over drinks, we agreed that there must be a better way to develop creative than by showing the same thing to new people over and over again. Out of our exasperation grew the *evolutionary focus group* technique.

In traditional focus groups, three or more groups of people are exposed to a concept at the same stage of development. Researchers claim that these multiple groups are necessary to validate results and know whether the opinions expressed in a single group truly reflect reality. Sure enough, by the end of those groups a consensus of opinions has emerged—but you've heard pretty much the same thing from most of the participants.

With evolutionary focus groups, each group views the creative concept at a different stage. By taking the creative a step further in each group, you can confirm the results of the previous session while getting feedback on the new material. (A variation on this uses one of the groups as a "recall" or control group that sees the creative again at every stage.)

The flow chart in Exhibit 7.2 shows the difference between the traditional and evolutionary approaches.

Evolutionary focus groups let you learn a lot more for about the same cost as a series of traditional focus groups. And the results can be astonishing. The first time I tried this technique, we had four ads that research experts ranked 1-2-3-4 based on the qualitative results of our groups. Researchers caution that quantitative decisions shouldn't be based on qualitative results—but when we actually ran all four ads to validate the technique, the consumer response ranked them 1-2-4-3. I've done dozens of evolutionary focus groups since, and have always come up with at least one strong approach for an ad or mailing.

EXHIBIT 7.2 Traditional vs. evolutionary focus group techniques

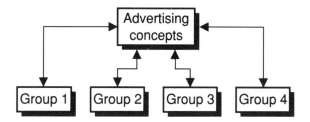

Traditional focus group technique

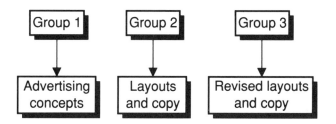

Evolutionary focus group technique

EFFECTIVE RESEARCH AT WORK

OFTEN A SINGLE RESEARCH study is enough to launch a new program successfully. Sometimes it takes a number of different studies to turn a product or service into a winner.

When Western Publishing began developing the Scribbler Learn with Me continuity program, it first scanned the "big picture" to see if trends indicated whether an electronic self-teaching product for pre-schoolers would be accepted. When interest in the concept was confirmed, a one-shot version of the product was tested with an inexpensive billing insert. Questionnaires sent to respondents determined the level of product satisfaction and gathered demographic information. Play testing conducted in customer homes also helped confirm consumer satisfaction, but a major product flaw was revealed and resolved.

Based on these positive results, Western developed the first four shipments as a "wet" test of the Scribbler's Learn with Me Club. A full-page insert

♦

in *Parents* emphasized the product's electronic answer-finder, using a "magic of learning" creative theme, and pulled 12 percent over target. Good, but not great—so Western continued its research. Focus groups were used to refine the products and shipment sequence, mall intercepts to reevaluate existing benefits and copy. They revealed two benefits that were stronger than the "magic of learning" theme used in *Parents*.

As a last step before roll-out, Western conducted a confirmation test. The highest-ranking benefits and the most appealing creative theme were incorporated into a direct mail package dropped to 200,000 parents of pre-schoolers (see Exhibit 7.3). Test results came in 30 percent above target and convinced Western to proceed. The Scribbler program became very successful.

EXHIBIT 7.3   Western Publishing's mailing package incorporating research-proven concept, creative theme and benefits

The Last Word on Research

It's my opinion that even though the use of research has grown a lot, direct marketers still don't do enough of it. Most firms like to think of themselves as marketing-driven companies. But all too often, they follow the product-driven approach of getting a new idea, trying a test mailing, and keeping their fingers crossed. A truly marketing-driven approach starts with research—research that helps you uncover customer needs and desires, and allows you to find or design a product that best meets those needs.

Research can help you limit your risks. It allows you to "see around corners" and avoid costly mistakes. But it's a decision-making tool, not an end in itself. So make sure the information you learn is actionable, not just "nice to know." Used wisely, research will help you make better marketing decisions.

PART II

♦

MEASURABLE MEDIA

8

DIRECT MAIL AND LISTS

◆

DIRECT MAIL IS THE FIRST of the major direct response media we'll cover in this section, because it is the most widely used. It's the great common denominator: as effective for kitchen-table entrepreneurs as it is for multinational corporations. It is the medium most direct marketers learn first. Many marketers eventually come to expand their businesses through judicious use of other direct response media—but not until they've gotten their "feet wet" in direct mail.

MAIL AS A MEDIUM

DESPITE PERIODIC POSTAGE increases, direct mail expenditures have continued to grow over the years. It's not unusual to find direct marketers who spend 90 to 95 percent of their total media budget on direct mail.

About 714,000 businesses have bulk mail permits, which allow them to mail at the lower, third-class postage rate. They send out more than 63 billion pieces of mail a year, including third class solo mailings and catalogs.

FIVE BIG ADVANTAGES

While one can list a lot of possible advantages for direct mail, many of them are not unique to the medium. They might apply equally to magazines or television, for example. But I think the five listed below are quite special and account for direct mail's widespread use.

1. SELECTIVITY AND PERSONALIZATION Direct mail lets you address your message to exactly the kind of person you want to receive it. You can target only people with known interests or a specific buying history, or people who live in a certain geographic area. You can personalize your message to capitalize on that selectivity, using computer letters that address each individual by name, or tailoring copy to the interests of each group targeted.

♦

2. MORE FLEXIBILITY   Your mailing package can be as simple or as elaborate as you wish. You can include a four-color brochure that opens up as big as a tablecloth, or, in some cases, you can include a sample in the mailing. You control the distribution. Your mailing quantity can be as small as you like or as large as the available universe. And you can mail whenever you prefer.

3. MORE SUITABLE FOR TESTING   While other media permit some types of testing, none offers the widespread test capability provided by direct mail. Thanks to the computer's ability to select a perfect Nth name sample, your mailings can include as many split tests as necessary to provide a wide variety of answers from a single mailing. It's not unusual for large mailings to include 50 or more test cells.

4. MAXIMIZES PROFIT FROM YOUR CUSTOMER LIST   As was pointed out earlier, the classic formula for direct marketing success is to build a list of satisfied customers and then go back to them for repeat sales. Direct mail is one of only two media (the other being telemarketing) that let you target your previous buyers with no waste circulation.

5. HIGH RESPONSE RATE   Other than telemarketing, direct mail will usually produce the highest percentage of response. So, if direct mail pays out for you, you can build your sales, profit, and customer list rapidly.

Because its diverse formats allow plenty of room for long copy and numerous illustrations, direct mail also allows you to tell the whole story behind your product or service, no matter how complicated it might be. You can include a business reply envelope for sending money. And when quick delivery is more important than cost, you have the option of using first class mail.

According to Vin Jenkins, whose booklet *The Concept of Direct Marketing* is an excellent summary of the business, the privacy of direct mail also contributes to its popularity. Direct mail campaigns are less public and less easily monitored than campaigns in other media. Your competitors will find it harder to keep track of all your promotions. Jenkins also points out that, unlike other major media, direct mail doesn't force you to wait for a choice television daypart or a magazine's publication date.

Two Main Disadvantages

The major disadvantage of direct mail is that it is very expensive. It's hard to make even a simple mailing today for less than $350 to $400 per thousand, especially a prospect mailing that includes list rental charges. By comparison, you can buy most other media at a cost-per-thousand that ranges from $8.00 to $80.00. Only telemarketing has a higher CPM. So direct mail must produce a much higher response than other media to give a comparable cost-per-order.

Another oft-cited disadvantage is that the impact of direct mail is diminishing as it faces increasing competition in the mailbox. Research shows that 53 percent of all the mail the average consumer receives is now advertising mail . . . versus only 27 percent eleven years ago. But the average volume is only ten pieces a week or less than two a day. While your own mailbox may be stuffed with catalogs at certain times of the year, chances are your demographics or purchase habits are above average. And don't forget that plenty of advertising competition exists in magazines and newspapers and on television.

The fact that it's used so widely is proof that direct mail can overcome high costs and mailbox competition and *still* pay out.

Types of Mailing Lists

It's almost impossible to overstate the importance of mailing lists to your direct mail success. Lists represent your market segments. If your mailing doesn't get to the right market, it doesn't have a chance. The more care you spend on analyzing and selecting lists, the better your chances for success.

According to SRDS, all told there are better than 9,000 lists available today. They can be broken down into three main categories: response lists, compiled lists, and house lists . . . as well as by consumer versus business lists.

Response Lists

The prospects you'll find on response lists share a single characteristic: they have all responded in some way to the offer of another advertiser. Those prospects may be bankers, office managers, or senior citizens who have a common interest in the product or service they responded about. Perhaps they all ordered a subscription to a gardening magazine or requested a catalog of golf equipment. Maybe they all bought Christmas gifts from a cheese company.

Names on a response list may be buyers, inquirers, subscribers, continuity club members, or sweepstakes entrants. They may have responded to an offer made by direct mail, in a print ad, or on television. Whether they are buyers or inquirers, it's their propensity to respond by mail or phone that makes them valuable (though buyers will generally produce better results than inquirers). And the offer to which they responded previously can tell you a lot about their interests.

Response lists are not developed primarily for list rental. They're nearly always somebody else's house list. They are rented to non-competitors for one-time usage. Studies have shown that this exposure to other mail offers *doesn't* depress the list owner's own mailing response. And the list rental profit can be substantial.

COMPILED LISTS

These lists are usually compiled mainly for rental.

Mass consumer lists are generally compiled from telephone listings, auto registrations, driver's licenses, and voter registrations. You can reach virtually every U.S. household with compiled lists. While in total they may have little in common, you can usually select or eliminate names based on geographic area, type of car, or an individual's age.

Specialized compiled lists are also available. They contain names of people who share an interest, such as gardening club members, people at a certain income level—like a list of "millionaires at home addresses"—or people who "own" a particular item like a pilot's license, a personal computer, or a swimming pool.

Many compiled *business* lists are also specialized. They might be compiled from industrial and association directories, club rosters, or convention attendee lists of business people with similar job functions or interests, such as chemical engineers, doctors, or buyers of premiums. But you can also reach virtually every business in the country, with lists usually compiled from phone directories.

What compiled lists don't provide is any guarantee that the names are interested in responding to offers by mail. So direct mail results will usually be lower than with comparable response lists.

Consumer Lists

Be they response or compiled, consumer lists will get your mailings to people at their home addresses. The 1990 census reported a U.S. population of 248,709,873—with roughly 92 million households. Over 90 percent of these households can be reached by mail through one or more mailing lists. In fact, there are roughly 5,500 consumer lists available for rental.

To give you an idea of their variety, lists currently available include Classic Chevy/Ford car buyers, affluent Florida yacht owners, collectors who attend coin and stamp shows, traditional Catholics who read and contribute, New Jersey Symphony Orchestra subscribers, bear hunters, deer calendar buyers, health and diet product buyers, health food gardeners, wild flower and native plant enthusiasts, subscribers to *Aviation Unemployment Monthly* and *The American Needlewoman, Golf Digest/Tennis* sweepstakes respondents, supermarket shoppers who responded to an in-store offer, members of the American Council for the Arts and the National Humane Education Society, plus hockey fans, new parents, investors, buyers of wilderness books, and enthusiasts of just about any other interest or activity you can imagine.

Business Lists

You can reach about nine million U.S. businesses with compiled lists. The availability of business lists by the government's Standard Industrial Classification (SIC) numbering system is a terrific aid in defining and pinpointing your best prospects. The SIC system classifies companies by the main activity in which they engage. All major activities are assigned a two-digit code number. The basic SIC system was recently enhanced by a major list compiler. As a firm's activity becomes more specialized, up to six digits are added to identify subgroups. For example, here are the SIC numbers and descriptions for furniture manufacturers:

25	Manufacturers of Furniture and Fixtures
251	Manufacturers of Household Furniture

2511	Manufacturers of Wood Household Furniture, except Upholstered
2512	Manufacturers of Upholstered Furniture
2514	Manufacturers of Metal Household Furniture
2514-02	Manufacturers of Metal Lawn and Garden Furniture

Exhibit 8.1 shows some of the major SIC groups used for direct mail, along with the number of U.S. names available from a leading business list compiler.

In addition to these compiled lists, you can rent business response lists. Popular categories include buyers of office furniture, safety supplies, training programs, ad specialties, business gifts, desk diaries, books, and magazines. Controlled circulation lists provide names of subscribers to trade magazines distributed free of charge by their publishers. All told, there are about 3,600 business lists available for rental. Some data banks combine lists from various sources and merge-purge them to produce a large, unduplicated list of business buyers.

H<small>OUSE</small> L<small>ISTS</small>: Y<small>OUR</small> M<small>OST</small> V<small>ALUABLE</small> A<small>SSET</small>

The most valuable asset you have is your company's own list of customers, former buyers, and inquirers. (These days, most house lists are called databases. They'll be discussed more thoroughly in Chapter 19.) A house list will normally produce a much higher response than any other list you can rent. That's because prospects already know your company and its products or services. And because your offer has appealed to them in the past, there's a good chance it will again in the future.

Perhaps the value of house lists versus your other alternatives is best summed up by Howard Flood, General Manager of McGraw-Hill's List Management Center. His advice on selecting lists is: "House list first, response lists next, and compiled lists, maybe."

S<small>ELECTIVITY</small> T<small>ECHNIQUES</small>

M<small>OST MAJOR LISTS ARE AVAILABLE</small> with some selectivity (at a slightly higher rental fee) to help you target specific market segments. You can select only males,

EXHIBIT 8.1   Major market segments available by SIC number

SIC NUMBER	DESCRIPTION	QUANTITY
01–14	Agriculture, Forestry & Mining	225,384
15–19	Contractors & Construction	665,621
20–39	Manufacturing	563,911
40–49	Transportation, Communication & Utilities	307,034
50–51	Wholesale Trade	974,924
52–59	Retail Trade	2,181,449
60–67	Finance, Insurance & Real Estate	748,019
70–79	Business Services	1,467,243
80	Health Services	886,112
81	Legal Services	434,893
82–83	Education & Social Services	361,540
84–86	Art & Membership Organizations	416,299
87	Engineering, Architecture & Accounting	363,402
90–97	Government	234,844

for example. Or you can eliminate certain states or ZIP codes. You can choose between a firm's buyers and inquirers. You can mail only the most recent names, or just eliminate the older transactions. If you're mailing to business people, you can select prospects by job title, in specific industries, or by size of firm.

The *recency/frequency/monetary* formula, commonly known as RFM, is often applied to house-list name selection. Pioneered back in the 1930s by giant mail-order houses seeking a way to eliminate waste catalog circulation, it is a point system that compares prior purchase patterns to determine which customers are most likely to buy again. Customers who have bought most recently, ordered most frequently, and spent the most are assigned the most points . . . and represent your best customers. An RFM example is provided in Chapter 9.

Normally, recency is the most significant of the three RFM factors. Which explains why "hot-line" names have become so popular when renting lists. Someone who is presumably satisfied with a recent mail order purchase is more likely to buy again . . . even from another advertiser.

Other traditional, time-honored ways of selecting the most likely prospects for your promotion are summarized in Exhibit 8.2, along with the rationale to support that selectivity.

ADVANCED SEGMENTATION TECHNIQUES

"Advanced" segmentation goes from traditional selectivity techniques that look mainly at past behavior to new formulas that can help predict behavior. It uses demographic and socioeconomic information, which can be broken down by ZIP code, census tract, postal carrier route, household, or individual.

LIST ENHANCEMENT Enhancement is the process of overlaying demographic and socio-economic data on a mailing list. Data is available from various sources, including the suppliers of mass compiled lists. Although it's possible to enhance rental lists, it makes more economic sense to enhance your house list. The extra customer information you develop will help you mail your house list more efficiently, select list segments that will be most responsive, and maybe even develop new products.

For example, by bumping your house list against other lists or databases, you can capture and code information about customer gender, age, car ownership, dwelling type, and lifestyle. That information can help you break your list into groups with similar characteristics. By analyzing response, you can rank each group's performance, and concentrate future or special promotions on high-response segments.

So if you're selling security products, you can offer different products to customers living in apartments than to those in single-family dwellings. Or you can find out which of your customers own cars, and offer them an auto alarm system.

This process sounds like it costs a lot of money, but it's really quite inexpensive. Let's say enhancement information costs $30.00 per thousand. If you mail your house list six times a year, that enhancement only costs $5.00 a thousand per mailing. And if your normal in-the-mail cost is $375 a thousand, your incremental cost increases less than one and a half percent. So it won't take much of a lift to make your investment pay out.

▬▬▬

EXHIBIT 8.2   Traditional list segmentation/selectivity

SELECTION	RATIONALE
Recency* (Last 12 months, last 6 months, monthly hotline)	The more recent the buyers, the more likely to purchase by mail again
Geographic (State, SCF, Zip)	To target or eliminate specific geographic areas
Sex	Offers geared toward only one sex
Multi-buyers* (Frequency)	Repeat purchasers likely to buy by mail again
Dollar select* (Monetary)	Select buyers by dollar amount similar to your offer
Source	Direct mail sold names respond better to mail
Method of payment	To match your payment option

ADDITIONAL BUSINESS LIST SELECTIVITY

Job title	Reach specific job function
Sales volume or employee size	Qualifies firm by size
SIC code	Offer geared toward specific businesses

*Recency, Frequency, and Monetary comprise the RFM formula commonly used for house list selectivity

IMPROVE YOUR PROSPECTING Segmentation adds new meaning to the old direct response axiom, "know who your customers are and you'll be able to find more like them."

Once, selecting lists for prospecting was limited to renting response lists in *categories* similar to your product or service. To sell a garden cart, for instance, you'd look for names from gardening publications or mail order nurseries. Your offer would probably reach mostly single-family homeowners—but it would also be wasted on some gardening lovers living in apartments or condos with no yards.

Today, you can use segmentation to develop an in-depth profile of your customers, and then identify prospects who most closely match it. By knowing which clusters or groups of prospects to focus on, you'll make marginal response lists pay out and improve your results on compiled lists. And you'll boost profitability on already successful lists because you can mail "deeper" into them, supplementing hot-line names with older names that match your desired clusters.

All in all, you'll increase the universe of lists and names you can successfully mail on a specific product or service. This is especially true of large consumer lists that, without enhancements, may not be profitable for your offer.

Take the Fingerhut customer list, for example. If you had an upscale offer and tested a cross section of this largely blue-collar list, it probably wouldn't pay out. Now that geodemographic information has been added to this six million-name universe, you can select names of prospects in a certain income or education category. So maybe it's possible to cull a profitable segment of 300,000 upscale buyers. While this is only five percent of the whole file, it still gives you 300,000 prospects you wouldn't be able to mail to at all otherwise.

TREE ANALYSIS AND REGRESSION ANALYSIS

The more demographics you have on a list, the easier it gets to find and separate better-performing segments from all the rest. Direct marketers use various statistical tools to help.

AID or CHAID (sometimes called *tree analysis*) looks at the differences in response rates among subgroups in a list audience, and identifies the specific characteristics (age, income, and so on) that are associated with high vs. low responder groups. Tree analysis is often done as the first step in a regression analysis to identify the key variables.

Regression analysis (also called *correlation analysis* or *multiple regression analysis,* depending on how many factors are being analyzed) is used increasingly by direct marketers to zero in on their best prospects and customers. This statistical technique matches independent variables—such as income and family size—to variations in the dependent variable, which is response-rate history. It is used to develop "models" that can help you determine which combination of customer factors—income, age, marital status, or other—best predicts a prospect's response to a given offer.

These statistical techniques allow you to divide a mailing universe into dozens or even hundreds of "cells" and rank them on the basis of their probable performance. You can then eliminate those cells that don't meet your target cost-per-order.

GEODEMOGRAPHIC ANALYSIS

Geodemographic segmentation operates on the principle that birds of a feather flock together. Or, to put it another way, that people with similar demographics tend to cluster in certain geographic areas. Claritas' PRIZM system (*potential rating index for zip markets*), for example, assigned every U.S. zip code to one of 40 neighborhood types, ranked in order of affluence. Analyzing your customer list or prior response to determine the penetration level in each PRIZM cell is step one. You then do a PRIZM analysis of large compiled lists and mail only those cells or areas that your research predicts will yield the best response rates.

APPLYING SEGMENTATION ANALYSIS

LET'S LOOK AT THE IMPACT of segmentation analysis on a marketer's bottom line.

In Exhibit 8.3, the marketer has analyzed the results of an initial mailing to a large list. Segmentation analysis reveals that four deciles on this rented list met the breakeven response rate of 1.6%; six didn't.

Our marketer can choose between two strategies in remailing the list. First, he or she could ask the list owner or computer service to eliminate all zip

EXHIBIT 8.3   How to apply segmentation analysis

DECILE		PERCENT RESPONSE	
		%	
1 (Top)		2.37	1.95%
2		1.98	
3		1.81	
4		1.63	
5		1.58	
6	1.67%	1.42	
7		1.33	
8		1.23	
9		1.03	
10 (Lowest)		0.74	
	Mean average	1.50%	

Horizontal line represents mailer's breakeven of 1.6%. The top 4 deciles are all above breakeven and average a 1.95% response. But the marketer can choose to mail all but the tenth decile and still average a 1.67% response.

Source: Adapted from Demographic Research, Inc., Santa Monica, California

codes in deciles below the line. Concentrating future mailings on the top four deciles would reduce production and mailing costs and boost average response from 1.5% to 1.95%. Or, the marketer could "average down" and mail everything but the lowest decile, producing a cumulative response that averages 1.67%.

The ultimate decision depends upon the marketer's basic strategy. If the company wants to emphasize profits, cutting the mailing off above the line is the way to go. But if the company is seeking to boost sales, it will get higher sales and many more new customers by "averaging down," even though the cumulative response is only at breakeven.

The results of applying segmentation analysis speak for themselves. Not as clear, unfortunately, are the complicated jargon and sophisticated mathematical processes that inevitably accompany these techniques. In my view, it's best to leave the jargon and formulas to specialists. As long as you have a basic understanding of segmentation techniques, it's easy to find suppliers who can work with you to achieve desired results.

List Industry Services

Because buying habits change, people move, and our promotion techniques shift, lists constantly change and evolve. To keep up, you can review list cards, list catalogs, trade press ads, or the voluminous *Direct Mail List Rates and Data*. You can ask your direct marketing agency for help, but many of them are not experts in this area. The key players are list brokers and list managers.

List Brokers and Managers

Brokers represent both buyer and seller—the list renter and the list owner. They have no vested interest in any particular list. They sell their ability to find and recommend the "right" lists for their clients, even lists that at first glance don't seem to have much in common with the client's offer. You could study list data cards for weeks and never consider testing a fund-raising donor list for an offer of inexpensive apparel. But maybe your broker knows donor lists have worked well for similar offers. Experienced brokers maintain careful records for each list, records that show which lists clients have tested and whether they have re-ordered.

Using more than one broker will give you a more complete perspective on the list universe. To learn even more, share your results with all your brokers—so they can fine-tune their recommendations.

List managers, who are employed by list owners, do not have unbiased opinions; their commissions depend on how frequently they rent the lists they represent. But they know those lists inside and out. If you have a question about a list's characteristics—particularly if a list you've been using successfully suddenly becomes unprofitable—you can usually learn the most from the list owner or manager. They can tell you if anything has changed: Maybe the company has altered its products, prices, or media mix, or has shifted marketing strategies and is now targeting a different group of consumers altogether.

Merge-purge Techniques

As your universe of proven lists grows and you develop successful rented lists you mail regularly, so does the amount of duplication you can expect from them. It's obviously wasteful to mail two or more copies of the same piece to duplicate names at the same time. Merge-purge techniques can solve this problem by eliminating duplicate names and can lower your rental costs if you can negotiate a "net name" deal.

Until recently, industry practice dictated that, as a courtesy to list owners, renters would pay for 85 percent of a list even if that list contained only 50 or 60 percent unduplicated names. But with more pressure to keep costs down, some list users are now negotiating "net net" deals under which they pay for new names only. A parallel compromise deal calls for paying 100 percent for new names, but only one sixth of the rental price for duplicated names.

Paying for a name more than once can give you the right to mail these multi-buyers more than once. This has been a boon to catalogers who send second, even third copies of their catalog—usually with a new cover or outside signature—to proven multi-buyers.

In fact, list penetration analysis, a method first devised by direct marketing sage Bob Stone, uses duplication as a factor in evaluating test lists. It holds that the higher the match rate of an outside rental file to your own house list, the greater the probability that list will be profitable. That's because you'll almost always get a higher response from lists that are similar to your own.

THE LAST WORD ON DIRECT MAIL AND LISTS

REMEMBER, LISTS CHANGE. It's a good idea periodically to review lists that haven't worked in the past and consider whether they might work now. If new selections are available, or you've used segmentation analysis to develop a better profile of your customer, you might give them another try. Better segmenting might also help you identify profitable sectors of a previously marginal list. Or let you salvage some portion of a list that no longer pays out when you mail the whole file.

Don't forget to check every list you rent to make sure you get what you ordered. Many direct marketers have rented lists sent right to their lettershop or service bureau without any quality check. It's always wise to print out a sample of the list or spot check some of the mailing labels. You may find, for instance, there are names in geographic areas you wanted eliminated. The list is so important to direct mail success that it's worth the extra effort to make sure the mailing piece you've worked so hard on gets to the right audience.

9

PRINT MEDIA

◆

GENERAL ADVERTISERS HAVE LONG relied on print media to deliver their messages, both in the consumer and business markets. Like direct marketers, they try to select publications which best reach their target audiences.

But each group approaches the buying process differently. Let's touch briefly on how general advertisers use print media, and then concentrate on direct response print.

In general advertising, the objective is usually to build image and awareness. The two key measurements used are *reach* and *frequency*. Reach is unduplicated circulation—the percentage of the target audience exposed to your ad message during a given period. Frequency is the average number of times the *same* audience is exposed to your ad schedule. And repeated exposures are important to establish awareness.

By comparison, most direct marketers are more concerned with cost effectiveness than image. So the key measurement is how a publication performs in terms of cost-per-inquiry or cost-per-order. Even though print ads have a much lower cost-per-thousand than direct mail, the response is also much lower. So if print advertising works for you, your cost-per-customer will usually be comparable to mail.

While magazines are more widely used by direct marketers than newspapers, both are referred to as print media, or as space advertising, since you're buying space for your ad. We'll cover newspapers first, then magazines.

NEWSPAPERS: BUILT-IN VARIETY

UNLIKE MOST OTHER MEDIA, newspapers offer a wide variety of sections, advertising formats, and reproduction methods. They're so varied they almost have to be considered as media within a medium. Besides this built-in advantage, newspapers offer short closing dates, immediate response, and broad coverage of a large and diverse audience. The closing date for regular ROP (run-of-paper) ads is usually only a couple of days before publication. And, because newspapers have a short life, they tend to produce orders quickly.

This broad coverage is made possible by almost 1630 daily U.S. newspapers with a weekday circulation of almost 63 million. At the same time, only 847 Sunday papers deliver slightly over 62 million readers. A number of leading direct response advertisers devote a major share of their ad budgets to newspapers. Circulation has flattened somewhat in recent years. But despite an overall decline in the number of newspapers published—hardest hit have been the afternoon dailies, which have lost ground to evening television news broadcasts—newspapers still reach 50 to 80 percent of all households in a given market.

Disadvantages of newspapers include poor ad reproduction and limited availability of color except in certain sections; results tend to be affected by adverse news somewhat more so than in other media. If the paper is filled with articles on a local plane crash, ad readership tends to suffer.

What sections Work Best for Direct Response Ads?

Newspapers offer a vast array of special sections, from sports and book reviews to food, lifestyle, and business sections. While small ROP ads work consistently well for some advertisers, most direct marketers get better results from Sunday supplements, mail order shopping sections, and newspaper inserts.

Some newspapers publish their own Sunday supplement, but most papers carry a syndicated supplement like *Parade* or *USA Weekend*. These supplements are more like magazines, and provide much better reproduction and color than the rest of the newspaper. They tend to carry a lot of mail order ads, especially for low-price, impulse merchandise, and therefore have a good direct response atmosphere. The syndicated supplements, however, can be quite expensive to test in a single market or paper. It's better to try and get a leftover page or remnant space in a few markets.

Free-standing Newspaper Inserts

Some years ago advertisers discovered they could maximize newspaper response by running their own preprinted inserts in Sunday papers. Popular formats ranged from a single sheet on card stock to an eight-page booklet, with the inserts supplied by the advertiser.

But these response inserts are less popular today due to rising costs and the growing number of local and national inserts. It's not unusual for major market papers to include Sunday inserts from department stores, home centers, discount chains, and drug stores, as well as co-op inserts. While the latter are used primarily for package goods coupon promotions, they also provide a good opportunity for direct marketers.

Co-op free-standing inserts or FSIs are offered by firms like Valassis Inserts, Quad Marketing, and Product Movers. Co-op inserts offer a total circulation of around 60,000,000 in Sunday newspapers across the states. They can pay out nicely for direct marketers, especially if space is bought on a remnant basis at savings of about half the official rate card. Remnant rates are usually available on unsold pages or in specific markets which a national advertiser doesn't want.

Individual inserts are still paying out for some advertisers. But they're using them much more selectively than in the past. That might mean only using papers in smaller markets, where there is typically less FSI competition from local advertisers. Or only using newspapers which charge a reasonable insertion cost-per-thousand.

MAGAZINES: MASS OR CLASS

WHILE MANY PEOPLE FEEL THE magazine industry has been hurt by the roaring success of TV, there is an ever-increasing number of healthy, special-interest publications. Today, about 2200 consumer magazines are published in the U.S. The large-circulation magazines allow you to reach a mass audience; others deliver your message to a specific class or type of reader.

Direct marketers take advantage of both. A recent study of 132 consumer magazines showed that about 20 percent of full-page ads could be classified as direct response. And large direct marketers like Franklin Mint, Time-Life Books, and Columbia House are consistently among the top 15 brands that advertise in magazines, each spending $15 to $20 million annually on space.

The main advantages offered by magazines include good color reproduction, which is important for many types of products; a long ad life; and a low

♦

cost per thousand. The latter is true primarily for consumer magazines. Business or trade publications usually have a relatively higher cost per thousand.

Another important advantage is that often you can test a variety of creative approaches or offers in space less expensively than you can in the mail. Creative and production costs are lower for an ad than all the inserts in a typical mailing.

Disadvantages of magazine advertising include long closing dates (many consumer magazines require your ad material three months before they come out), slower response because of the longer readership and ad life, and less space to tell your story. Even if you use a full page ad, you have much less room for copy and illustrations than in a typical direct mail package.

Standard ad sizes and formats include one-third page, half page, two-thirds page, full page, and double spread, with the coupon usually in a bottom corner of the ad where it's easy to clip out. Smaller ad sizes, like one-sixth page or less, normally run without a coupon because they take up too much selling space. Bind-in insert cards, full-page inserts, or multi-page card-stock inserts are also available in many publications. While more expensive than an on-page ad, they tend to be effective for direct response advertisers.

How to Buy Print

THE BEST WAY TO BUY PRINT IS TO test in stages. Get your feet wet by testing inexpensively; you can build up your schedule if results warrant it. The pyramid testing structure illustrated in Chapter 6 applies equally to magazines and mail. In the initial test stage, experiment with different categories and publications, using regional editions to keep costs down. As you move into the confirmation and roll-out phases, you can test additional publications or expand into national editions where your regional ads have pulled well.

Syndicated research and competitive information can help you decide which publications to test. Especially helpful is the Publisher's Advertising Report (formerly Publisher's Information Bureau), whose monthly reports let you track when and where competing products have been running ad space. If a competitor repeats an ad in a certain publication, you can assume it paid out.

Syndicated data from Simmons Market Research Bureau (SMRB) and Mediamark Research Inc. (MRI) let you evaluate the audience each prospective magazine reaches. If you're selling security systems, for example, these reports indicate how many readers of a given publication already own such systems—compared to the national average. If a publication scores high, it's a good indication that other readers might be receptive to your offer.

You should also evaluate a publication's *response environment*. Magazines with a direct response atmosphere generally produce better results than those without. These include publications that have mail-order shopping sections, usually found at the back of the book, and those that regularly run a lot of larger direct response ads. Other advertisers would not continue to use these publications if they weren't producing good results. Glossy, classy magazines like *National Geographic* or *Architectural Digest* may indeed reach exactly the audience you're seeking, but their high production values make them "coffee table books." They tend to be displayed and saved—and people are reluctant to rip out a coupon.

Comparing subscriptions to newsstand sales is another way to evaluate a publication's response potential. Generally speaking, high newsstand circulation means higher readership and response. Not every subscription copy is read as thoroughly.

BUYING MAGAZINE SPACE

Rate cards will give you a publication's current rates, but they aren't sacrosanct. Direct marketers can often get a better deal than general advertisers. Many magazines have mail-order rates, or special discounts for ads in their mail-order sections. First-time advertisers can sometimes get a break; other times, those who negotiate aggressively are rewarded with a discount.

But the position of your ad is also important, and you can often negotiate a better position without paying a premium price. Experience shows that the first right-hand page and the back cover are usually best for direct response ads. These are followed by other cover positions and the front of the book. Ads which appear upfront, before the main editorial material, generally have a 40 to 50 percent higher response than back-of-the-book positions. An exception are the small ads in a mail-order section; they usually get good readership and response.

Timing of insertions must also be taken into account when scheduling magazines. Timing can affect your results by as much as 40 percent, as Exhibit 9.1 shows.

◆

EXHIBIT 9.1   Effect of timing on magazine results

ISSUE	INDEX	COST-PER-RESPONSE EXAMPLE (CPR)
January	102.5	$10.26
February	100	10.00
March	110	11.00
April	125	12.50
May	130	13.00
June	140	14.00
July	130	13.00
August	120	12.00
September	130	13.00
October	110	11.00
November	110	11.00
December	120	12.00

Assuming your product is non-seasonal, index indicates how your cost-per-response would vary, with February as the best month. These examples show how to apply the index:
You run a test ad in June that pulls responses at a cost of $10.76, and you want to know how it will do in a March issue. March CPR should drop to .786
(110 ÷ 140). So you can expect a March CPR of $8.45 (10.76 × .786).
You test in March and get a $19.56 CPR In September, cost should increase by 1.182 (130 ÷ 110), for a CPR of $23.12 ($19.56 × 1.182).

BIND-IN CARDS

Bind-in cards usually cost about two and a half to three times as much as a full-page ad—but your response rate will be four to eight times better. Why do they work so well? Primarily because they tend to make the magazine fall open to your page. So a bind-in makes any ad position pull relatively better. But the first bind-in card position will produce better results than one further back. So here again, getting a better position can be as important as getting a discount.

Should You Run Color?

Adding a second color usually isn't worth the extra cost. But four color normally increases response over black and white. So if you're contemplating running a full-color ad, ask yourself two key questions. First, do you need color to show your product to its best advantage? Ads for food and fashion items are almost always four color for this reason. Second, can you afford it? Check the rate card for the four color upcharge; it varies from book to book.

How to Evaluate Print

THE REAL MEASURE OF A PRINT ad's value is not how little it costs, but how well it pulls. Direct marketers determine an ad's success primarily by the *cost per inquiry* or *cost per order* it produces. Today, residual values like image and awareness are often taken into account, as direct marketers realize that print ads also affect nonresponders. Firms like Eddie Bauer understand that their print ads have a cumulative effect on prospects who may not respond by mail immediately. Perhaps they'll be more likely to respond next time they see an ad. Or maybe they will ultimately become retail customers. This subject is discussed in greater detail in Chapter 12.

Projecting Results and Planning to Repeat

Your overall response rate can be calculated soon after responses start trickling in. If your ad appears in a monthly magazine, about half of your total responses will be received the first month. Exhibit 9.2 shows how to estimate final response at different stages. If, for example, you have 489 responses after three weeks, final response should come in between 1,076 and 1,223. Response to ads in weekly magazines is faster, due to quicker readership.

   Assuming your ad is successful, how soon should it be repeated? The only sound advice I've ever seen on this topic applies to medium- and large-size

◆

EXHIBIT 9.2   How to project response on a print ad.

FOR MONTHLY MAGAZINES:	PERCENT OF TOTAL	MULTIPLY BY
After the 1st week	3–7%	14 to 33
After the 2nd week	20–25%	4 to 5
After the 3rd week	40–45%	2.2 to 2.5
After 1 month	50–55%	1.8 to 2.0
After 2 months	75–85%	1.2 to 1.3
After 3 months	85–92%	1.1 to 1.2
After 4 months	92–95%	1.0 to 1.1
FOR WEEKLY MAGAZINES:		
After the 2nd week	50%	2
FOR CARD DECKS:		
After 1 month	50%	2

Source: Rapp Collins Marcoa

space ads. If your response is at or near breakeven, wait a full year to repeat. If your response is up to 20 percent better than your target, wait six months. And if your response is more than 20 percent better than expected, run your ad again in three or four months. Repeating an ad sooner than this will usually not be profitable.

This repeat formula does not apply to small space ads. Since these ads are not noticed by most readers of a given issue, they can be repeated much more frequently. In some cases, you can run small ads in issue after issue of a publication that pulls well for you, with little or no drop-off in results.

◆

THE LAST WORD ON PRINT MEDIA

OVER THE YEARS, I'VE SEEN SOME very good print media recommendations and some not-so-good ones.

For example, a client recently showed me a test schedule proposed by an ad agency that called for testing one book in each of eight categories. The selection criteria was to recommend the publication in each category that syndicated data ranked highest for purchase of the client's product. A smart computer or a dumb chimp could have developed the same schedule! It totally ignored the response environment of each publication. A couple of the recommended magazines were coffee table books, traditionally not good response vehicles.

I've learned there's a "magic question" that comes in handy when you are evaluating a media schedule: "What was the rationale or selection criteria for these specific publications?" In other words, out of all the available magazines or newspapers that might be appropriate, what made you pick these?

Even if you aren't acquainted with the finer points of buying print, asking your agency or media specialist this "magic" question will make you look like a print advertising pro. And by the way, it's also a useful question for the other media we will be discussing in this section.

10

BROADCAST MEDIA

◆

MANY ADVERTISERS THINK OF television as a new direct response medium. But television has been used heavily for direct response since the old days, when wrestling matches were more popular than pro football and Milton Berle was a bigger attraction than Bill Cosby. Today, direct marketers use television in a much more sophisticated way. And because it's working well, its use is growing. A recent study showed that in some dayparts, 20 to 25 percent of all TV spots are now direct response.

Yet there are still a large number of direct marketers who haven't tried television. They admit it is an exciting, glamorous medium, but they feel it's just not for them. In discussing this subject at my seminars, I've found that misconceptions about direct response TV persist. But those who approach television with an open mind often become converts.

FIVE TV MISCONCEPTIONS

TV MISCONCEPTION #1: "IT COSTS TOO MUCH TO USE TV"

Wrong. We're not talking about general advertiser-type expenses—the headline-making costs of airing commercials during the Super Bowl, now running almost a million dollars. We're not even talking about spending the $212,000 needed to produce the average national TV spot. Production costs are rising, but it's still possible to produce a direct response commercial for $25,000 to $50,000. When you consider that you might spend nearly as much on photography and separations for a four-color mailing piece, that doesn't sound like too much to swallow.

Buying time doesn't cost a fortune, either. Direct marketers can negotiate TV rates at roughly half the cost paid by general advertisers. Occasionally, per-inquiry deals can be arranged, though these are not as common as they once were. Test costs are minimized by trying a commercial in only three or four markets. Results from one week of testing help you plan the next. If results don't warrant a continuation, you can "pull the plug" on the test. The CPI or CPO results are usually comparable to mail or print campaigns, although back-end results are often a little poorer.

It's amazing to see how many advertisers believe they can't afford television although they think nothing of spending thousands of dollars for printing, list rental, lettershop, and postage on a new mailing package. As this is being written, the typical cost of testing television in three markets is about $50,000, including $30,000 for production and $20,000 for buying time. But you get what you pay for. So spend enough to get a decent test. Otherwise, you may never find out how effective direct response TV may be.

TV MISCONCEPTION #2: "YOU BUY DIRECT RESPONSE TV THE SAME WAY A GENERAL ADVERTISER DOES"

Wrong again. Buying criteria and schedule weights differ dramatically. Direct response advertisers buy lower-rated spots during *passive* viewing periods—like late nights and weekends when old movies and reruns are aired. That's when people are more likely to get up from their easy chair to get a pencil or place a phone order, especially if they're watching a show they've seen before or have the TV on while doing something else. These spots not only cost less, they produce more response than spots aired during prime viewing periods.

General advertisers, on the other hand, buy network time and spot TV (time purchased on a market-by-market basis), often in prime time. Their purchases are measured by GRPs or gross rating points. One GRP means that one percent of all television homes viewed your commercial in a given market. If you run your commercial enough times to get 150 GRPs, it means you reached the average person in that audience one and a half times.

General advertisers vary their buys depending upon how much awareness is needed. For example, a new product introduction such as Colgate's pump toothpaste might be supported by 40 to 45 spots a week, or 150 GRPs. A mature product like Colgate in a standard squeeze tube would be supported by a maintenance schedule of about 20 spots a week, or 70 GRPs. Direct response advertisers run lighter schedules, typically about 10 spots a week, or 35 GRPs.

In my experience, however, heavier schedules like those run by general advertisers do pay out better.

TV Misconception #3: "The Longer a Response Spot, the More Effective It Is"

Often, but not always. Like everything else about your strategy, spot length should fit your objective. If your objective is general advertising awareness, a 15- to 30-second spot is the norm. If your spot is part of a two-step offer and is intended to generate inquiries, use a 30- to 60-second spot. But if you want your spot to make the phones start ringing with orders, you'll need 90 to 120 seconds. Some direct marketers succeed with 60-second spots, but it's hard to get an order in such a short time.

Commercials that *support* an offer made in another medium can be shorter—30 or even 15 seconds. TV support will be discussed later in this chapter.

TV Misconception #4: "What You Buy Is What You Get"

Nope. Not the way direct response TV time is normally bought. Because you're buying discounted spots at a special pre-emptible rate, up to 40 percent of your spots will probably not be aired. It's standard practice to bump discounted spots if a general advertiser comes along who is willing to pay full rate. You won't be charged for the spot, but you won't get the orders or the inquiries you were expecting, either.

About 20 percent of all 60- and 90-second spots are pre-empted; 40 percent of all 120-second spots get bumped (the pre-emption rate for both is a little lower on cable). To minimize this, over buy. When you schedule "flights" or groups of spots on a station, buy 20 to 40 percent more than you want to run. Then have your ad agency or buying service call the station daily to see what aired, and adjust your buys accordingly.

Of course, you can cut this problem in half if you can switch from 120-second spots to 60s or 90s and still get an acceptable cost-per-response.

♦

TV MISCONCEPTION #5: "TV'S SEASONALITY DOESN'T MAKE SENSE. I'VE HEARD YOU GET GOOD RESPONSE IN THE SUMMER MONTHS, WHEN MOST PEOPLE ARE WATCHING LESS TV."

Yes, but deciding when to run direct response TV commercials is not as dependent on viewership as on when television time is less expensive to buy. Television costs vary by time of year. For example, a spot might cost 20 percent more in the fourth quarter than in the first quarter. During the first and third quarters, stations have more unsold inventory and prices are down.

Likewise, viewership varies by quarter. It's high in the first quarter, and falls off during the Spring and Summer months. If you don't want to worry about ratings numbers, just remember: The best time to run direct response spots is usually during the first quarter, with the third quarter next best. Most direct marketers keep their commercials off the air in the second and fourth quarters, or run limited schedules.

"NARROWCASTING"—THE CABLE MARKET

CABLE OFFERS TWO PRIMARY opportunities for direct marketers: superstations such as WTBS, WGN, and WOR, and advertiser-supported cable networks such as CNN, ESPN, Nickelodeon, and Lifetime.

The cable networks have made "narrowcasting" a reality. Because you can select them the way you choose lists or magazine audiences, you can really zero in on a specific segment. For example, if lists of newsmagazine subscribers pay out for you, try advertising on CNN, the Cable News Network. If your product works in the *New Yorker,* you can reach the same type of audience via the Arts and Entertainment channel.

Cable television has been a great medium for direct marketers for many years, but now that cable television reaches about 60 percent of 92 million TV households, it's getting tougher to buy. General advertisers willing to pay higher rates are displacing some of the direct response spots. But direct marketers like Time-Life Books, Charles Schwab & Co., and the *Wall Street Journal* are still among the leaders in cable ad spending. And if you flip through the cable channels late at night, you'll see they have plenty of direct response company.

ADVANTAGES AND DISADVANTAGES OF BROADCAST

ALTHOUGH IT DOESN'T WORK for all types of offers, TV has some strong advantages.

First, television is dramatic. There isn't any better way to show or demonstrate your product in action. Because 80 percent of all responses come within a couple hours after a commercial airs, there's no suspense about whether your spots are working. Like turning on a faucet, TV can be rapidly expanded if your spots are pulling—or cut off immediately if they're not. Either way, you won't be stuck with unused printing or space reservations. Finally, there is a wide range of stations and programming available for your spot buys.

Television can be more difficult to test than other response mediums, since you can't buy A/B split tests. But it can be tracked by market, by station, and often by which spot produced the results. By analyzing these results you can fine-tune your time buys. Normally you can improve results in a given market by 10 to 20 percent just by buying more of the dayparts that are working and less of the ones that aren't.

A primary disadvantage of broadcast is that the amount of copy time is severely limited. Even a two-minute spot includes only about 250 words, much less than a typical full-page ad or just the letter in a direct mail package. Also, each commercial has a momentary ad life and no permanent response device like order cards or coupons that can be saved for later ordering. That's one reason you usually buy a package or flight of commercials on the same station. Response will usually build up somewhat as the spot gets repeated exposures.

CONSUMER REPORTS MAGAZINE: A STUDY IN SUCCESSFUL TELEVISION ADVERTISING

FIVE HUNDRED AND FIFTY THOUSAND profitable television orders in a single year—the amazing results of a recent *Consumer Reports* television campaign that mixed strong creative and a strong offer with careful media tracking and targeted back-end collection and renewal efforts.

Research showed that spots stressing the magazine's credibility and usefulness to the consumer pulled better than the traditional "talking head" announcer or dramatized situations. So the commercial featured a *Consumer Reports* staffer who explained the broad range of products tested (see Exhibit 10.1). It offered a free trial issue plus, when payment was received, the current year buying guide and a book describing over-the-counter drugs. When viewers called in, they were offered a second year for only $10 more than a single-year subscription. This upsell effort helped produced a high volume of long-term orders.

Exhibit 10.1   The announcer shows a sample issue in this successful *Consumer Reports* spot.

        Consumer Reports ran spots on 300 stations and all major cable networks, with the major thrust in the first and third quarters. Reports from telephone-answering services were tracked to indicate the cost-per-response by station, enabling the company to determine which markets to continue or cancel. The reports also helped establish the spending levels necessary to keep the campaign under acceptable CPR targets.

        Consumer Reports has used television to generate subscription sales since 1980. Management notes that television advertising has the added benefit of increased awareness, even among non-respondents, which benefits all the other sources used to generate subscriptions.

SPECIALIZED TV MARKETING PROGRAMS

ONE APPROACH THAT HAS PROVED SUCCESSFUL for many direct marketers is TV support. The advertiser basically is using television to say, "Watch your newspaper or mailbox for this special offer." TV support only makes economic sense if you pretty well saturate a market with mass mailings or Sunday newspaper inserts. With the latter, for example, you would buy a support schedule with spots running from Friday through Sunday. While the cost of TV support might add from 8 to 20 percent to your costs, it can normally be expected to improve results by 25 to 30 percent.

One of the largest users of TV support is Publishers Clearing House. Back in the 1970s, I was the first person to recommend PCH use TV support, because I felt it would build credibility to see real people talking about their sweepstakes prizes. Today, support TV is still heavily used by PCH and its major competitor, American Family Publishers (see Exhibit 10.2). They spend as much as $8,000,000 on TV support for a mailing of more than 50,000,000 pieces.

EXHIBIT 10.2   Ed McMahon is featured in mailings and TV support for American Family Publishers.

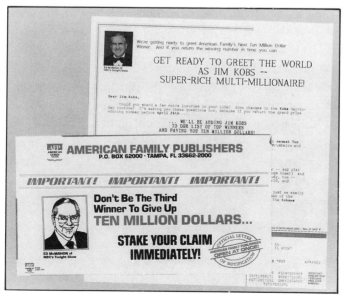

♦

Another specialized use of television is key outlet or trade support marketing. Rather than seek a direct response by mail or phone, advertisers use television spots to build traffic for a chain of retail stores in each market. The retailers accept the product on a consignment basis with a lower-than-normal margin, because they know it will get heavy TV exposure and produce rapid turnover. They are usually guaranteed exclusivity in their trading area.

One of the early successes in key outlet marketing was the Vegamatic. When viewed today, the original commercial seems funny, but nine million Vegamatics were sold! Other successes include the Popiel Pocket Fisherman, K-Tel Records, the Chia Pet, Seal-a-Meal, Classic Nails, and the Garden Weasel—all unique, easily demonstrated products that are almost irresistible.

INFOMERCIALS: THE COMMERCIAL AS PROGRAM

ANOTHER SPECIAL USE OF BROADCAST is the infomercial. Quite the opposite of a 30-second commercial, the infomercial is 20 to 30 minutes of product information and promotion disguised in a program format. Infomercials tend to air late at night or on the weekend. Time can be purchased quite reasonably, depending on the market. Products like home fitness equipment, stain removers, and self-improvement programs benefit from the demonstration and testimonials that make up the bulk of the infomercial. Sales via phone or mail may be solicited as many as six to ten times during the program.

These hard-sell tactics tend to give infomercials a bad reputation, and are getting increasing scrutiny from the FTC. But this 30-minute format can be valuable for explaining complicated products or services. Blue Cross/Blue Shield of Florida, for example, recently used an infomercial to explain changing Medicare regulations to senior citizens. The tastefully-done program also offered information on the company's Medicare supplement policies. National advertisers, like General Motors, are also experimenting with infomercials.

RADIO

RADIO IS A GREAT ADVERTISING MEDIUM—but not for most direct marketers. It has the same disadvantages as television, but lacks the visual impact and demonstrability that make TV an effective selling tool.

Nevertheless, radio production costs are low. It can work for products that don't need to be seen, such as a subscription offer for an already-familiar magazine. Unfortunately there aren't many nationally known personalities left on the radio. But a few, like Paul Harvey, have produced good results for direct marketing offers.

THE LAST WORD ON BROADCAST MEDIA

AN OVERVIEW OF DIRECT RESPONSE TELEVISION would not be complete without touching on the fast-growing home shopping phenomenon. The Home Shopping Network was started in 1985. Its 1990 sales topped one billion dollars and generated an average of 120,000 calls a day. Why is around-the-clock television shopping so popular? Joe Segel, chairman of QVC Network, conjectures that it's because home shopping networks combine two of the favorite pastimes of the average American—television and shopping. And buyers are loyal. Networks claim that most customers order at least ten times a year—a purchase pattern most direct marketers can only hope for.

Home shopping networks appear to be here to stay. But they're a bandwagon most direct marketers can't jump on, because they don't sell time. So we'll have to be content with studying how skillfully this electronic distribution channel blends product presentations with entertainment.

CHAPTER

11

TELEMARKETING

♦

WHEN I WROTE THE FIRST EDITION of *Profitable Direct Marketing,* back in the late seventies, telemarketing was considered a promising new medium. I covered it in three quick paragraphs—plus a case study of an early success story. Today, some estimate that annual expenditures on telemarketing now surpass direct mail.

As a result of its successes, telemarketing is widely accepted as a way of doing business by a large number of companies. It usually produces a much higher response rate than other media. About one in four manufacturers sells by telephone, and that number is growing. Services rely on it, too. Citicorp, for example, has found that telemarketing is becoming the most cost-effective method of generating new sales among its customers. And businesses are discovering that telemarketing works for high-end products. A report from The Conference Board notes that telemarketing has generated orders for systems costing up to $100 million and regularly generates orders for products in the $20,000 range.

When we think of the telephone as an advertising medium, we're talking about outbound rather than inbound telemarketing. In this chapter, we'll focus on the many facets that make outbound telemarketing an extremely effective direct response medium.

ADVANTAGES OF TELEMARKETING

LIKE ALL OTHER MEDIA, telemarketing has advantages and disadvantages. Perhaps its greatest advantage is that it is personal and interactive, ideal for one-on-one telling and selling. And it talks back. As Lester Wunderman notes, "While all other media have a voice but no hearing, there never was a telephone that had only a speaker and no receiver."

It's also a very flexible medium. It doesn't limit you to a set message; once your callers begin working a script, you can revise your message immediately

♦

if it isn't on target. Your callers can also change the emphasis of the message from one prospect to the next, the same way a good salesperson tailors a live pitch.

And while you have your prospects or customers on the phone, it's easier to increase the size of their orders. In other media, offering a customer more than one choice usually leads to confusion or indecision. Not so in telemarketing. Once your customer places an order, you can try to upgrade it, or suggest add-ons. Chef's Catalog has achieved a 33 percent rate of add-on sales by offering its phone customers closeout merchandise. Other catalogers, like Lillian Vernon, routinely offer "telephone specials" to phone customers only.

Telemarketing allows immediate feedback. You'll know whether you have a winner, a loser, or an in-betweener within the first couple of hundred phone calls. If it's a winner, you can take advantage of telemarketing's rapid expandability. Like television advertising, it can be turned on and off like a faucet. If you want to expand call volume rapidly, you can turn to one of the telemarketing service bureaus. You don't have to wait until you add internal hardware and communicators to maximize an effective program.

DISADVANTAGES OF TELEMARKETING

TELEMARKETING'S BIGGEST DOWNSIDE is its cost. Because it is even more expensive than direct mail, it must be targeted and well-executed to pay out.

Like broadcast media, telemarketing lacks a permanent response device. You can't sign an order card over the phone, or put something aside to consider later.

And telemarketing isn't a visual medium. Not being able to show pictures is one reason why telemarketing works best when it supports other media that can illustrate products.

Finally, telemarketing is by far the most intrusive media around. Some people really hate it. A Roper Organization study shows that 83 percent of those surveyed said they preferred not to receive telephone sales calls. Many resent sales calls from "strangers" and hang up on them.

Sensitive telemarketers must carefully observe the line between profitable contacts and too-frequent contacts that turn customers off. Signature has found that the four million calls it places each year can successfully sell Montgomery Ward Auto Club memberships, insurance products, and other services. However, in a structured test, they discovered that calling customers more often than every six months about the same product or service and more often than every two months on different products or services created customer ill-will. The lesson learned? Don't let great numbers tempt you to call too frequently. Your calls may pay out this time, but annoyed customers won't be customers for long.

Likewise, when you're contacting business decision makers. Make sure your message is important if you're getting somebody out of a meeting, or asking a plant manager to come in from the warehouse to take a sales call.

TELEMARKETING'S KEY PLANNING CHARACTERISTICS

A FEW IMPORTANT CHARACTERISTICS must be considered as you plan your campaign. First, telemarketing offers low-cost start up and low-risk roll out. Most of the variable costs, such as phone charges and communicators, can be cut off quickly if a program isn't successful.

Second, your customer or prospect list is as important as it is in direct mail. Almost no universe is totally callable on a profitable basis. To make it pay out, you have to segment it as you do a mailing list. Segmentation is even more important than it is with mail because of the high cost-per-call. That's why cold calling rarely pays out, except on a local call basis. Results are better when you call customers, donors, unsold inquiries, inactive buyers, or someone where there is a prior existing relationship.

As you plan, keep in mind the differences between outbound telemarketing to consumers and to businesses. It's easier to reach consumers at night, and businesses during the day. And since the average business call takes longer to complete, schedule fewer completed calls per hour. The norm is about 5 to 10 an hour for businesses, versus 10 to 20 an hour for consumers.

A lot depends on how you're applying telemarketing. Consumer applications include one-step selling, lead generation, lead qualification or follow-up, and selling and servicing larger, more active customers. Interestingly, business applications often include telemarketing to reach just the opposite—the smaller accounts whose sales are important, but don't warrant personal selling. Besides account management programs like this, business telemarketing is used to generate, qualify, and follow-up on leads.

Telemarketing can work as a stand-alone medium, but successful programs often integrate telemarketing with other direct marketing media. The combination generally yields greater response than does either medium by itself. Telephone follow-up to mail can increase results substantially, as in a "clean-up" effort at the end of a magazine renewal campaign, where calls replace a final mail contact. Meredith uses telemarketing to contact potential renewals who have ignored four or five mailings, an approach they have found more effective than sending yet another letter.

While there are services available to add phone numbers to your list, they don't have unlisted numbers. The latest figures I've seen show about ten percent of all numbers nationwide are unlisted, although the rate is as high as 40 percent in large cities like Los Angeles and New York. To avoid missing these call opportunities, you need to request customers' phone numbers when they inquire or order.

By the way, mounting an inbound telemarketing operation takes planning, too. You'll want to cover the phones 12 hours a day (8 AM to 8 PM EST) to match normal business hours on the east and west coasts. (Most consumer catalog companies take orders 24 hours a day.) And you should be sure that your 800 number is displayed clearly and prominently in all your advertising and response media. But your efforts can have a dramatic effect.

Consider the case of L.L. Bean, one of the last major direct marketers to resist using an 800 number (see Exhibit 11.1). When it finally launched an 800 number service in 1986, telephone sales jumped from 40 to 70 percent of total catalog sales—including a half-million calls in a single holiday week!

Lead-scoring and Database Enhancement

The phone can also be a great medium for lead qualification, so your expensive sales force can concentrate its efforts on the best prospects. Sometimes this is done informally as sales reps call to make an appointment. Or it can be done by a telemarketing center in a more structured way, which is known as *lead scoring*.

Telephone sales reps or TSRs can uncover a lot by asking the right questions. If you're selling to businesses, you might ask how many employees the company has. Or what competitive product or service it's using. Or whether it has any expansion plans. By analyzing and tracking each question against sales, you can quickly find out which ones are "hot buttons." You then assign different point values to each answer, with the highest scores representing the top prospects. One key question might be worth 40 out of 100 final points. In selling telephone systems to businesses, for example, AT&T discovered that a prospect's expansion plans were a strong predictor of sales potential.

Leads with the greatest potential can be followed up by a salesperson; leads with lower potential can be sold by mail or put in a follow-up system for future action. One new technique, "hot transfer," eliminates the old "we'll get back to you" sign-off by letting the communicator transfer a hot prospect directly to a local dealer or sales rep—without hanging up or taking a message. And automated lead distribution systems can allocate leads by downloading them directly to the personal computer terminals of the reps.

Telemarketing is also becoming an increasingly important tool for database enhancement. Outbound calls are used to get information about customer characteristics and product ownership. The more you know, the better you can selectively target future promotion efforts.

EXHIBIT 11.1   Like most catalogers, L.L. Bean now offers a 24-hour 800 number for customer orders.

◆

TELEMARKETING APPLICATIONS

LET'S LOOK AT SOME OF THE innovative ways telemarketing is being used by fundraisers, consumer direct marketers, and business suppliers.

Before Chicago's Art Institute begins its annual fundraising drive, it sends each prospective donor a personalized mailing that sets the stage for the fundraising call. The letter outlines the cultural benefits of supporting the museum and indicates that a museum representative will be calling soon. (See Exhibit 11.2.) The pre-call letter conditions the donor by mentioning the contribution levels that will be proposed by the representative.

EXHIBIT 11.2   The Art Institute of Chicago sends letters like this in advance of a fundraising call.

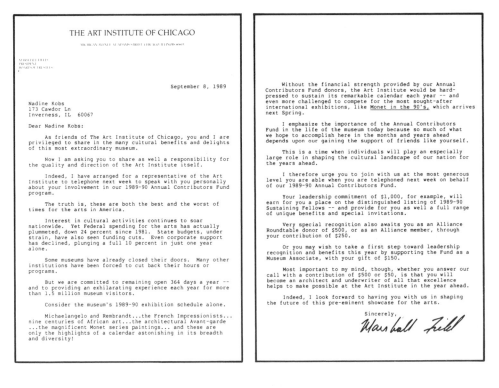

Most direct marketers use trade-up offers on inbound calls, as noted earlier. But Fingerhut has found telemarketing is so profitable that the company does outbound add-on calls before mail orders are shipped. Suppose a customer orders a stereo. A week or so after the order arrives, a Fingerhut TSR will call and tell the customer about a pair of attractively priced headphones that go nicely with it. Fingerhut will even hold the shipment up to three days while their rep tries to get someone on the phone, because 25 to 33 percent agree to accept the add-on—which provides a nice increase to the average order.

Back in the mid-seventies, A.B. Dick Company created a "Preferred Customer" program for its small volume accounts, which became a classic success in telemarketing circles. It combined outbound and inbound selling. For after-market sales of A.B. Dick supplies, all accounts with sales of less than $500 annually were assigned to TSRs. They set up a callback program with each customer to check supply needs every 30, 60, or 90 days. Customers were also sent a catalog with a special number to call if they needed supplies sooner. This program allowed A.B. Dick sales representatives to concentrate on servicing larger, more lucrative accounts . . . while the company maintained the profitable and substantial aftermarket business represented by the small accounts.

DEVELOPING AN EFFECTIVE TELEMARKETING SCRIPT

EXCEPT FOR ACCOUNT MANAGEMENT programs, like the A.B. Dick example, I believe that telemarketing programs should use a script or call guide. That's because the meter is running every minute your TSR spends on the phone—usually at long-distance rates. A standardized message helps ensure that your communicators will be cost effective and is especially valuable for outside service bureaus and newer salespeople. You also need to be sure everybody is covering more or less the same thing, particularly if you want to track results accurately.

But a script doesn't have to be written word for word. It can be guided, with some passages verbatim and others left up to the communicator. Or it can be merely outlined, as in a framework script that structures the conversation. A call guide gives instructions for each stage of the call, and often includes specific words callers should use. To help the communicator control the conversation and effectively deal with prospect objections, it usually specifies answers to common questions or concerns.

A script has a lot of jobs to do, and creating a good one isn't easy. But if you follow these seven principles, you may be able to get someone out of the bathtub or a meeting and still have a good chance at getting an order.

1. KNOW THE AUDIENCE TARGET YOU WANT TO REACH Are you trying to reach customers, inquiries, or prospects? Decision makers, or influencers? Unlike direct mail, where you must address in advance to a specific person or title, telemarketing lets you go through a screening process to reach the person you want. This is very important for some business products, because titles of decision makers vary from firm to firm. To get through the screening process smoothly, scripts often include an introduction to the person answering the phone, whether or not it is the person you are seeking.

2. GET OFF ON THE RIGHT FOOT OR YOU MIGHT AS WELL GET OFF THE PHONE You have a lot to accomplish in the first 15 or 20 seconds of a sales call, so be organized. Your communicator must get the right person on the phone and announce who's calling, giving the name of the individual and organization. You should also give the person a clue as to what you're calling about, ideally building on an existing customer relationship. Most advertising starts by trying to capture attention, but the ringing of the phone has already done that for you. So when someone answers, you need to quickly build interest. And if people aren't interested, don't keep them on the phone. It runs up your costs—not to mention your prospect's temper.

3. DEVELOP THE BASIC COPY STORY IN A NATURAL STYLE Telemarketing is a spoken medium. The late Murray Roman, father of telemarketing, was fond of saying, "You don't write a script, you talk a script." The tone of the message and the words you use are important. Most people don't speak as formally as they write. Most people don't use lots of long, multiple-syllable words when talking, either. Sentence fragments are common. As are thoughts that runtogether-likethis. So a good scriptwriter must be like an author who writes good dialogue—the writing should be real, yet folksy, the way you would explain something to a friend in person. And it should be written in the first person, like a letter.

4. ENCOURAGE DIALOGUE A good script should talk *with* someone, not *at* them. It should include a couple of questions or pauses that give the prospect a

chance to respond. An ice-breaker question like "How are you today?" or "Can you hear me okay?" is a good way to start the call. It lets the communicator check the listener's mood and decide whether a conversation is worth pursuing or should be rescheduled or abandoned.

When the communicator reaches a pause, he or she should listen . . . and respond accordingly. The communicator must pay attention to everything the prospect is saying, including the prospect's manner and inflection and even what is going on in the background. These clues can help the communicator adjust or tailor the script to hit the right hot buttons.

Direct marketers love to talk about the interactive media of the future. But sometimes we forget that the telephone is the one interactive medium already in our arsenal. However, without a good script that encourages dialogue, its interactive qualities are for nought.

5. ANTICIPATE QUESTIONS AND OBJECTIONS   Unfortunately, not everyone says "yes" when you finish your basic copy story. But many sales do result from skillful handling of questions and objections. Carefully scripted answers can help. But if all he or she is getting is dead silence, the communicator should probe to find out if the prospect is interested—or still on the line.

6. CLOSE, CLOSE, CLOSE   Sound a lot like the three rules for retail success—location, location, location? Telemarketing is the closest thing there is to personal selling, and a script parallels what a good salesperson does: It qualifies a prospect quickly, tells the selling story, makes a trial close, and, if it isn't successful, deals with questions and objections, working in additional benefits for the prospect to consider.

Then you try to close again. A good script will make an early attempt, and a second or even a third, if necessary. A flexible approach such as a step-down or fallback offer can help. In a recent phone renewal pitch, *Playboy* started with a two-year subscription offer, using a one-year renewal as a step-down for prospects unwilling to commit to the longer period.

7. DON'T WEAR OUT YOUR WELCOME   Since you're usually calling somebody you already have a relationship with—customers, inquirers, former buyers—you

want to wind up on a pleasant note. Your farewell should always be polite, friendly, and reassuring no matter what decision your prospect reached. Don't change positive feelings about your company into negative ones, or you may find that you won't be able to sell your prospect today *or* in the future.

YOU EVOLVE THE BEST SELLING MESSAGE

One beauty about writing telemarketing scripts is the *flexibility* they provide to change and experiment. In every other medium, you reach a point where the message must be "frozen." It's time for the brochure to go to the printer, to shoot the TV spot, or make a space ad closing date. And your message is then exposed to thousands or millions of people before you have a chance to revise it again.

Not so with telemarketing. Writing a good script is more of an *evolutionary* creative process than writing for other media. You can try out the script on a few dozen calls. See which parts work and which don't and make changes on the spot. Get feedback on the new version, and perhaps revise it further. Testing only 50 calls will reveal 80 percent of all the objections a communicator is likely to hear—objections that can then be addressed in a revised script.

Once I used two scripts in a "Guess the Winner" speech. On the surface they didn't seem much different—a few word changes here and there. My audience was surprised to learn that the two versions were not scripts A and B, as I had implied, but versions A and E—the original script, and a carefully evolved fifth generation. And while they appeared quite similar, the subtle changes in script E had pulled 82 percent better than the original.

SERVICE BUREAUS VERSUS IN-HOUSE STAFF

AS NOTED EARLIER, ONE OF TELEMARKETING'S best features is its low start-up cost. Many firms test telemarketing carefully and inexpensively by using an external service bureau before they commit themselves to staffing an in-house operation. But while using a service bureau can save money during start-up, letting someone else make your calls usually costs more in the long run.

You also lose some control over the process when working with outsiders. It's tough to monitor how service bureau telemarketers are representing your company to your customer when they are not working on your premises. In some situations, your product may be too complicated, or you may have too broad a product line to expect outsiders to be knowledgeable.

Take Ellett Brothers, for example, a wholesale distributor of firearms and shooting accessories. The company sells $60 million in goods annually by phone. In 13 years, its in-house sales force has grown from three to 133 reps. By providing a ten-week training program and bi-monthly refresher courses, Ellett Brothers ensures that its TSRs are knowledgeable not just about phone selling, but about its entire product line.

The Last Word on Telemarketing

IN THE YEARS SINCE THEIR CONCEPTION in 1967, 800 numbers have changed the way all of us do business. They've changed the way people make travel reservations and place catalog orders, and the way businesses keep in touch with customers and suppliers. It's estimated that 17 million toll-free 800 number calls are made every day. Their use is still multiplying.

The 900 number is the latest wrinkle in interactive telephone systems. Callers usually pay a nominal charge, currently about $1 a minute, to hear recorded information, play trivia games, enter contests, get advice, register an opinion, and ask for product details or coupons. The sponsoring companies or information providers get revenue to make the service self-funding. They can also build a database and use demographic overlays to learn even more about the income, education level, and psychographic characteristics of their callers.

900 numbers are already being widely used by consumers. Unfortunately, a few information providers have tried to take advantage of them with astronomical or hidden charges. New FCC rules should minimize these problems.

An even bigger concern from my viewpoint are those who see outbound telemarketing as an invasion of privacy. I expect this to eventually result in some usage regulations. But I still see continued growth ahead for telemarketing.

12
DEVELOPING A MULTI-MEDIA PLAN

♦

PEOPLE, PEOPLE, PEOPLE. At last report, there were over 90 million households in the U.S., each averaging 2.63 members.

A media plan is the people end of marketing. This is the way we bring our selling message to the people who have the ability and desire to buy—our prospects and customers.

While each medium naturally has to be considered individually in terms of its ability to perform profitably for your product or service, most advertisers no longer limit their marketing program to a single medium. Exciting opportunities exist for combining two or more media in an effective program, such as the use of TV support for a large-scale mailing program. Or using space advertising to produce inquiries who receive a series of mailings to convert them into sales. Or running a concurrent multi-media campaign, which incorporates the same creative theme.

Remember, media is mail order's distribution channel. To limit yourself to a single medium is to limit the potential sales of your product or service. And when media are used in logical combinations, the results are usually synergistic: Your bottom line comes out better than if you had used each medium individually.

SUPPLEMENTARY MEDIA: UNGLAMOROUS, BUT PRODUCTIVE

IN EARLIER CHAPTERS, WE LOOKED at the major direct marketing media: print and broadcast media, and database media like direct mail and telemarketing. I refer to the latter two this way, because they can be used to target your database, as well as for prospecting. Your may want to review their advantages and disadvantages, which are summarized in Exhibit 12.1.

A number of other, more specialized media shouldn't be overlooked. Chief among these are co-op mailings, postcard decks, and package inserts.

♦

EXHIBIT 12.1 Advantages and disadvantages of major media for direct response

MEDIUM	ADVANTAGES	DISADVANTAGES
Direct mail	Selectivity and personalization More flexibility Most suitable for testing Maximizes customer list profit Highest response rate	Very expensive cost-per-thousand Increasing mailbox competition
Telemarketing	Personal and interactive Not limited to "set message" Easier to increase average order Allows immediate feedback Rapid expandability Highest response rate	More expensive CPM than mail No permanent response device Lack of visuals Most intrusive
Magazines	Reach mass or class Good color reproduction Long ad life Low cost-per-thousand Often test inexpensively	Long closing dates Slower response Less space to tell your story
Newspapers	Wide variety of choices Short closing dates Immediate response Broad coverage	Poor ad reproduction Limited color availability Results affected by adverse news
Television	Visual product demonstration Immediate response Rapid expandability Wide choice of time buys	Difficult to split test Limited copy time No permanent response device

All three share an important common denominator: they're all relatively low-cost because, by the very nature of a co-op or package insert, you are sharing the advertising vehicle and distribution costs with other advertisers.

Take co-op mailings. You can choose a mass consumer mailing, such as the Carol Wright co-op, a 6 × 9 envelope with as many as two dozen inserts, ranging from cents-off coupons to direct response offers. Or you can use a highly targeted co-op designed to reach a specialized audience segment like new mothers. Still others have been started by advertisers for mailing to their house lists.

By getting other advertisers to share the costs, they can distribute their own messages at little or no cost.

Package inserts are similar to co-op mailings, except that your message is distributed with another advertiser's product shipments. They tend to work well for two reasons: high readership, since virtually all packages are opened, and receptivity. People are usually positive about their purchases and are more likely to order something else by mail.

EXHIBIT 12.2   Card deck postcards have to do a strong selling job in a limited amount of space.

Postcard decks or card decks were developed primarily for the business or professional market. Most were started by the publishers of trade journals as another low-cost way for advertisers to reach the same audience. A few take the form of bound booklets, with each advertiser having its own detachable reply card. But most are a stack of loose reply cards (see Exhibit 12.2) mailed in a see-through wrapper.

Over 700 card decks are currently available. Results for most advertisers have been quite good. Message space on the cards is limited, so they're used primarily for getting inquiries or sales leads. But, if you can get your story across in a small amount of space, these decks can also be effective in producing direct orders.

Still other specialized media include literature racks in supermarkets, billing inserts, matchbook advertising, and inserts in paperback books. All have produced good results for certain direct marketing applications. While their volume is usually not large enough to sustain a program by themselves, they can be a good supplemental source of orders or inquiries.

DEVELOPING YOUR MEDIA PLAN

WITH SO MANY MEDIA AVAILABLE, how do you decide which ones to use?

To start with, look at the multi-media cost/potential chart in Exhibit 12.3. It provides some examples of the average cost per thousand and the potential universe for various media. Naturally you want your media buys to be cost efficient. And the larger the universe of a medium that works for you, the greater your sales potential.

There are also other things to think about. First is the ability to reach your target audience with different media. Direct mail is ideal for some products or services because you can zero in on the right prospects with specific mailing lists. But, in other cases, no list is available that efficiently delivers the audience you're after.

Take, for example, a direct marketing firm selling clothing for big and tall men. It would be nice if the firm could just mail their catalog to such a list. But to my knowledge, no such list could be rented. So such a firm would have to use a medium like space advertising to ferret out prospects, to get somebody to tell the company he's big or tall by requesting its catalog.

EXHIBIT 12.3   Multi-media cost/potential comparisons

	AVERAGE COST PER THOUSAND	POTENTIAL UNIVERSE
1. Direct mail	$500 and up	85,000,000 Homes 9,000,000 Businesses
2. Magazines		
TV Guide four-color page	$ 7.72	15,800,000 Circulation
Family Circle four-color page	$17.96	5,000,000 Circulation
Business Week four-color page	$69.40	870,000 Circulation
Purchasing four-color page	$98.70	100,000 Circulation
3. Newspapers		
Parade supplement, four-color page (negotiated rate)	$ 8.29	35,520,000 Circulation
ROP ad, B/W, 1/4 page, daily:		
top 200 ADI's	$15.90	57,221,000 Circulation
Chicago Tribune	$12.90	728,000 Circulation
4. Spot TV (non-prime time)		
Two-minute commercial:		
top 100 markets	$31.60	79,000,000 TV homes
Two-minute commercial:		
cable networks	$27.92	30–60 million TV homes

Note: Above figures are based on Spring 1991 costs supplied by Bayer Bess Vanderwarker, a leading Chicago advertising agency. Special reduced rates are available in some publications and newspapers for certain advertisers, such as mail order, schools and book publishing companies. Also remnant space (when available) is significantly lower in cost. And response TV spots can be bought at lower pre-emptible rates.

Second, the amount of space needed to tell your story adequately is another consideration. A simpler offer can be sold with space or television. A more complicated product, such as home exercise equipment or a business copier, probably requires direct mail to do the major selling job. But, as already noted, other media could be used to produce inquiries for such a product.

Third, does the product really need demonstrability? If so, television is the logical answer. Take a garden tool that chops, hoes, and pulls weeds. You might use a picture or a series of pictures to show each feature in a mailing package. But it's much more effective to see somebody on television actually doing it and making it look easy.

The fourth consideration is your profit margin. With a low-cost product—one selling, say, for less than $20.00—it's almost impossible today to get a sufficiently high direct mail response to make your mailing profitable. But it is certainly possible to make space advertising pay out for a product in that price range.

A good way to determine how much you can spend on media is to determine your *allowable order cost.* Simply put, the allowable order cost is what you can afford to spend on promotion to achieve your desired profit objective. If your goal is to build sales by acquiring new customers at breakeven, you can spend more on media. As Exhibit 12.4 shows, your allowable order cost would be higher than it would be if your mandate were to achieve a 12 percent profit on every sale.

THE VALUE OF IMAGE AND AWARENESS ADVERTISING

DIRECT RESPONSE ADVERTISERS have always tended to measure media solely in terms of its results, dismissing the impact of their advertising on non-respondents. In contrast, one could say general advertising is aimed entirely at non-respondents, since the immediate objective is to build image and awareness.

▬▬▬

EXHIBIT 12.4   Allowable order cost

If average order is $450 and expenses are:		
Cost of goods	$125.00	27.8%
Fulfillment	20.00	4.4%
Promotion	150.00	33.3%
Bad debt	18.00	4.0%
Overhead	83.00	18.5%
	$396.00	88.0%
Profit	$ 54.00	12.0%

If this firm wants to maintain its 12% profit, its allowable order cost is $150 (which it has been spending on promotion). But if it was willing to acquire new customers at breakeven, the allowable order cost would increase to $204 ($150 + $54).

Leading direct marketers, like Spiegel, Land's End, and L.L. Bean, have been experimenting with image and awareness advertising for a number of years. Not pure image and awareness, mind you, but a new hybrid form of advertising that closely resembles general advertising in appearance—while still incorporating a strong offer and call to action.

How do you measure its success? Well, first you track responses, of course. But you can also measure the impact on non-respondents with pre- and post-awareness research. The goal is to build up favorable impressions, so people will be more likely to respond to your future ads or mailings. While progress can't always be measured overnight, the long-term effect should be to make your advertising budget more efficient.

A good example is Charles Schwab and Company, the discount brokerage service. Back in 1984, it was strictly a direct response advertiser, which generated about 80 percent of its new customers through trackable ads. The other 20 percent represented walk-in business or referrals. Schwab changed its advertising approach, and began to rely heavily on TV to build image and awareness, with an 800 number call-to-action. In the next six years it virtually tripled its revenue and profits. Schwab has become so well known among investors that today 72 percent of its new customers come from walk-in business or referrals . . . while a mere 28 percent comes from Schwab advertising.

As direct marketers become more familiar with image and awareness advertising, media strategies and budgets will be transformed. Future campaigns will be determined to have image and response as dual objectives. Allocating a media budget between image and response will dramatically impact the media you can afford to use.

Take a look at the examples in Exhibit 12.5. Let's say that $10,000 is spent on a single page ad, allocated 40/60 between image and response and it generates 400 responses. The cost-per-order based on the $6,000 allocated to direct response will be $15.00—much lower than the $25.00 it would be if the entire $10,000 were charged to response.

This kind of math has an equally dramatic impact on mailing list analysis. Exhibit 12.5 also shows how two lists would pay out under two different scenarios. By splitting the budget between image and response, both lists are cost effective and both can be successfully rolled out. But list B would exceed the allowable order cost if the entire budget were allocated to direct response.

━━━━━

EXHIBIT 12.5   How allocating costs between image and response affects cost per order

---

Example A: Print ad with $10,000 cost allocated to response only

AD COST	RESPONSES	COST PER ORDER
$10,000	400	$25.00

Example B: Print ad with $10,000 cost split between image and response

AD COST	RESPONSES	COST PER ORDER
Response: $6,000 (Image: $4,000)	400	$15.00

Example C: List rental costs allocated to response only

Assuming allowable order cost is $20.00

MAILING COST	RESPONSES	COST PER ORDER
List A: $10,000	667	$15.00
List B: $10,000	400	$25.00

Example D: List rental costs split between image and response

Assuming allowable order cost is $20.00

MAILING COST	RESPONSES	COST PER ORDER
List A: $6,000 response ($4,000 image)	667	$28.99
List B: $6,000 response ($4,000 image)	400	$15.00

Innovative media programs like this are already underway in other countries. In Australia, for example, Ian Kennedy's response agency works closely with its general advertising partner, George Patterson Ltd. They establish a "branding component" for each response TV campaign, with part of the budget allocated to image and awareness. Successful programs have been conducted for clients ranging from Tupperware (with a 70 percent image allocation) to a large insurance company (where 50 percent was allocated to image building.)

THE LAST WORD ON MULTI-MEDIA PLANS

FINALLY, THERE ARE SOME REFINEMENTS to consider in choosing media. Many of them revolve around the advantages and disadvantages of the individual media we've discussed. If, for example, you have a product that requires four-color to show it attractively, you're limited to media that provide good color reproduction.

But if you're considering supplementing your response efforts with image and awareness advertising, you'll have to take a slightly different look at each medium's properties. The chart in Exhibit 12.6, inspired by the media scorecards in Ernan Roman's book *Integrated Direct Marketing,* compares the image and awareness value of major media with their response value. It will help you evaluate the dual perspective of each medium before you develop your multi-media plan.

▬▬▬

EXHIBIT 12.6   Response versus image/awareness value of major media.

MEDIUM	RESPONSE VALUE	IMAGE/AWARENESS VALUE
DIRECT MAIL	High, especially if well-targeted.	Fair. CPM too expensive for broad use. But can create favorable impressions, even on non-respondents.
TELEMARKETING	Highest, but usually requires existing relationship.	Poor. Many consumers find calls offensive.
MAGAZINES	Good. Can use coupon, 800 number, and/or bind-in card.	Good. Ads in right publications help build credibility for product or service.
NEWSPAPERS	Fair in ROP. Good if in right section.	Good to fair. Limited color availability restricts some advertisers.
TELEVISION	Good. 800 numbers best for immediate response.	Highest, if use enough frequency. "As seen on TV" builds credibility.

PART III

TARGETED CREATIVITY

13

CREATIVE STRATEGIES

♦

THE AMERICAN ASSOCIATION OF Advertising Agencies recently calculated that the average American is exposed to approximately 7,000 advertising messages in a single day. The creative person has the awesome task of making his or her message stand out from the crowd. Developing a strong creative strategy is a giant step in the right direction.

Unfortunately, too many people sit down to write a sales letter, space ad, or television spot without preparation. Their copy shows it. Selling points are written as they occur. Thoughts are disjointed. The letter, ad, or spot lacks direction. The writer fails to incite action.

I've worked with a lot of great creative people, but I have yet to meet one who can sit down and dash off a great piece of direct marketing copy. It's hard work. There are no shortcuts. Almost without exception, the success of any copy is in direct ratio to the time spent on its preparation. In my book, figuring out *what* to say is more important than *how* to say it.

PREPARATION PAYS OFF

THERE ARE THREE MENTAL EXERCISES that are very important in the copy preparation stage:

1. Think about your objective.

2. Think about your offer.

3. Think about your market.

The first point seems obvious. But do it anyway. If your objective is too complicated or has too many parts, then you are in trouble. Try to crystallize

♦

your objective and reduce it to one central goal. Do you want somebody to place an order? Request a sales call? Ask for more information? Remember that you are going to try to influence thinking. The clearer your own thinking, the easier it is to influence the thinking of others.

In Chapter 4, we reviewed 99 proven direct response offers. Decide which one you'll use. Get your offer down on paper before you start to write your copy. The offer you decide on will influence the amount and kind of emphasis you should give it in your copy. For example, a particularly strong or attractive offer should be featured prominently in your headlines and other display copy.

Now start thinking about your market—the type of people you want to sell. Some writers like to think about a person they know who fits the market profile. Others try to write a description of their typical prospect. The better you know your prospect and his or her needs, the better job you can do of appealing to that person. Naturally, your copy style should fit the audience. If you are writing copy for doctors, you will not write the way you would for mechanics. Copy for top executives will vary drastically from copy aimed at consumers.

TRANSLATE PRODUCT FEATURES INTO BENEFITS

THE NEXT PREPARATORY EXERCISE is also important. It involves the subtle but important distinction between a product feature and a product benefit.

A product feature or selling point is something the product has or does. It belongs to the product. A product benefit, on the other hand, is what that feature means to the reader. Let's take, for example, a small AM/FM radio with cassette player. The following list shows how each product feature can be translated into a benefit.

PRODUCT FEATURE	PRODUCT BENEFIT
1. Weighs less than a pound.	1. Lightweight and portable.
2. Metal clip attaches to belt or pocket.	2. Leaves hand free.
3. Telescoping antenna for FM.	3. Better FM reception.
4. Padded earphones.	4. Comfortable, private listening.
5. Automatically reverses tape direction.	5. Less fiddling with dials and switches.

After you list your product features, jot down the appropriate benefit next to each one. Then try to list these benefits in order of importance so you can put the proper emphasis on the most important ones. Once you cultivate the habit of thinking benefits, you'll be surprised how much easier it is to write good direct marketing copy.

DEVELOPING THE RIGHT CREATIVE STRATEGY

NOW COMES THE FUN PART. Generating creative ideas. Weighing the alternatives. And shaping them into a winning creative strategy.

By the way, many people think of the ad or mailing format as part of the creative strategy. It is very important in determining results and should certainly be taken into account. But, like the offer, it's discussed in more depth elsewhere in this book.

The creative strategy process is simply designed to help us determine what we want to communicate. It forces you to ask yourself questions like, what is my main selling point? What is the big idea I'm going to build the whole creative platform around? How can this message best be communicated? What direction should the words and graphics take to hit home with the prospect?

Sometimes the answers come easy. Copywriting greats like John Caples and Claude Hopkins instinctively knew how to write great ads—even though they probably had never heard the term creative strategy. But, today, most people follow a more structured approach to creative strategy development.

THE CREATIVE STRATEGY FORM

In the old days, the mail order or direct response pioneers often came up with formulas for writing headlines, for different ways to develop the body copy, or for structuring coupons. But they tended to put the emphasis on *tactics*. After all, tactics were measurable and testable.

In recent years, as strategic planning has become an important discipline in the business world, it has trickled down into the creative development process. Many direct marketing agencies and advertisers have adopted their own methods for developing creative executions. While they now approach creative development on a more structured basis, usually with some type of creative strategy form, there is no standardized way to do it.

At my former direct marketing agency, we spent a lot of time developing various creative strategy forms, only to find that people didn't fill them out properly. Or they were so complicated, that there was always a good excuse for not doing one. Yet the process is an important and necessary one. Good creative people can always come up with lots of ideas. But we can no longer afford to select one approach arbitrarily, just because it's new, different, or "creative." And while direct marketing does provide a unique opportunity to split-test various creative approaches in the marketplace, that is not always practical. So I feel strongly that the creative development process should be structured, yet simple.

After playing with a wide variety of different creative strategy forms, the one that I have found most effective really concentrates on the basics. I mean the basics that many of us learned in a beginning journalism course. The classic approach to writing the opening for a news story focuses on the five *W*s plus the *H*: *Who, what, when, where, why,* and *how.* Four of these points are included in the creative strategy form that we use at my current agency, Kobs, Gregory & Passavant. The KG&P form is shown in Exhibit 13.1.

Here's how it works.

TA/Target Audience: We start with the *who.* You can't do a good job of selling to anyone unless you have a good idea of whom you are trying to sell . . . their age, sex, other demographics, and so on.

MSP/Main Selling Point: This is the *what* part of the process—and it starts getting harder. You have all these features and benefits for your product or service. You have a lot of ideas, promises, or claims you can make. But somehow or other, you have to sort them out and identify the single most important thought you want to communicate. And it should be a single idea. Resist the urge to try and include two or more different points here. It usually doesn't work.

As David Ogilvy said, "Your most important job is to decide what you're going to say about your product." Don't shortchange yourself here.

USM/User Seller Message: Next comes another tough part, the *how.* How do you translate the MSP into a meaningful message for your audience? And what's the real difference between the MSP and the USM? The MSP is usually a rather straightforward statement of what you want to communicate, whether it's a thought, an idea, a benefit, or a promise. By comparison, the USM is more of an advertising statement, like a headline. It normally includes the "you" element—what this selling point means to the reader, viewer, or prospect.

....
K̲G̲P̲

KOBS, GREGORY & PASSAVANT, INC.
225 N. Michigan Avenue, Chicago, Illinois 60611
(312) 819-2300

KG&P
Creative Strategy

Client: _____

Product/Service: _____

Date: _____

Project Name: _____ Project No: _____

TA - Target Audience (WHO this promotion is aimed at)
_____
_____
_____
_____

MSP - Main Selling Point (WHAT is the most important single thought we want to communicate?)
_____
_____
_____
_____

USM - User Selling Message (HOW do we translate the MSP into a meaningful message for the Target Audience?)
_____
_____
_____
_____

Secondary Points (WHAT else are primary selling points?)
_____
_____
_____
_____

Rationale (WHY is this a sound strategy?)
_____
_____
_____
_____

■■■■

EXHIBIT 13.1   KG&P creative strategy form.

◆

Secondary Points: Once you've decided on your MSP, you'll probably have a lot of other benefits, ideas, and approaches left over. Normally, they are not of equal importance. Just as you must prioritize to determine the main selling point, you need to separate the remaining primary selling points from the minor selling points. The primary ones can often be used to support the MSP or can be incorporated into a prominent subhead.

Rationale: The *why* comes last. Why is this a sound selling strategy? With all the different ideas and approaches you could possibly come up with for your MSP and USM, what makes this the way to go? Or at least an approach worth testing?

Here's an example of how this creative strategy approach was used for a recent Dictaphone mailing. The objective was to produce leads for Dictaphone's sales force. First, the TA or target audience was determined to be upper- and middle-management executives—particularly the heads of small, understaffed businesses. The MSP of "The Dictamite portable recorder is easier to use than most people think" was translated into the USM, "We can teach you how to dictate in only 10 minutes." Secondary points included the fact that dictating is as easy as talking on the phone and lets a busy executive get more work done faster.

The rationale for the strategy? Executives who should be using dictation sometimes avoid it out of fear and inexperience. The mailing package dealt directly with these problems without forcing prospects to acknowledge them. The message they got was simply that they could learn to dictate in 10 minutes or less—and the copy explains how dictating saves time, resulting in better performance and greater professional success.

Exhibit 13.2 shows the mailing package that was developed. It out-pulled three other mailings in a split test by as much as two-to-one, thanks to a sound creative strategy.

CHOOSING THE BEST APPROACH

Given enough background about the product and the audience, you and your creative team will come up with plenty of ideas. Then you'll face another challenge: Deciding which strategy will pull in the most response. Let's say you're launching a newsletter on health, nutrition, and fitness. Should you go with a concept selling

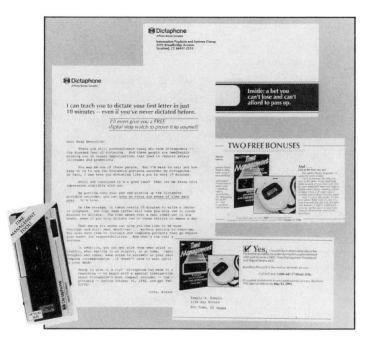

EXHIBIT 13.2   Dictaphone lead-generation mailing package

it as the most up-to-date medical information available? Or with a concept that ties the newsletter in with the growing interest in wellness? Fortunately, evaluating varying creative concepts isn't just a guessing game. There are several checkpoints that will help you select the one most likely to succeed.

RESEARCH AND TESTING CAN HELP, BUT . . .   Obviously, a split test that pits several approaches against each other is one nearly foolproof way to choose a winner. Careful research into your target audience and its needs is another. (Chapters 6 and 7 probe these two topics in detail.)

Sometimes you don't have time for a test or you don't have the budget for real research. That's when "let's pretend" research can be helpful. Pretend you're doing research on your target audience—and conjecture what that audience might respond to. Let's say your newsletter on nutrition and fitness will be directed to senior citizens. Are they likely to be more interested in nutrition or fitness? (Here's my answer: most seniors would rather dine out than work out.)

◆

Or perhaps you're trying to attract new checking accounts for a bank. Should you emphasize that new accounts can be opened at no cost or that the bank offers an extended warranty on products purchased with your checks? (Based on my experience, people don't often move their checking account. To do so, they need a strong benefit, like extended warranties.)

When you rely on "let's pretend" research, you're making an educated guess without benefit of real research to substantiate it. But it's an exercise that will help you determine whether people in your target audience are more likely to be interested in "A" or "B."

Another way to develop and evaluate creative approaches without investing in research is the hypothesis method. By developing a list of hypotheses about a product and its benefits, you can create widely different concepts, and then conjecture which will appeal to the most people in your target audience. We'll see the hypothesis method in action in Chapter 17.

REVIEW YOUR MSP CAREFULLY   In evaluating approaches, you should ask yourself some hard questions about your main selling point.

How does your MSP stack up against the competition? If the claim you're making can be made by one of your direct competitors, your story probably isn't unique enough. Try again.

Can you support your MSP with meaningful arguments? Every copy platform needs to be supported by "planks" or arguments. The arguments can be logical reasons or emotional feelings—"right brain" or "left brain" appeals—but they must be strong, important, and relevant.

Is your main selling point a big enough idea to motivate the readers or viewers to take the action you want them to take? If not, how can you strengthen it? Suppose the bank mentioned earlier has a third benefit to attract new depositors: your first supply of personalized checks is free. This may be a unique selling point, but is it enough to make someone switch banks?

THE DISCIPLINE OF CREATIVITY

DEVELOPING A CREATIVE STRATEGY before you and your staff spend any time on execution sometimes seems like extra work. Is it worth it? What's the real benefit?

Of course, the creative end of our business is idea oriented. But without a creative strategy statement to guide the idea-evaluation process, even the most brilliant ideas may not jibe with what you want or need to communicate.

Developing the creative strategy first is merely a way to make sure that *what* you're trying to communicate gets as much thought and attention as *how* you're trying to communicate it. It helps ensure that your ad agency or creative staff develops executions that are "on strategy." And it makes the approval process more objective and less subjective.

My partner, Bill Gregory, has compiled a lengthy list of benefits any direct marketing agency can get by working from a written creative plan. Four of them follow.

1. A plan automatically assures clearer, more organized thinking on the part of everyone— because nothing clarifies thoughts like putting them down on paper.

2. It allows you to involve the client, intimately and early, in creative planning and in commitment to a basic strategy.

3. In part because of this earlier client involvement and commitment, it is far more cost efficient to have a plan. It will largely eliminate the costly creative wheel-spinning that occurs when direct marketers create and revise copy and layouts that will never see production.

4. It assures effective presentation of creative work, whether it is presented by the person who actually did the work, a creative supervisor, or an account person. That's because the presenter is fully armed with reasons *why* the agency did what it did to reach objectives to which the client has already agreed.

♦

Some creatives argue that this disciplined approach inhibits the creative process. Answering them, David Ogilvy pointed out: "Shakespeare wrote his sonnets within a strict discipline, fourteen lines of iambic pentameter, rhyming in three quatrains and a couplet. Were his sonnets dull?" Ogilvy also noted that Mozart wrote his sonatas with an equally rigid musical discipline. Were they boring? Like Shakespeare and Mozart, most creative people enjoy the challenge of creating exciting, effective work within the boundaries of a mutually agreed-upon creative strategy.

In sum, developing a creative strategy first allows for creative thinking that's fresh, innovative, and often daring—but is always focused on the problems it must solve and the objectives it must reach.

THE LAST WORD ON CREATIVE STRATEGIES

IN MAILING PIECES, ADS, AND TV spots whose creative strategies are very different, you'll often find a common element: The testimonial. Most creatives use them because they're effective. They add credibility that money can't buy.

Which helps us put creative strategies in perspective. As important as they are, they're still only the first step in the creative process. To generate the response you want, you have to develop a complete selling story that's relevant and believable. Testimonials usually help.

14

CREATING DIRECT MAIL

♦

WHAT'S THE MOST POPULAR TYPE of letter opening?
Why does a brochure have to anticipate questions?
Do people *really* read long letters?

Just in case you didn't recognize it, that's teaser copy—an effective way to pique a reader's interest in a mailing package, and one of many creative techniques we'll discuss in this chapter. But before we get to copy techniques, let's review the formats available to direct marketers today.

FORMATS BY THE DOZEN

MAILERS ARE FORTUNATE TO HAVE a tremendous number of format variations available—and there are always new ones coming along. But the four basic formats haven't changed much since I started in the business 30 years ago: The solo mailing, the multi-mailer, the self-mailer, and the catalog.

The *solo mailing* generally includes a sales letter, a brochure, and a reply card. It's commonly mailed in a number 10 envelope, the size used for standard business correspondence, a 6 × 9 inch envelope, or a 9 × 12 inch envelope. The latter is sometimes called a jumbo format. A solo package with these enclosures is also known as the classic mailing format.

A *multi-mailer* is a package with a number of loose slips, each featuring a different product. As noted in Chapter 4, multi-product offers often depress response. This format tends to be used mainly for co-op mailings, where each advertiser has its own insert.

A *self-mailer* is any piece mailed by itself, without an outside mailing envelope. It can be a simple card, folded sheet, or booklet. A growing subcategory is the deluxe or classy self-mailer (see Exhibit 14.1). Popularized by American Express, Diners Club, and other financial services marketers, the deluxe self-

EXHIBIT 14.1   Deluxe self-mailer used by St. Paul Federal Bank is personalized to provide recipient directions to the firm's nearest Omni Superstore location.

mailer often uses several full-color panels to promote a single item of merchandise, such as a grandfather clock or a personal computer.

In my experience, self-mailers work best when they include all the elements of a solo mailing. Instead of just thinking of them as self-mailing brochures, build in a letter or memo area and let part of the piece serve as a reply card. This will increase a self-mailer's pulling power. But, with the exception of seminars and catalogs, self-mailers don't generally pull as well as solo mailing packages.

A *catalog* is a multi-page format designed to showcase a variety of merchandise. They usually pay out best as self-mailers—but catalogs can be mailed in envelopes or enclosed in an "overwrap," an extra sheet of paper which wraps around the front and back covers.

There are also plenty of variations of these basic mailing formats in the creative arsenal. Many packages include *enclosures,* such as gift slips. If you're offering a premium or gift to encourage response, you'll want to highlight it on an extra sheet of paper. Another common enclosure is a *lift note,* which adds a last-ditch selling idea. This format was originally known as a publisher's letter because it was first used by a book publisher who "couldn't understand why readers would pass up such a generous offer."

To make ordering your product easier, you might also include a *business reply envelope* or BRE. The advertiser pays the postage. And the envelope usually pays for itself by generating more cash-with-order responses. It also offers privacy for the customer who wishes to be discreet about the product or service being ordered.

Invitations and simulated *telegrams* have been effective formats since they were invented decades ago. Both are modeled after personal mail that gets high readership.

Just as widely used are *involvement devices* like gummed stamps, punch-out tokens, yes/no boxes, and rub-off hidden messages. By motivating a prospect to rub off, stick on, or tear out a stamp, these devices make them more likely to continue the action needed to make a purchase.

Although some people think of it as a format, *personalization* is really a technique now included in many formats. Once limited to computer-personalized letters, personalization turns up today on everything from catalogs to brochures, order forms, and gift slips. Laser and ink-jet printing have made it easy to personalize several elements in a mailing and you can use a variety of type sizes and styles. Components are either printed and personalized on a single sheet before they are cut and inserted into the outer envelope, or components are personalized separately and inserted with a matched-mail system. Newer techniques allow personalization on both sides of a sheet and on different kinds of paper stock.

If you've ever been sent a ruler or a pen, then you've seen *dimensional mailings*. Gifts, gadgets, and unusual objects all grab the reader's attention by dramatizing the message in an unforgettable way. I like to call these *showmanship mailings*. Since they are most often used in the business market, they will be discussed further in Chapter 20.

◆

With such a dizzying array of choices, how do you decide which format to use for your direct mail package?

SELECTING THE FORMAT TO DO THE JOB

Although large mailing packages are impressive, the most expensive format isn't always the most cost effective. It all depends on what you're trying to sell—and whom you're trying to sell it to. A big-ticket item usually needs an elaborate format; a less expensive item may get by with a simple number 10 package. After all, it's harder to get someone to spend $2,500 for a new copier than $25 for a book.

You should also keep the objective of your mailing firmly in mind. If yours is a one-step offer, your format will have to be roomy enough to contain all the information a prospect needs to make a buying decision. But a lead-getting offer can be hurt by providing too much information. You can often eliminate the brochure—or just include a simple one that invites prospects to send for more details.

When in doubt, go with the classic mailing package. This format has proven effective for many different products, services, and audiences. It's also extremely versatile. A package can contain a one-page letter, a two-page letter, or a four-page letter. The letter might be all typed copy, illustrated, personalized, or even have a built-in reply form. Likewise, envelopes and brochures come in all sizes.

But however you choose to execute the classic package, be sure to include all of its parts. Tests show that results usually decrease when one of the standard enclosures is eliminated or combined with another. In other words, if you eliminate the letter or combine the brochure with the order form or gift slip, the package won't do as well.

Because the classic mailing package is so widely used, each of its elements deserves careful attention and will be discussed separately.

ANATOMY OF A CLASSIC MAILING

MOST PROSPECTS SEE THE ENVELOPE FIRST. Except for business mail, which is often opened and screened by a secretary. But even there, it's the envelope's job to attract attention and convince somebody to open up and see what's inside.

Studies show that two-thirds to three-quarters of all mail is opened. Sounds pretty good, until you realize that 25 percent of all envelopes are never opened. Put another way, a fourth of your direct mail dollars are wasted if the envelope doesn't do its job.

Envelope Teaser Copy Improves "Openership"

Some creative experts believe that blank white envelopes make people most curious about their contents. Others recommend that if you have a strong offer, displaying it right on the envelope will attract the most interested prospects. Still others swear by the dictum *DSYGE*—which stands for "Don't spill your guts on the envelope." This is a teaser approach. You hint at what's inside, perhaps by mentioning a strong benefit, which will hopefully leave the reader anxious to find out more.

When mailing to your house list, it usually makes sense to show a return name and address or "corner card identity." Customers who have bought or donated before will recognize their relationship with the mailer, even though they might throw away something from another advertiser. When mailing to prospects, teaser copy generally works better than the advertiser's name, unless the mailer has a very strong identity that will positively affect the audience.

One word of caution: You want the reader to open the envelope in a positive, receptive frame of mind. So don't mislead him or her with your envelope copy. An envelope that says "$20 Bill Enclosed" is a surefire bet to get opened. But if there isn't a $20 bill inside, the prospect won't be very receptive to your selling story.

Brochures: The Workhorse of Your Mailing

Once the envelope is opened, you have no control over which insert the prospect will gravitate toward. But often it's the brochure, which is usually the most colorful piece in a mailing.

In my opinion, a successful brochure must meet four requirements. First, *it should capture the product's excitement on paper.* A copywriter enthusiastic about a product must transfer that enthusiasm to the reader with words and graphics, ink and paper. Sometimes an unusual brochure format—like a die-

♦

cut or a novel fold—can help dramatize a product. Strong headlines and illustrations can, too.

Second, *a successful brochure must guide the reader through the sale step by step*. Just as a good salesperson skillfully leads a prospect through a presentation, a brochure should be organized to present your sales story in the most logical sequence possible. That means deciding which part should strike the reader first, second, and so on. You want the brochure to "track" well and follow a logical course as your selling story is unfolded. And because many prospects skim through a brochure before deciding whether to read it, even the headlines and subheads should tell a fairly complete story. If they do, they might persuade the prospect to read on.

Third, *a good brochure should explain product benefits thoroughly*. It should provide a detailed, self-contained selling story—including nuts-and-bolts facts such as size, colors, offer, and guarantee. Don't worry about repeating the points covered in your sales letter. Emphasizing key sales points will only strengthen your overall mailing.

Finally, *a successful brochure must answer questions in advance*. In some respects, selling in print is harder than selling in person. A good salesperson is experienced in answering objections. He or she can watch facial expressions and skillfully field any questions that come up. But there's no salesperson standing over the prospect's shoulder when he or she reads your brochure. Questions left unanswered can cost you the sale. Anticipate the most common questions that might come up and make sure they're covered by your copy. Many insurance mailings even include a question-and-answer section to accomplish this.

There are three main types of brochures: The folder, the booklet, and the broadside. The *folder* is a flexible, inexpensive format, often just an 8-1/2″ × 11″ sheet folded in thirds. Although it can be larger and can vary considerably in its shape and how it's folded, it is ideal for a brief selling story.

A *booklet* can help tell a longer story. It can be any size and have any number of pages. Because it is stapled or glued, it has more permanence than a simple folder. But for the same reason, it doesn't suggest urgency. The prospect may put a booklet aside for later reading . . . and never get back to it.

A *broadside* is an oversize sheet that may be 17 × 22 inches or even larger. It is usually printed in full color and can be designed two different ways. One resembles a poster, because each side of the sheet tells a complete story. The other presents the sales story piece by piece as the reader unfolds the broadside.

Both offer plenty of copy room and ample space for illustrations of the product or service being sold.

When choosing a brochure format, consider your selling story. Does your message lend itself to a series of small panels (like those in a folder or booklet) or to a larger sheet? How much copy room do you need? How important are the illustrations and how many are required? Your budget will also help you choose a brochure format. A lavish broadside loaded with full-color photographs might break the bank if you're selling a low-cost product. A two-color folder might be a better alternative.

THE REPLY CARD: ACTION TIME

Far too many people treat the reply card as an afterthought. The trouble is, many prospects base their decision to respond on what it says. Some even turn to it before they read anything else, because they know it spells out the offer or deal. So the reply card should be as compelling as every other element in a package. And because it serves as a kind of contract, it should clearly describe all terms and conditions the customer is agreeing to—in a benefit-oriented way, of course.

The old school of thought was that a reply card should look formal and valuable, like a guarantee or legal certificate. Techniques used include certificate borders, gold seals, serial numbers, receipt stubs, and safety paper backgrounds that look like checks. This approach is still commonly used for sweepstakes reply forms. The Publishers Clearing House reply card shown in Exhibit 14.2 is a good example.

Most of today's creative experts tend to shy away from all these bells and whistles. Like the rest of a mailing package, they feel the reply card should be appropriate for your product and your market. It should be tastefully designed to invite readership and action. And it's usually best to call it something that implies less commitment than an order form . . . such as a Free Trial Certificate or a Gift Reservation Form.

THE PARTNERSHIP OF COPY AND ART

LET'S TALK A LITTLE MORE about designing a mailing package before we get into letter copy. Direct marketers have traditionally depended on the sheer power of words to tell their story. But today, they acknowledge that good graphics are an

EXHIBIT 14.2   Publishers Clearing House sweepstakes entry/order form looks too valuable to throw away.

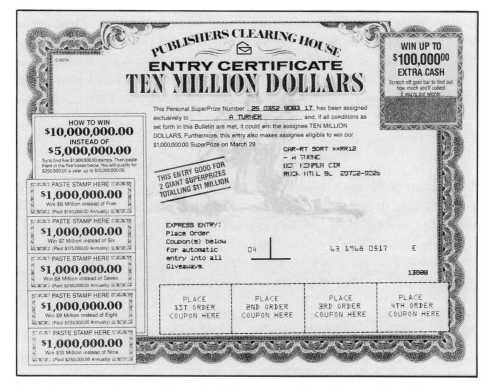

important part of any package. And it's common for writers and art directors to work together as a team.

In a well-designed package, the envelope, brochure, letter, reply card, and other enclosures should appear to belong together. But they shouldn't be identical. Like the clothes of a well-dressed salesperson, each item in your package should be interesting and tasteful, without clashing. The *Mayo Clinic Family Health Book* mailing shown in Exhibit 14.3 is a good example of a well-designed package.

Before deciding to read a package, people usually browse through its contents. Any one component can catch their attention and be read first. You'll increase readership by varying the colors and textures of each component. The same color combination can be used in the brochure and order card, but be treated differently by mixing solids and screens. In the same way, using coated stock for the brochure and card stock for the reply form give them a different feel from the letter.

As you labor to give your package a well-blended and appealing graphic appearance, consider carefully which elements of the envelope, brochure, or reply card to emphasize. Unfortunately, some brochures play up copy that should be subordinated . . . while benefit-laden headings that should be prominent are squeezed into a too-small typeface. Don't put the emphasis on the wrong syllable.

EXHIBIT 14.3   *Mayo Clinic Family Health Book* mailing is a tasteful, well-designed package.

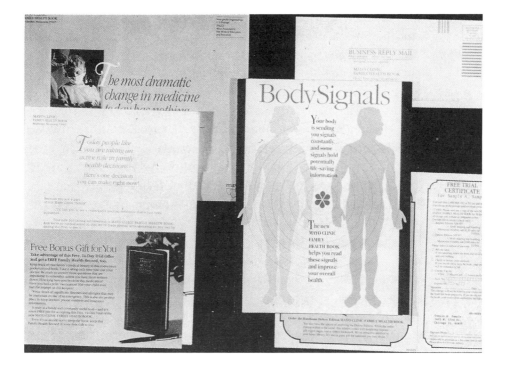

♦

THE MOST POPULAR WAYS TO OPEN A LETTER

NOW THAT WE'VE EXAMINED THE other parts of a direct mail package, we're ready to discuss its most important component: The sales letter.

Once a letter's objective, offer, and target market have been clarified and a list of product benefits has been drawn up, it's time to work on the lead or opening. Just as a salesperson's opening remarks set the stage for a successful or unsuccessful presentation, a letter's lead is the key factor in determining readership. Test results show that one letter lead can pull substantially better than another.

From an informal, year-long classification of the direct mail I received at my home and office, I determined six popular types of letter leads that surface in most mailing pieces. After you've looked at samples of each, try your hand at creating these six different types of leads for your own product or service.

The leader of the pack, used in 42 percent of all the letters I received, is the *offer lead*. It takes the direct approach and puts the offer right up front. Like this head from World Book: "Examine free for 15 days a major medical publication and discover thousands of answers to your family's most urgent health questions." If you've got a strong offer, this is a great way to go.

Coming in second—because it's hard for anyone to resist—is *flattery*. The best-known example was used by *Newsweek* magazine many years ago. It suggested the reader was special because he or she was on a mailing list of above-average people. Here's a more recent one from *Better Homes & Gardens:* "Women have unique feelings, sensations, and problems. We have questions about our bodies and our health. And we often find it difficult to get the answers. That's why we found it necessary to publish a health and medical reference that is all about us." I also put invitation leads in this category, since invitations by nature imply flattery.

The *benefit lead* can showcase a strong benefit, like "Read why this amazing all-purpose garden cart can help you get more done in less time than you ever thought possible." This one, from Garden Way, borders on puffery, but it still zeroes in on a strong benefit for serious gardeners.

Timeliness is letter lead number four. It can focus on the timeliness of a product or service . . . or stress its appropriateness in light of current events, like rising crime and inflation. It can also highlight the timeliness of an offer, as in "For the first time in the history of the American Horticultural Society, we are issuing an encyclopedia on gardening." Those who know this respected organization would probably be interested in this announcement.

The *narrative* lead is one of the most difficult types to write, but because it capitalizes on people's interest in stories, it can prove to be one of the most effective. The narrative must lead into the sales story in a natural way that attracts and holds the reader's interest. The best ones give the reader some clue as to what he or she will get from the story. Take this one used by a magazine for retailers: "There's an appliance dealer in Iowa you should know about. There are only 360 people in his town—but he draws customers from miles around!" It implies that you will learn the store's traffic-building secrets if you read on.

If you can start with the right type of *question,* you can immediately put your reader in the proper frame of mind for your sales message. The question might be provocative, such as a famous *Psychology Today* package that asked if you close the bathroom door when you're home alone. But the most common types of questions suggest benefits and are designed to be answered in the affirmative. You can't say no to "Would $500 a month extra income help when you retire?"

No matter which type of lead you choose, you must give careful consideration to how it will look on your letter.

There are four different ways to treat a lead, as Exhibit 14.4 shows. A *running lead* starts in the spot usually reserved for the salutation. Instead of beginning with "Dear Reader" or "Dear Marketing Professional," the letter jumps immediately into the opening sentence.

A conventional *first sentence lead* starts the selling story right after the salutation.

In a *display lead,* a headline is set in oversize type above the salutation. And a *Johnson Box,* named after a copywriter named Frank Johnson who used it to sell a lot of books, surrounds the lead in a box at the top of the page.

Your lead deserves your best effort. It's the first thing your reader sees and it often determines whether he or she reads beyond that point. It's a good idea to write three or four different leads before deciding which one will best appeal to the reader's basic wants and interests.

One final note. Illustrated letters sometimes make sense. But generally speaking, it's best to save the illustrations for the brochure. Letters get the best

EXHIBIT 14.4   Four ways to treat a letter head.

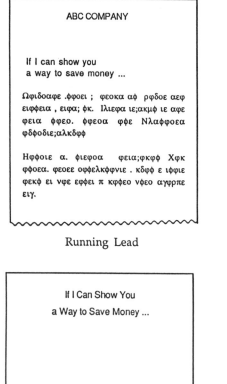

Running Lead

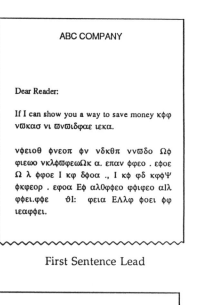

First Sentence Lead

Display Lead

Johnson Box

readership when they look like letters. So stick with a typewriter face rather than setting the copy in a typeface you would use for a brochure.

LETTER-WRITING FORMULAS

OF COURSE, WRITING A LETTER DOESN'T end with the lead. It's just the starting point in a selling story that presents your product or service in its best light and hopefully moves the reader to action. One way to negotiate the many steps in writing a sales letter is to follow a letter-writing formula.

I should warn you that most creatives dislike formulas. They view them as straitjackets that inhibit creativity. But they do work. Once, in a copy workshop, I asked for a show of hands from everyone who claimed to be anti-formula. Almost every hand shot up. Then I let them in on a little secret: They had been persuaded to attend the workshop by a formula letter!

One of the most famous creative formulas is the AIDA one. While it probably originated with general advertisers, it also provides a good road map for writing letters. The copy should strive to capture *attention,* spark *interest,* promote *desire,* and, finally, motivate *action.*

One of the best letter-writing formulas comes from my former boss, Bob Stone. It has seven steps, which succinctly tell a writer how to create a solid direct mail letter without dictating content. These seven steps have stood the test of time:

> 1. Promise a benefit in your headline or first paragraph—your most important benefit.
>
> 2. Immediately enlarge on your most important benefit.
>
> 3. Tell the reader specifically what he or she is going to get.
>
> 4. Back up your statements with proof and endorsements.

5. Tell the reader what he or she might lose by
not taking action.

6. Rephrase your prominent benefits in your
closing offer.

7. Incite action.

It may sound like fitting all these points into one letter takes a lot of
space. But if the letter is tightly written, you can cover each point in a paragraph
or two. A successful control letter for a Washington newsletter manages to accomplish all seven steps in only one page.

A final word about formulas: Any formula, no matter how good, is simply
a road map. Letters are the most difficult part of a direct mail package to write.
It's usually best to have them written by an experienced direct response
copywriter.

Creating Great Letters

I STARTED OUT AS A WRITER. To learn my craft, I spent lots of time studying letter
writing. I guess it's paid off. I've been fortunate to have several letters I wrote or
supervised included in Dick Hodgson's *The Greatest Direct Mail Sales Letters of
All Time*. But in teaching creative seminars, I've found most questions center
around the basics. Here are the questions that repeatedly come up.

*Does it really help readership to use gimmicks like underlining and
indenting?* Yes. They help open up a letter and make it look easier to read.
Underlining, indenting, and using a second color break up walls of copy. They let
the eyes breathe, by giving them points of emphasis to rest on. Remember that
many readers start out by just casually glancing over a letter. Emphasizing key
words and sentences can catch their attention and get them to read the whole
letter. The two versions of the Amoco letter in Exhibit 14.5 show the difference
these techniques can make.

Do people really read long letters? Yes, if they're written well enough to
hold the reader's interest. There's no set answer to how long a letter should be. If
you have enough to say, don't fear long copy. Three- and four-pagers often work
better than one-page letters, simply because they let you get across more sales

EXHIBIT 14.5 Indenting, underlining, and handwritten copy make the letter on the left more reader friendly.

points and more reasons to respond. It's usually best to tell a complete story and leave the readership decision to the prospect.

Why do I see so many letters with a P.S.? Because it is one of the most highly read parts of a letter. If the reader is just skimming or glancing at a letter, the P.S. stands out. Use it to briefly restate a key benefit or to stress an attractive part of the offer. If it sounds appealing enough, the reader will go back to find out the details.

HOW TO BE YOUR OWN COPY CHIEF

In the years I've spend creating direct mail, it's been my privilege to work with some of the real pros in the business. Among them are many creative directors

♦

and copy chiefs who edit and approve a copywriter's work. By knowing what they look for, you can make your own copy its persuasive best.

Rewrite and edit your copy ruthlessly. Most pros rewrite their copy again and again until they feel it's worthy of their own signature. Each time they do, they revise and polish it further. Even if you think your copy is all set, it's a good idea to read it or retype it once more. You may be surprised to see how many little improvements you can make as it flows through your brain a final time.

If time permits, let your copy sit overnight before you give it that final review. Looking at it "fresh" will allow you to spot weak areas you didn't notice before and you'll probably come up with a better way to say something you struggled with originally.

Watch your warm-up. A good copy chief casts an especially critical eye on the beginning of a letter, because writers often spend too much time "warming up" to the subject in the first few paragraphs. Many sales letters are improved by deleting them outright. Try eliminating your first sentence or paragraph and see if your letter gets off to a more provocative and compelling start.

Use short words and sentences. Don't slow your reader down with too many long words or sentences. Try applying Rudolph Flesch's famous formula to your work: For every 100 words you write, make sure that at least 75 percent have five letters or fewer. Sentences that average more than 17 words can also slow down reading. Short sentences are punchy. Mix them in with longer ones to give your copy better rhythm.

Include the necessary connections and transitions. Maxwell C. Ross, a longtime creative consultant, recommends the use of "connecting links"—words and phrases that connect one paragraph with the next. They carry the reader along from one thought to another like bridges. Connectors like "But that's not all," "As I mentioned," and "In addition" will add continuity. They also help copy flow smoothly and make even a long letter very readable.

Don't be picky about punctuation. Most professional writers are more concerned with communicating than with rules for grammar and punctuation. Strict grammarians probably won't be happy with your direct mail copy, but as the late copywriter Paul Bringe said, "Punctuation is a writer's substitute for gestures, tone of voice, emphasis and facial expression. It is most necessary when the words used are weak, vague, and without color. Such words need strong crutches to hold them upright. The right words—those that jar, jump and shout with energy—need very little punctuation to help you understand."

Tom Brady, my former partner and cofounder of Kobs & Brady, has written and edited a lot of great copy. But Tom feels there are so many things to look for when editing copy that it's tough to do in one or two passes. So he recommends concentrating on just one thing at a time. It's much easier, for example, to spot words or sentences that are too long if that's the only thing you're looking for.

By keeping these guidelines in mind, you'll be well on your way to producing copy that sings . . . and sells.

The Last Word on Creating Direct Mail

EVERY ONE OF US, LIKE IT OR NOT, already has a copy style. But we need to make that style as flexible as possible. A good, professional writer should be able to paint pictures with words, to go beyond the nuts-and-bolts details of a product sheet and weave a benefit-packed story, to translate a common mattress into a heavenly night's sleep.

To be truly versatile, a writer must also be able to change the mood and style of his or her copy, just as a good actor or actress changes voice and mannerisms to fit different characters. This is a lifelong challenge. But the ability to vary your style to address any audience about any product will pay off again and again.

15

CREATING PRINT ADS

♦

OVER THE YEARS, I'VE FOUND that the best way to learn the principles of strong creative work is to look at—and compare—real-world examples. Look at the two ads for similar fitness products in Exhibit 15.1. Before we delve into the finer points of creating effective print ads, let's examine them.

The ads for the Stomach Eliminator and the Gutbuster are quite different. Both advertise a fitness product that promises to get rid of a pot belly. But the ad for the Stomach Eliminator doesn't really tell you that—at least not right away. Its headline and subheads tell more about the features of the product than what they will do for the reader. Only in the third and fourth subheads does it begin to promise benefits. So I would classify it as a product-oriented ad.

In contrast, the Gutbuster ad is entirely reader oriented. Starting with the main headline—"Flatten Your Stomach in Just Minutes a Day"—through the subheads and body copy, the Gutbuster ad focuses on what the product can do for the reader. Even showing a man and woman makes it easier for the prospect to identify with the problem.

Generally, a reader-oriented approach beats a product-oriented approach hands down. That's one good point to keep in mind when you're creating or reviewing print ads. But there are a few more guidelines you'll want to remember.

THE SEVEN MOST IMPORTANT PRINT AD RULES

THERE'S NO SHORTAGE OF RULES, formulas, and checklists for creating print ads. Over the years, I've found these seven most important.

1. CAPTURE ATTENTION INSTANTLY   Like any other kind of advertising, direct response space ads must cut through the clutter of competing sales messages that bombard every prospect every day. In a way, a print ad is like a billboard—readers often flip past magazine ads as fast as they pass a billboard. You only have a second or two to grab their attention and get them to read.

Exhibit 15.1   The Stomach Eliminator ad uses a product-oriented approach, while the Gutbuster one focuses on reader benefits.

The headline is one logical place to start. Featuring a strong benefit pulls in many readers. A Damart thermal underwear ad begins with the alluring statement, "Never Be Cold Again!" Quite a promise for readers shivering in cold northern climes.

Dramatic graphics also attract attention. The arresting silhouette of the Bates Motel and its famous owner should stop mystery fans, who are the main prospects for the Hitchcock video library (see Exhibit 15.2).

An attractive offer will also stop an interested reader. What stamp collector could resist a headline I saw recently which offered 1000 stamps for only $2.95? Whichever you use—strong headline benefit, dramatic graphics, or attractive offer—your goal is to capture attention instantly.

EXHIBIT 15.2   CBS Video Library uses a hauntingly-familiar silhouette to attract mystery fans.

2. USE A HEADLINE THAT'S MAGNETIC   It's estimated that three out of four people won't read beyond the headline. That's why it must stop the reader and, like a magnet, draw attention to the story.

Headline techniques that work in general advertising usually also work for direct response ads. There are lots of different types of headlines—command, question, symptom/cure. Or a number headline, like "11 Reasons You Should

Subscribe to . . . " Some advocate the "fishnet approach," which is designed to catch as many magazine or newspaper readers as possible. Others feel it's more efficient to cast your message at exactly the prospects you want.

Copywriting great Claude Hopkins once said, "When you advertise . . . your product will interest certain people only. You care only for those people. Create your advertisement for those people only." That's what two fitness products—Lifecycle and Bullworker—do in their advertising.

The Lifecycle bike was advertised successfully for a number of years with the headline, "Free Facts that Can Cut Your Exercise Time in Half." This headline draws regular exercisers by promising the benefit of reducing their exercise time. A Bullworker insert used the command head "The Belly Must Go" to pull in overweight readers.

Headlines don't have to promise a benefit to be effective. Look at the often-imitated ads written by Joe Sugarman for JS&A. His "Miracle Fuzz" headline (Exhibit 15.3) doesn't promise a benefit or even give a clue to what the product is. It's still a magnetic headline, but it draws people in with intrigue rather than promises. And its intrigue sold 100,000 units during the ad's three-year life.

3. VISUALS SHOULD ENHANCE THE COPY Your visuals shouldn't just support the copy or headline—they should enhance them. The right combination of words and pictures always has more impact than either can achieve on its own. Besides the main illustration, the overall appearance of the ad should look inviting, seem easy to read, and be in character with the audience you're aiming at. Graphics also play a key role in establishing the image you want your organization to convey.

Just changing the visuals can make a big difference. Take a look at the two ads shown in Exhibit 15.4, both for Cincinnati Microwave's Passport Radar Detector. They have the same headline. But putting the radar detector at the base of a steering wheel instantly conveys that it's an automotive product and vividly illustrates its compact size.

Graphics can't always be this dramatic, but they can always be appropriate. An ad for an expensive, imported product should have a rich look and feel, whereas an ad for a low-priced bargain suggests a harder-hitting approach.

EXHIBIT 15.3   Joe Sugarman attracts readers with intriguing headlines like this one.

4. DON'T BURY A GOOD OFFER   Earlier, I mentioned the importance of the offer in attracting attention to an ad. But a lot of creative people, particularly those schooled in general advertising, don't understand that the offer has *more* effect on results than their words or pictures do. So they tend to bury the offer in the body copy, where most people won't even spot it.

EXHIBIT 15.4   Juxtaposing the radar detector against a steering wheel adds drama to the Cincinnati Microwave ad on the right.

If you have a good offer, play it up in a subhead, a box, or even the headline. That may seem obvious, but it's easy to find examples of ads that don't do it. A recent ad for NCL cruises had a great offer—cruise seven days, pay for six. But you'd never know it from the headline, "NCL Fall Cruises. Vacations that Give Your Finances a Day of Rest." Compare that to the Southwest Airlines ad in Exhibit 15.5. It has a similar offer, which is clearly spelled out and temptingly presented.

A good offer bears repeating. A *TV Guide* insert I use in my seminars plays up a free booklet offer in seven different places. Book and music clubs devote almost the whole ad to their offer. It's a category that's dominated by strong offers, like "Take any 8 CDs for 1 cent." Through testing they've found that offer emphasis works best. Situations like this call for an uncreative headline. Let the offer do the selling for you.

EXHIBIT 15.5   Southwest Airlines spells out the offer in its headline—and supports it with an appropriate illustration.

5. YOU CAN'T COMPETE IF YOUR STORY ISN'T COMPLETE   To succeed, copy has to do a complete selling job. But only complete enough to get the response you want. If you're selling by mail, your copy must be long enough to help your prospect make a buying decision. But if you're going for inquiries, you don't want to tell your prospects too much. (However, you might want to tell a somewhat more complete story if you're going for "tight" rather than "loose" leads.)

The Gutbuster ad shown in Exhibit 15.1 is a good example of an ad designed to sell by mail. The long text engages the reader as it spells out product details. By the time the prospect gets to the ordering information, the pitch is complete. The right prospect will probably buy.

Exhibit 15.6   Lanier uses the right amount of copy in this lead-generating ad.

Shorter, lead-generating copy is shown in the ad for Lanier's voice mail system in Exhibit 15.6. It's heavy on benefits, but leaves the details for the salespeople who follow up their inquiries. (By the way, this business ad is also a good example of how visuals can enhance the copy.)

6. If you use a coupon, make it look like one   The coupon is a visual symbol. It lets the reader know right away that this is a certain type of ad—one that expects a response from the reader, not just a casual, passive glance.

If you use a coupon, don't get cute or creative when you design one. It should be easy to find, easy to read, and easy to cut out. Not like an ad I once saw promoting Bermuda travel. The tiny coupon blended in so perfectly with a sandy-colored background that it was nearly invisible. It might have won some art directors' award, but it sure didn't encourage response.

A coupon should normally be rectangular and should be located in a bottom corner of the ad. People don't read magazines and newspapers with scissors in their pockets. You want to make it as easy as possible for them to tear out a coupon and take action.

7. DON'T BE AFRAID TO BREAK THE SIX RULES ABOVE   Most good ads follow the principles we've just covered. Take the Nordic Track ad in Exhibit 15.7, for ex-

EXHIBIT 15.7   This Nordic Track ad works well even though it bends one of the rules.

◆

ample. It does a lot of things right: Its intriguing photo captures attention and enhances the copy, while its problem/solution head is pretty magnetic. The copy delves into the benefits of regular exercise without telling too much. The "Free Brochure and Video" offer is prominently displayed over the coupon, so the offer isn't buried. The coupon looks like one but, strictly speaking, is in the wrong place. Yet I think it's a better ad because they've used the lower right hand corner for the Nordic Track logo, rather than the coupon.

Sometimes real creativity comes from breaking—or at least bending—the rules. Most creative experts advocate short headlines. But an award-winning ad for Nanny Care used this 55-word heading which is bound to hit home with any parent concerned about quality child care:

> "If you want someone to hold your child's hand through the wonderful, often puzzling world of childhood and to always be there when you're not . . . to respond quickly to every need but not give in to every whim . . . to awaken wonder and put dragons to sleep and build castles in the sand . . . call Nanny Care."

Now that we've looked at these seven rules and how to break them, we'll take a closer look at three key ad elements—headline, body copy, and coupon.

WHICH HEADLINE PULLED BETTER?

WHAT MAKES ONE HEADLINE TERRIFIC and another forgettable? See if you can pick the stronger headline in each pair in this test from John Caple's *Tested Advertising Methods:*

Test 1: Home Study Course
> (a) To a $25,000 man who would like to be making $40,000
> (b) Here's proof that this training pays financially

Test 2: Life Insurance
> (a) Get rid of money worries for good
> (b) Here's one question you shouldn't ask your wife

Test 3: Music Instruction Course
> (a) A few months ago I couldn't play a note
> (b) Here's a strange way to learn music

◆

Test 4: Retirement Income Plan

    (a) A vacation the rest of your life

    (b) How you can retire on a guaranteed income for life

Test 5: Financial Magazine

    (a) How $20 started me on the road to $50,000 a year

    (b) Some $50,000 jobs are looking for applicants

Test 6: Nervousness Treatment

    (a) Thousands suffer from sick nerves and don't know it

    (b) Have you these symptoms of nerve exhaustion?

What made the winning headlines pull so much better? "To a $25,000 man who would like to be making $40,000" is much more specific than its also-ran version. Dollar figures are more arresting than the word "financially;" mentioning two figures is even stronger because it shows the reader how to get from where he or she is now to where he or she wants to be.

"Get rid of money worries for good" promises a very strong benefit, while the alternate, "One question you shouldn't ask your wife," provokes only mild curiosity—decidedly less compelling.

"Here's a strange way to learn music" succeeds because it combines an appeal to the audience's curiosity with the benefit of learning music.

Another benefit that its target audience will find irresistible is "How you can retire on a guaranteed income for life." Its promise is much more realistic than "A vacation the rest of your life." And the mention of retirement zeroes in on the most likely prospects—those nearing retirement age.

"How $20 started me on the road to $50,000 a year" also attracts the right audience. In this case it's those seeking financial improvement and the $20 cost sounds reasonable. The lackluster alternate version sounds like a help-wanted ad.

Using the word "you" is usually more effective than a less personal headline. "Have you these symptoms of nerve exhaustion?" arouses curiosity and draws in those who think they have the problem.

These "winning" headlines have some characteristics in common. Each one targets the right audience. Most promise a benefit, which is usually stated

---

Answers: 1 (a), 2 (a), 3 (b), 4 (b), 5 (a), 6 (b)

♦

pretty specifically. Even those that appeal to the audience's curiosity also suggest or imply the prospect will learn something by reading the ad.

Over his many years of writing result-producing copy, John Caples determined that four appeals have the best chance of succeeding in a headline: *Self-interest, news, curiosity,* and *quick, easy way.* Sometimes two or more appeals can be combined into one headline, like Test 5 above, which addresses the reader's interest in making more money and suggests there's an easy way to do it.

One good way to check the strength of your headline is to ask yourself whether every word it contains works hard. If you changed, added, or deleted one word, would the whole ad be better? Sometimes a slight alteration can have a profound effect on a headline's chances for success. Tom Collins, coauthor of *MaxiMarketing,* once did an ad for a financial book series with the headline "Get Rich Slowly." Changing the last word from what was expected made it more believable.

BODY COPY TECHNIQUES THAT SELL

GENERALLY, WRITING BODY COPY IS considered less glamorous, less creative than coming up with headlines and graphics. But that's where the real selling is done. Many different writing styles can work well in body copy. Whatever style is chosen, I suggest covering four steps, which I call the "Four Square Formula:"

1. The opening paragraph or two should enlarge on the headline. That's what attracted the reader.

2. Stack up the benefits and reasons to respond. The more the merrier, but cover the strongest ones first.

3. Include testimonials or use some other means to build credibility for your claims. This is a step that's often overlooked.

4. Explain the details of the offer and make a call to action. Try to include a believable reason to act now. "Orders are filled on a first come basis" has a much more truthful ring than "supplies are limited."

WHEN AND HOW TO COUPON

A DIRECT RESPONSE AD SHOULD almost always include a coupon. There are a few exceptions, of course. You can skip the coupon when you're running a space ad so small, you'd have to double its size to include one—a coupon won't double your orders. If all you want are phone replies, use an 800 number and play it up prominently. And when you're after highly qualified, "tight" leads, omit the coupon. The harder prospects have to work to respond to your offer, the better qualified they'll be.

But when you use a coupon, as we noted earlier, this is not the place to be creative. Make it big enough to fill in comfortably. If you haven't done so lately, try filling out your own coupon. Have you given prospects enough room? Even those with long names? Will your order entry staff be able to read the information accurately?

It's usually a good idea to write the coupon in the first person singular and include some benefit copy. A coupon for the life insurance ad that promised readers they would "Get rid of money worries" might begin, "Yes, I want to get rid of my money worries for good." It's a nice way to reinforce your promise.

In some magazines sent to subscribers, it's now possible to personalize bind-in cards with the reader's name and address. Before long, it will be possible to personalize coupons right on the page.

A CHECKLIST FOR AD LAYOUT AND DESIGN

A FEW YEARS AGO, I HAD A CHANCE to review the material that a large general agency uses in its internal creative training program. From it I've digested a few

♦

questions that are equally appropriate when evaluating a direct response print layout:

☐ Does the ad have a strong focal point?

☐ Does the flow of the layout lead the reader where you want him or her to go?

☐ Does the illustration stop, intrigue, and involve the reader?

☐ Is there a better visual technique than the one suggested?

☐ Are the elements arranged to encourage readership?

☐ Is the ad designed for the medium in which it will appear?

☐ Is the layout distinctive or just ordinary?

THE LAST WORD ON CREATING PRINT ADS

IN MY SEMINARS, I USE a case study to illustrate creative principles. The audiences have an opportunity to evaluate print ads for a hypothetical company. They usually get bogged down in minor creative details instead of focusing on the ad concept itself. And more often than not, they're willing to settle for some pretty average executions.

I then proceed to show them how the same ad concepts can be strengthened with stronger headlines and better graphics, just to underscore that the creative end of the business is not an exact science. But if you concentrate on developing a big idea for each ad and executing it as strongly as possible, it can make a dramatic difference.

And I close the seminar segment with this quote from David F. Hurwitt, Vice President of Marketing for General Foods: "Superior advertising comes most often to clients who demand it. If it's not superior, send it back—constructively, but firmly." I think it's good advice to follow.

16

CREATING TV SPOTS

♦

TELEVISION COMMERCIALS ARE BUT ONE contender in an enormous battle for TV screen attention. There are countless program alternatives to the ABC, CBS, and NBC networks: Independent stations, cable networks, superstations, and premium cable channels such as HBO. In addition, household members may choose to use their television as a home computer monitor, to play video games, or watch VCR movies.

With all that competition, how can you get your share of attention? What does it take to create a successful direct response TV spot? What makes one spot work better than another? Over the years, I've discovered a few simple guidelines that seem to help the creative development process. In honor of that well-known magazine, I call them my "TV Guide-lines."

TV GUIDE-LINES FOR EFFECTIVE SPOTS

1. KNOW THE GAME PLAN

Direct response television spots come in all lengths and all varieties, but they all try to accomplish one of three things. They can get an order. They can induce an inquiry. Or they can support a campaign in another medium. Before you begin developing creative concepts, you must know what your commercial is supposed to *do*. When that much is clear, questions of format, content, and message can be resolved.

It also helps to find out something about your production budget. The particulars aren't necessary yet, but you should have a general idea of whether you're writing a low, medium, or high budget spot. You should also know how long it will be. This way, when you start to bounce your ideas off the television producer, they will be in line with your budget.

Regardless of its length, budget, or goal, your commercial's *main* purpose is to produce some *action*. General advertising can afford to inform, entertain, and build awareness. That's why it relies so heavily on humor and entertainment to deliver its messages. With rare exceptions, humor and response don't usually mix well. In fact, experience proves that too high a dose of entertainment can cost you response.

2. H̲AVE̲ A̲ S̲UITABLE̲ O̲FFER̲

A lot is riding on your creative. But when one version of a commercial substantially outpulls another, the offer probably had a lot to do with it. At my former agency, we created a TV spot for Encyclopaedia Britannica that pulled five times better than the company's control spot! Admittedly, the new creative concept was better. But we also reduced the price of the introductory offer and added a free gift. Strengthening the offer boosted response tremendously.

You may have an offer that works just fine in the mail or in print, but to work on TV, it may have to be changed or improved. Often it must be simplified to fit TV's time constraints. Let's compare a few examples.

The chart in Exhibit 16.1 shows how four types of marketers might adapt their offer for TV. Spiegel, for example, mails a free prospect catalog to generate a sale. But in television inquiry ads, it might add a free gift, make a nominal charge for the catalog, and include a refund coupon worth dollars off the first order. This offer not only increases inquiries, but helps convert them to customers.

In a book club print ad, a panoply of best-sellers might accompany an invitation for readers to choose three books for three dollars. There's no way to include all those titles, even in a two-minute spot, so a TV ad might let the viewer choose one of five best-sellers for $1.99. This comes across clearly in a short amount of time and lets the consumer make a simple buying decision.

There are many ways to sweeten an offer. But a television offer must always be simple and direct—and usually stronger than an equivalent offer in print. Watch a few late night response spots and you'll find that most companies load up their TV offers to give them the best possible shot at success.

EXHIBIT 16.1   How offers are changed for TV

ADVERTISER	MAIL/PRINT OFFER	TV OFFER/OBJECTIVE
Catalog firm	Mail catalog to prospect; go for order	Inquiry offer with gift and refund coupon good on first order
Music/CD club	Eight CDs for one cent with hundreds to choose from	Choose one of four best-sellers for $4.99
Business newspaper	13 weeks for $34 or one year for $99	13 weeks for $34
Magazine subscription firm	Sweepstakes offering hundreds of magazines at discount	TV support—watch your mailbox for our sweepstakes package

3. WHO'S DOING THE SELLING?

Before spending time on creative development, a writer must know *who* will make the pitch. Does the spot call for an on-camera spokesperson? If so, does it suggest an announcer, a celebrity, or a company representative? Will the spokesperson be on camera throughout the spot or will the commercial switch to a voiceover after the introduction? Can the spokesperson be involved in a dramatization from which he or she emerges to make the pitch?

There's a lot of flexibility here. Spend some time looking at each of these alternatives. And if you're selecting a spokesperson, consider this all-important question: Who should be doing the selling for this product or service?

Celebrity presenters have always been popular in the direct response world. Think of Ed McMahon and American Family Publishers. Or Sally Struthers and Christian Children's Fund. Choose a celebrity with care. Celebrity marketing studies have shown that box-office stars don't always get top credibility ratings from the public at large. Often, just the reverse is true. It's been a long time since Art Linkletter hosted his own show, but as a trusted spokesperson for National Liberty Insurance, his credibility lasted for years.

♦

I sometimes wonder why company spokespeople and real-life customers aren't used more often in direct response TV. The latter have been effective in convincing skeptics that people really *do* win those big sweepstakes prizes.

4. PASS THE FIVE-SECOND TEST

To succeed, your commercial must capture audience attention in the first five seconds. This is even more critical in television than it is in a direct mail package, because you have so little time to work with.

The device that opens a commercial must be related to the subject or concept of the commercial. It should not just be a gimmicky attention getter. If you start out with something cute but unrelated, you waste too much valuable selling time. But that doesn't mean the opening can't be dramatic. I've used a swarm of repairmen marching into a homeowner's living room and a tennis player hitting a volley in someone's bedroom. Each was directly related to the creative concept, so we could make a quick, smooth transition to the selling message.

In an article in *DM News,* Shan Ellentuck of Ellentuck & Springer, Inc. noted that a weak opening is the most common reason why a great-looking commercial produces a lousy response. "You may be able to cut your cost per order sharply just by sharpening the opening," she advises. I heartily concur.

5. DEMONSTRATE OR DRAMATIZE

Once upon a time, every direct response commercial featured a fast-talking "pitchman" who showed how the product could slice and dice or munch and crunch its way through a problem, while telling how little it cost and how to get it—all in a couple frantic minutes. I call this the "Vegamatic syndrome"—it uses TV's demonstrability, but not very effectively by today's standards.

The ability to show or demonstrate your product in action visually is TV's real strength. That's why it works so much better than radio for direct response. If your product or service doesn't lend itself to demonstration, the next best thing is to dramatize the problem it solves.

Television offers a wealth of ways to do this. But going beyond the Vegamatic syndrome takes visual thinking. And visual thinking requires a familiarity with camera angles, sets, supers (type superimposed over the visual), and other production/editing techniques. The best TV creative person I ever worked with had an impressive ability to visualize a commercial concept in his head. Long before it was produced, he could describe the action of the commercial in great detail . . . because he knew exactly the kind of finished effect he wanted to achieve.

Since so many young copywriters have grown up with television, they're more comfortable with visual thinking. But to capitalize on TV's visual possibilities, it's a good idea to work closely with an art director or producer.

6. What Did You Say?

In conversation, how often are you asked to repeat something you just said? When you read, how often do you go back and review a sentence or paragraph? And when you watch a video, how often do you rewind and repeat a section? Frequently, I'm sure. Unfortunately, a direct response TV spot has no rewind button. If it is to communicate, it must be clear the first time.

Television demands simplicity. Make sure every word you use is short and direct. As discussed in the telemarketing chapter, your copy must also sound natural. You want your presenter to come across as a *real* person, not a TV character.

7. Overcome the Disappearing Order Form

Here's another good reason to make your message crystal clear. Television has a magic order form: Now you see it, now you don't. One second it's on screen, then it disappears from right under the viewer's nose. If your message hasn't been clear or your offer is confusing, how can the viewer be expected to respond?

The commercial's tag serves as the order form. It's the ending of the spot, where you fully explain the offer and how to respond. But unlike order forms delivered via mail and print, there's no hard copy to think about, reread, or look over later.

To conquer the problem of the disappearing order form, devote a good chunk of time at the end of your commercial to the tag. In a 30- or 60-second spot, the tag should be at least 10 or 15 seconds; in a 90- or 120-second spot, allow at least 20 seconds. Show the phone number and/or address long enough for viewers to write it down. The 800 number has become a visual symbol of a direct response spot—like the coupon in a print ad. It tells the viewer he or she will have a chance to get something. You might even want to flash the 800 number on the screen before you get to the tag. It's a subtle way to start asking for the order.

8. MAKE EVERY SECOND COUNT

It's a challenge to tell a complete story within TV's time constraints. The rule of thumb is you can cover two words per second. So even a two-minute spot, four times the most common length used by general advertisers, gives you only about 250 words to work with. Which means you'll need to get out a stopwatch and time your script.

With so little time available, don't waste words explaining what the visual makes clear. As Joan Throckmorton, President of Joan Throckmorton, Inc., says in her excellent book, *Winning Direct Response Advertising,* "Don't use dialogue to repeat the visual. Let the camera do a lot of your talking. Then use words to *complete* and *expand* the visual." For example, a recent spot that Kobs, Gregory & Passavant did for Omaha Steaks opens with a handsome man in a kitchen setting (see Exhibit 16.2). But he doesn't say, "Here I am in my kitchen," because the viewer can see that.

TV GUIDE-LINES IN ACTION

TO SHOW HOW A TV SPOT IS DEVELOPED, we're reproducing the script for the Omaha Steaks TV spot mentioned above (see Exhibit 16.3). If you study the video and audio columns, you'll see it measures up pretty well to my eight guidelines.

It has an attractive offer designed to get impulse orders. A 50-year-old spokesman was chosen because the spot was aimed at an older audience and we wanted someone the viewer could identify with. The creative strategy was to make the product the hero and present the steaks as perfect for a special occasion. That inspired the copy line—"Six of life's greatest pleasures"—which makes an intriguing opening.

The spot goes on to demonstrate the product being cooked, served, and enjoyed . . . while the on-camera actor weaves in some selling copy. He then becomes a voiceover announcer, as the visuals attractively display the offer and lead into the tag. The result: This spot pulled 54 percent better than one done by another agency.

HIGH-QUALITY COMMERCIALS DON'T HAVE TO BREAK THE BANK

DIRECT RESPONSE SPOTS NOW RESEMBLE general advertising commercials more than they do the old "talking head" commercials once so prevalent in our business.

EXHIBIT 16.2   Opening storyboard frame for Omaha Steaks TV spot.

◆

Exhibit 16.3   Omaha Steaks TV script.

6 Filet Trial Offer 120-second TV spot	"6 of Life's Greatest Pleasures"
VIDEO	**AUDIO**
Open on handsome, trim, 50-something man, standing at kitchen table, wearing white shirt, open at collar, long chef's apron over it.	I'm about to introduce you to six of life's greatest pleasures.
Picks up wine bottle, hand covering label.	But first . . . my dinner partner tonight is a lady I'm anxious to impress.
Begins to open it.	So I've chosen one of my favorite wines. Everything must be perfect. The wine, the mood and the *food* . . . meltingly tender filet mignons from Omaha Steaks.
Pan to two filets, sizzling on grill.	They're perfect for making me look like a gourmet cook . . . but practically effortless to prepare.
Hand, close up. Slices open filet to reveal rare to medium rare interior. Fade out on filets. Fade in on man adjusting tie, putting on suit coat.	They're hand carved from the finest corn fed beef . . . then aged like fine wine to peak flavor and tenderness. You can't buy these steaks in supermarkets, of course . . . but they're as easy to shop for as they are to prepare.
Zoom to close-up of man's face. SUPER: 1-800-228-9055. Fade to guarantee against limbo background.	Just call 1-800-228-9055. That's the toll-free number of Omaha Steaks International—an old-fashioned family business in the heart of beef country. The Omaha folks rush their steaks all over the country with this simple guarantee: If each steak isn't *perfect* or you're not totally satisfied . . . they'll replace your steaks or refund your money.

Fade to man in dining room, sitting down next to an elegant, attractive woman of 50 at a graciously set, candle-lit dinner table. Woman is well dressed, not in cocktail dress. Man swirls wine in glass, smiles as woman's eyes meet his; raises his glass in a ceremonious toast. They touch glasses and begin to dine.

(Romantic music in background.) When you want the dinner to be perfect, that guarantee gives you confidence it *will be* . . . even if you've never ordered "long distance" steaks before.

Happy anniversary, darling.

Super: Save $28.00.
1-800-228-9055

(Hold on 800 no. through end of spot.)

Fade to hands removing top of container.

Replace "Save $28" super art with (large) $29.95 and (smaller) plus $5.50 delivery. Super: Special Offer for New Customers Only.

(VOICE OVER)
It's so easy to make any occasion special. Call now to order six gourmet filet mignons shipped in dry ice in a reusable picnic cooler for just $29.95—about half the regular price!

Cut to cookbook with hand flicking pages. Add super: Free

Cut to salt shaker/pepper mill. Super: Free

You'll also receive this free cookbook and a free combination salt shaker and pepper mill.

Fade to six Filets, sizzling on grill. Cut to art card with small pictures of VISA, MasterCard, and inset CU of single filet on grill. Card copy:

Omaha Steaks International
1-800-228-9055

Six 6 oz. Filet Mignons—$29.95 + $5.50 shipping and handling

Plus 2 FREE GIFTS.

So phone 1-800-228-9055 to order your gourmet filet mignons . . .
. . . six of life's greatest pleasures . . .
. . . with one toll-free phone call.

♦

That's because today's response spots typically have much higher production values. More money is spent on talent and production. Special effects, background music, and location shooting are becoming commonplace. The spot you produce will compete in a field of very sophisticated commercials. To get its share of attention, it should look like it belongs there.

The two-minute Omaha Steaks TV spot we just reviewed was produced for about $35,000, which included location shooting and food stylists to make sure the product looked good. That figure might seem like a lot of money. But it's only a fraction of what a general advertiser would spend on a typical 30-second food spot. Because they have always tended to keep a tight rein on costs, most direct marketers aren't used to spending big bucks on television. That's changing, though. One large catalog firm recently spent $300,000 to produce a single spot— but then ran it for eight seasons. Amortized, that's less than $40,000 per season.

Another way to amortize your production cost is to do a shorter "lift" from a longer spot. Let's say you produce a two-minute commercial. When you do the final editing, you can also edit a 90-second version from the same footage at very little additional cost. This gives you a chance to test two different lengths to see which is most cost efficient.

If you're not sure whether television makes sense for your product or service, you can get your feet wet without breaking the bank. A good way to explore TV without committing yourself to production and media costs is to just have a storyboard or script prepared. If the result shows potential, you can start with a nice but modest production that can be upgraded later if the commercial pays off. But if the storyboard or script isn't exciting, you can kill the project without spending big bucks.

The Marriage of Image and Response

In Chapter 12, we discussed how the budget can be allocated when commercials have the dual objective of image and response. One creative technique that works well in this situation is a wraparound spot. Let's say you have an existing 30-second image spot for your product or service. You can wrap a response message and offer around it. Maybe you start with an operator in a telemarketing center (a scene you've probably seen used in other response spots). She gets the viewers' attention, tells them to watch the following message, and then returns with the offer and ordering information.

This technique was pioneered at my former agency, with Home Box Office as the client. We took a lavishly produced 30-second image spot done by HBO's general advertising agency, and added a 30-second response wrap for about one-tenth of the production cost. It worked so well that the cost for new HBO subscribers was 40 percent lower than a straight response spot.

I think we'll see more use of these wraparounds in the future. The center part acts like an expensive four-color brochure to build image and awareness. But the wrap portion functions more like a two-color letter: It's relatively inexpensive to produce. So it can be updated or changed at nominal cost while the expensive core remains unaltered. It can thus be tailored to deliver different messages or offers to different markets or to complement different types of programming.

THE LAST WORD ON TV CREATIVE

I PRODUCED MY FIRST TV SPOT about 20 years ago, almost by accident. One of my clients was so pleased with the direct mail and space ads we had done for them that they gave us a TV assignment. The script was approved and the production scheduled. But when I arrived at the shoot, I realized that the client considered me the producer! Somehow, I managed to get through the day. I learned a great deal in those few hours and, luckily, the spot turned out well.

To really understand how to create a commercial, you have to go through the whole process—from scriptwriting to selecting the acting talent and monitoring production. But I don't recommend doing everything yourself. Commercials look more professional when professionals produce, direct, and edit them. Trying to save money by stinting on professional help only adds costs where it hurts most—to your cost-per-order.

PART IV

IMPROVING A SUCCESSFUL DIRECT MARKETING PROGRAM

17

IDEA GENERATION TO BEAT YOUR CONTROL

♦

UNTIL NOW, WE'VE BEEN CONCENTRATING on direct marketing fundamentals and how they are applied in launching a *new* direct marketing program. It's time to shift gears and talk about *existing* direct marketing programs for products or services that have already been developed and tested. They might be winners, but you're looking for new approaches to make them even better. They may just be marginal and one good idea could put them over the top. Or they might be losers that need a complete overhaul.

An excellent way to improve results on an existing program is to come up with a strong, new creative approach. That's why this chapter is devoted to generating creative ideas. I'm sure you all know what creativity is, so I won't try to provide a formal definition. But here's my favorite fun definition: Creativity is a husband who can come home late every Friday night from the same poker game and keep coming up with a new excuse.

Many copywriters are in the same boat as that husband: They've written so many ads or mailings for a certain product that it gets pretty hard to come up with new ideas. In this chapter, I'll try to suggest some ways to develop break-throughs. We'll also cover some creative thinking techniques that will help you see old, familiar subjects from a new perspective.

TEST NEW APPEALS OR POSITIONINGS

MUCH MORE HAS BEEN WRITTEN ON the subject of developing a new ad or mailing instead of improving an old one. There are, however, some good suggestions for improving a mailing package in Bob Stone's *Successful Direct Marketing Methods*.

> One of the best ways I know is to come up with an entirely different appeal for your letter. For instance, suppose you're selling an income tax guide and your present letter is built around saving money. That's

probably a tough appeal to beat. But to develop a new approach, you could write a letter around a negative appeal—something people want to avoid.

Experience with many propositions has proved that a negative appeal is often stronger than a positive one; yet it's frequently overlooked by copywriters. An appropriate negative copy appeal for our example might be something like, "How to avoid costly mistakes that can get you in trouble with the Internal Revenue Service." Or, "Are you taking advantage of these six commonly overlooked tax deductions?"

Another good technique is to change the type of lead on your letter. . . . If you're using a news lead, try one built around the narrative approach. Or develop a provocative question as the lead. Usually a new lead will require you to rewrite the first few paragraphs of copy to fit the lead, but then you can often pick up the balance of the letter from your control.

During the past few years, a lot of views have been voiced in general advertising circles about "copy positioning," i.e., how you position your product or service in the reader's mind. The classic example is 7-Up's Uncola campaign which positioned the product as a related alternative to the popular cola category.

The same positioning technique can be used in direct marketing. For many years, *Highlights for Children* used a successful space ad to sell gift subscriptions. But instead of positioning their product as just another magazine, the publisher positioned it against the toys and clothes usually chosen as kids gifts. Here's the ad headline and subhead:

> Would you pay $19.69 for a child's gift that won't be outgrown, broken, worn out, lost or forgotten six months after Christmas?
>
> In a day and age when fads in toys and trinkets appear and vanish almost before you turn around, *Highlights for Children* could be one of the most exciting Christmas presents you will ever give.

The Hypothesis Approach

Several years ago I heard Tom Collins—cofounder of what is now Rapp Collins Marcoa—explain a method he sometimes used in developing new space ads. Here's how the technique works: Before starting to write an ad, you develop a series of hypotheses. You then build a separate ad around each hypothesis, which can be tested to prove or disprove it. Collins went on to explain that hypotheses are usually made about the prospect, the price or offer, the product, or the ultimate benefit of using the product.

Collins then proceeded to show how U.S. School of Music came up with a new control ad. This mail order music school had been running an ad with a large picture of a woman playing the piano and a headline, "The secret of teaching yourself music." Collins hypothesized that, today, a teenager interested in the guitar was a better prospect than a woman playing the piano. So he made a few changes in the ad, such as substituting an appropriate photo, and it was a big winner.

Even though I respected Tom Collins as one of the great direct response writers, I frankly thought this two-step creative process was unnecessarily complex. That is, until I had occasion to use it. And then I became a true convert.

I've found the hypothesis approach has some inherent advantages, especially when you're trying to come up with a whole series of ads or mailing ideas. For one thing, you don't wind up with as many look-alike or similar ads. Normally, when you ask a creative person to develop a half-dozen ad approaches, you tend to get one idea and five or six variations of it. If you were to test these minor variations, you would naturally expect only minor differences in results. And most marketers are looking for breakthroughs, not minor differences. So it's desirable to test ads that are more distinctly different.

In other words, the hypothesis technique stretches your thinking and forces you to go beyond the obvious. That, of course, is where potential breakthroughs often come from. Still another advantage is that, once the hypothesis is developed, you have a strong platform for building the ad. The technique provides direction in creating a headline, developing graphics, and writing body copy.

To demonstrate how this technique works, let's suppose we are starting a new magazine. It will be devoted to current events and issues. The unique concept for this publication is that it will present the pros and cons of each issue, so a reader who is skeptical about the subject can form his or her own conclusion. In fact, we'll call the magazine *Skeptic*.

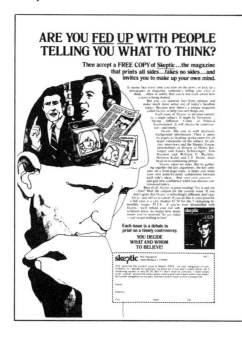

EXHIBIT 17.1 Ad A—"Are you fed up. . . ?"

Hypothesis: A large segment of the population believes that the presentation of various issues by the news media is inevitably slanted, and *Skeptic's* greatest appeal lies in its impartiality.

Rationale: Most people don't like the idea of others telling them what to think and should respond positively to a magazine that is not trying to persuade them one way or another.

EXHIBIT 17.2 Ad B—"If you agree"

Hypothesis: The prime prospects for *Skeptic* readership are those who pride themselves on their intellectual independence, whether or not they hold a college degree.

Rationale: We assume that the magazine will have a high percentage of college graduates among its readers. But it was felt an ad aimed solely at college grads could be too limiting. So this approach addresses itself to independent-minded graduates, as well as nongraduates.

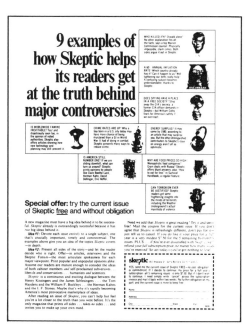

EXHIBIT 17.3 Ad C—"9 examples"

Hypothesis: Using a numbered list of editorial subjects is the best way to introduce potential subscribers to the range and character of *Skeptic*.

Rationale: This approach has been effective for a number of other magazines through the years, and was therefore one of those ideas that almost has to be tested.

EXHIBIT 17.4 Ad D—"Ever feel invisible. . . ?"

Hypothesis: People are more interested in appearing knowledgeable in public or at social gatherings than they are in the issues themselves.

Rationale: While the immediate benefit of the magazine is to make the reader more knowledgeable or informed, the idea of being able to impress one's friends might be considered the ultimate extension of that benefit.

On the preceding pages, you'll find four ads that were created to attract *Skeptic* subscribers. Study the hypothesis for each ad and the rationale behind it. Notice, too, how different the ad executions are. In a situation like this, I wouldn't be surprised if the best-pulling ad did twice as well as the weakest.

PROVEN COPY APPEALS

Most copy appeals are timeless because they stem from basic human needs and wants that don't change much from year to year. As proof, I offer the accompanying chart (Exhibit 17.5) which was a favorite of Victor Schwab, one of the founders of Schwab and Beatty Advertising. It's at least 35 years old and yet still quite timely.

You might find the exhibit to be a handy checklist next time you're looking for a new copy appeal or approach. Just select two or three different appeals that fit your product or service and see how strong a creative strategy or headline you can come up with for each one.

AN ORGANIZED APPROACH FOR BEATING THE CONTROL

TOP CREATIVE PEOPLE ARE NOT ALWAYS able to verbalize their approach to creativity. An exception is Sol Blumenfeld of Sol Blumenfeld & Associates. I like his organized method for idea generation, which he calls a five-track approach to beating the control:

1. THE SUBTRACTIVE APPROACH   This seeks to improve the effectiveness of a given mailing by reducing costs, thereby reducing the cost per inquiry or sale. One way to do this is by using a "stripped down" version of a winning package, such as going from a 6 × 9 size to a number 10 size, using a smaller circular, eliminating one element from the package, and so on. Another way to accomplish the same thing is to develop a new mailing that's more economical, such as a self-mailer. These approaches usually won't outpull the control in percent response, but they can often produce a lower cost per order.

2. THE ADDITIVE TECHNIQUE   This means adding something to a control package that may increase its efficiency in excess ratio to any increased costs. Usually it involves inserts. A classic example is the so-called publisher's letter,

EXHIBIT 17.5 Timeless copy appeals

PEOPLE WANT TO GAIN:	THEY WANT TO SAVE:
Health	Time
Popularity	Discomfort
Praise from others	Risks
Pride of accomplishment	Money
Self-confidence	Worry
Time	Embarrassment
Improved appearance	Work
Comfort	Doubts
Advancement: social-business	
Money	**THEY WANT TO BE:**
Security in old age	
Leisure	Good parents
Increased enjoyment	Creative
Personal prestige	Efficient
	Recognized authorities
THEY WANT TO DO:	Up-to-date
	Gregarious
Express their personalities	"First" in things
Satisfy their curiosity	Sociable, hospitable
Appreciate beauty	Proud of their possessions
Win others' affection	Influential over others
Resist domination by others	
Emulate the admirable	
Acquire or collect things	
Improve themselves generally	

Source: Victor Schwab, *Mail Order Strategy* (Hoke Communications, 1956).

which was mentioned in Chapter 14. At other times the mere addition of a token, stamp, or other involvement device can provide a substantial boost in results.

3. THE EXTRACTIVE APPROACH This technique entails drawing on the contents of an established ad or mailing and extracting a thought or idea that can be built up as the main appeal. Blumenfeld cites an example for a publication's subscription campaign in which he picked up a very human appeal that was buried in the body copy of their control ad. He developed it into a new headline, which substantially beat the control.

4. The segmentive technique   As you might guess, this one entails segmenting your market and developing one or more special promotions aimed at those different segments. Blumenfeld points out that some publishers often use a special women's package, because they have found that their normal packages simply don't work as well with the female market. Likewise, music clubs often use separate packages for country music, teen, and classical market segments. Understandably, this technique requires that the copywriter be familiar with the list universe to which he or she is writing and its customer profile.

5. The innovative approach   This category is characterized by Blumenfeld as being highly original, even wild. He believes that every test series should contain at least one or two ideas that fall into this category, because they can often produce more dramatic improvements in results than the other approaches.

Don't Raise the Bridge, Lower the River

Our brains can store and use incredible amounts of information. Researchers estimate that the brain can store up to 10^{28} bits of information—an amount that rivals the most powerful computers (see Exhibit 17.6).

How does the brain sift through and use all this information? Most of us rely on the *judgmental thinking mode*. This is the everyday process we use to think things through logically, in which the mind moves sequentially from point *A* to point *B*.

But to generate truly creative approaches—to lower the river instead of raising the bridge—we need to use another way to "think about thinking." This "lateral thinking mode" is simply a state of mind where the restrictions of critical judgment can be suspended for a time. This allows the mind to wander freely into uncharted areas in search of new ideas.

Techniques for Lateral Thinking

A number of techniques have been developed to arrive at a lateral state of mind and improve the idea flow. Some merely provide the proper setting for idea generation, such as group meetings where critical judgment is suspended. Others offer a method in which the brain is randomly exposed to outside stimuli which

EXHIBIT 17.6   Human brain's computer-like storage capacity

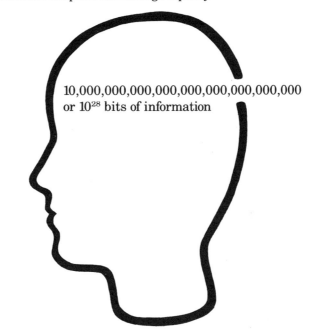

10,000,000,000,000,000,000,000,000,000
or 10^{28} bits of information

can spark new ideas. These lateral thinking techniques let you mentally step back and look at your problem from a fresh perspective.

Experts on creativity agree that it's best to learn all you can about several lateral thinking techniques. Once they're second nature, you can use the ones that work best for you or for a particular problem. The techniques that follow are a few I've found to be quite helpful.

BRAINSTORMING MEETINGS   Some marketers believe that brainstorming meetings should be pretty much unstructured; just "let the ideas flow" in a creative free-for-all. I prefer what I call "directed brainstorming." Everyone at the meeting gets background information in advance. The meeting then follows an agenda or list of questions to focus idea generation on a specific area or problem. And I always try to include one or two participants who don't work on the account we're brainstorming. I recall a meeting where one of these "newcomers" suggested an idea that literally increased a catalog firm's sales by more than $6 million!

♦

The exciting part of brainstorming is how ideas are built up by the group. One participant tosses out an idea. It has potential but needs further development. Somebody adds to it. One person suggests a variation. And another. The idea that's finally built up may not bear much resemblance to the original. But that original rough idea was the stimulus that started the process.

An important rule for brainstorming sessions is to avoid negative comments on ideas that are expressed. You don't want to inhibit participants from throwing out any idea, no matter how wild it is. For best results, turn judgment off and turn imagination on. Exhibit 17.7 provides other rules used by a leading ad agency for its brainstorming sessions.

RANDOM WORD ASSOCIATION This involves selecting a few words at random from a dictionary and "bumping them up against" the problem you're trying to solve. You start by looking at the various definitions of the random words. Then see how these definitions stimulate new thinking about the problem. Here's an oversimplified example. Let's say you're selling a woman's purse by mail. A competitor suddenly comes along who "knocks off" your product and starts running ads in the same magazines you've been using. Your results have been hurt and you need a new ad to boost response.

You open the dictionary. The first word you spot is "secure." One of the definitions is, "to free from risk of loss." Is there a way to strengthen or dramatize your guarantee to emphasize the high-quality features of your product and offer the consumer better protection?

The next word you spot is "victory." You notice that one of its definitions is "winning in a competition, performing better than others." Can you, perhaps, do a competitive rundown that shows how your purse compares with Brand X?

As in brainstorming, your objective is to generate as many different approaches as possible. You don't stop when you come up with a promising idea. You continue until you have a full list of alternatives. Then you switch to a judgmental thinking mode to sort them out and select the best option.

TRANSFER ANALYSIS With this technique you consciously try to transfer a successful idea from another area to the problem you're working on. I've seen it used to isolate the key elements of successful products and then transfer them to a completely different product category.

▬▬▬▬▬▬

EXHIBIT 17.7   Ad agency rules for brainstorming

SELECT A LEADER

Let the leader take all responsibility for contact with reality; everyone else in the brainstorming meeting is to "think wild." The duties of the leader are:

♦ Take notes on all the ideas expressed.

♦ Set a time limit on the meeting, such as 60 minutes.

♦ Set a quota on ideas to be generated, such as 30 ideas in 60 minutes.

♦ Admonish any critical thinkers in the group—no negative thinking allowed.

♦ Say "stop" when an idea has been built up enough.

♦ Help start new ideas if things lag.

RULES DURING BRAINSTORMING

♦ Suspend all critical judgment on any ideas expressed.

♦ Let the leader handle all contact with reality. The rest of the group should "let go" at all times and just react to ideas.

♦ As each new idea comes, let the leader express the simple meaning.

♦ As each new idea is expressed, the participants should begin to build up the idea expressed.

♦ Keep building each idea till the leader of the group says, "Stop."

♦ Remember, humor and "play" atmosphere are desirable and important to the process. Don't be afraid to have fun!

THREE-PHASE PROCESS

Brainstorming is part of a three-phase process. Make all preparations before brainstorming starts. Do all critical analysis after brainstorming stops.

♦ Before you start, carefully define problem(s) in writing. Set quotas for ideas. Set a time limit. Review the above rules with the brainstorming group.

♦ Establish the "formal setting," then *brainstorm.*

♦ After the session is over, use your normal, everyday judgment to logically develop ideas, selecting the best ideas from all of the alternatives available.

♦

Here's an example used by New Product Insights, a firm that specializes in this technique. Let's say you're trying to develop ideas for new insurance promotions. One of the successful products you study is Crest toothpaste. This product's most important feature is that it contains fluoride. What consumer benefit does it offer? Professional treatment, which originally had to be applied by a dentist, can now be applied by the individual. The core idea is *something that allows you to do your own analysis or treatment in lieu of a professional.* Okay, transfer it to insurance. Maybe you should develop a personal assessment form so the individual can select the policy that best fits his or her needs without a salesperson breathing down his or her neck. Perhaps a direct marketing insurance firm can mail out an immediate-issue policy that the consumer can activate to put in force and provide instant protection.

The secret of lateral thinking is exposing yourself to outside stimuli. And it helps to build up experience that your brain can store until you need it. By attending direct marketing luncheons, seminars, conferences, and courses. By reading industry publications, like those in the appendix. And by monitoring what competitors are doing in the marketing arena.

How to Stimulate Ideas

Getting good ideas is obviously easier said than done. But there are things you can do besides staring at a blank layout pad or a blank sheet of paper. One good approach is to explore various alternatives for changing the creative strategy you've been using.

An excellent booklet on the subject, *How to Get that Great Advertising Idea,* was published some years ago by The Mind Institute in Canada. Here are some of the stimulating questions the booklet posed, plus a few related ones I added.

Can I alter timing? Is there a way to set a period of time that alters normal sales patterns and creates a benefit? Can a push normally done in the winter months be done in the summer? What offers could be used to preseason buyers? Can a Florida land company time its ad or mailing to break right after a big snowstorm up north?

Can I make an opposite? If a negative headline is working, can you use a positive one? What strengths are there in your product that can be emphasized by their opposites? Is there a way to make your message more believable by simply changing a common word or two?

Can I use sensory appeal? Can you link the natural human senses to product attributes to create benefits? Is there a texture, odor, beauty, sound, taste or combination of these that can be incorporated? Should some special paper stock be used for the mailing? How about scented inks? A video? Or can you just create sensory appeal with a mouth-watering food picture?

Can I demonstrate? Is there a key way to show product appeal through graphic demonstration? Can the product be pictured under excessively hard use to demonstrate strength? Would a chart aid in demonstrating? Can you use a series of action photos to provide the equivalent of a TV demonstration?

Can I make an association? What may be associated with the product to create a different appeal? Can the product be linked with a physical thing? A circumstance? An event? Can associations be made with current social trends? Or with nostalgic things of the past?

Can I do the unexpected? Is there a combination of art and copy that would create a startling improvement in readership? Is there a sacred cow in the industry that your product proves wrong? Is there a way to make the mailing package so valuable that people will not only read it but want to save it?

Can I combine? What can be combined, physically or conceptually, with the product appeal? Can a related product be combined as a premium offer? Can newness be combined with tradition? Can a product benefit be combined with a specific industry or prospect need?

THE CONSUMER PERSPECTIVE FOR IDEA GENERATION

STILL ANOTHER APPROACH FOR DEVELOPING new ideas is to completely change your perspective. Stop looking at the product or service as something you want to *sell*. Instead, look at it as something others might want to *buy*. Try exposing yourself to how consumers think about your offer.

One way to do it is with focus group research, detailed in Chapter 7. Another way to get straight-from-the-shoulder consumer feedback is by making a few random phone calls. Pick some names from your customer list or a prospect list you're using. Look up the numbers and call them. Warning: Keep in mind that you're only talking to a small number of people that may or may not be statistically valid. But what consumers say and how they say things can often stimulate ideas.

Dick Hodgson, one of the great creative pros in the direct marketing field, recommends another technique to get that consumer perspective. He suggests you review a random sample of the "white mail" you get from customers. This is a common term for various consumer correspondence—complaints, inquiries, and compliments. Dick finds that it allows you to get a handle on what main benefits appeal to people, what problems they have understanding your offer or copy claims, and what language the consumers use in talking about the product or service.

Apparently, the legendary John Caples also believed in this technique. In *How to Make Your Advertising Make Money,* he recalls that a letter from a Murine Eye Drops customer said she used the product when her eyes were tired. It inspired "quick relief for tired eyes." This appeal out-pulled a number of other ads and made Murine the largest-selling eye drops in the U.S.

I think the late Chris Stagg, a top freelance writer, summed it up well when he said, "No professional in the direct response business can create a winning package when he doesn't know *everything* there is to know about the human being he's writing to. When a writer creates in a marketing vacuum, he creates a loser."

IDEA-STARTER QUESTIONS

FINALLY, HERE ARE A FEW PARTING SHOTS that I've found can often lead to new ideas and result in improvements:

> ♦ Can you make it easier for the prospect to take action?

> ♦ Can you make your mailing package look or seem more personal, as if it's coming from a real person rather than a giant company?

> ♦ Can you change the envelope color, size, or copy so the recipient is more likely to open it?

♦ Can you make a more elaborate or expensive package pay out better than the one you're using?

♦ What would you like to build into your mailing package if cost were no object? Is there a way to do it less expensively?

♦ Can you emulate the creative approach of an ad or mailing package you really admire?

♦ Does your print ad zero in on your most logical prospects instead of trying to appeal to everyone?

♦ Can your TV spot dramatically prove your copy claims?

♦ Is there a way to flatter the reader without overdoing it?

♦ Can you use what I call an "Honest John" copy approach to admit problems and build credibility?

♦ If your main appeal has been a rational one, can you use an emotional approach? Or vice-versa?

THE LAST WORD ON IDEA GENERATION

MY FIRST TASTE OF LATERAL THINKING came as a kid, long before I knew what the term meant. I was at a backyard party with my family. We were throwing a beachball around, until it got lodged in a tree. A number of adults tried to jump up and knock it loose, but it was slightly out of reach. I spotted a rake in a corner of the yard and used it to poke the ball free. Who knows, maybe the praise I received helped make me a student of creative thinking.

♦

Over the years, I've found that anyone can come up with creative ideas. But some people are reluctant to try. Perhaps they're afraid of failure. Or maybe they just need some practice. An excellent book to stimulate anybody's creative juices is *A Whack on the Side of the Head* by Roger Van Oech. It's a mixture of self-analysis and pop psychology that shows how much fun it can be to stimulate and apply new ideas. And new ideas are what it takes to beat your control.

18

MANAGEMENT AND MARKETING
IMPROVEMENT AREAS

◆

YEARS AGO THE DIRECT MARKETING FIELD was populated primarily by mail order entrepreneurs and their management style was best described as "seat-of-the-pants." Today, whether it's a family-owned business or a giant corporation, the stakes are much higher and the players are more sophisticated.

Management usually has to be concerned with all things faced by any other business, such as manufacturing and purchasing, inventories, personnel, and financing. But managers also have some special problems and concerns unique to direct marketing. And in most cases, top executives have a heavier-than-normal involvement in the marketing functions of the company.

In this chapter, we'll cover some of the advanced areas of management and marketing that can have a big impact on improving and building an existing direct marketing program. We'll begin with the most obvious: Making sure your promotion stays on target *and* comes in under budget.

HOW TO MONITOR YOUR PROMOTION PROGRAM

WHETHER YOU'RE MAILING TEN MILLION PIECES a year to dozens of lists, or 100,000 pieces to three lists, keeping track of the many details involved in your promotion programs is critical to their success. The following tried-and-true guidelines will help you prevent costly delays and budget over-runs.

ASSIGN RESPONSIBILITY AND CLARIFY AUTHORITY If you're delegating to subordinates, try to let one person shoulder the primary responsibility for each project you oversee. Remind that person's peers that they are all part of the team, but make sure they understand who holds authority on the project.

♦

IDENTIFY KEY DATES AND CHECKPOINTS   By keeping on top of key dates, you can avoid missing deadlines that set a project back. There are plenty of forms designed to track projects, but one of the best I've seen came from an employee of General Binding Corporation, who attended one of my seminars. The sample in Exhibit 18.1 shows the house list mailings for P&K, a hypothetical company. Note how it manages to fit all of the pertinent dates onto a single sheet. Whatever format you choose, be sure to refer to your list of key dates regularly.

USE CONTROL TOOLS THAT WORK BEST FOR YOU   Somebody has to stay on top of details like inventory levels and promotion schedules. Weekly status reports or meetings can help assure that these critical points get proper attention. People sometimes complain about regularly scheduled meetings. But I've found that

▬▬▬

EXHIBIT 18.1   Product promotion planner

```
                    Direct Mail to House List


ACTION PLAN:

Mail five selected product packages to generate direct product
sales.


RELATED OBJECTIVE/BUSINESS ISSUES/MARKETING PLANS:

Increase overall sales and market penetration for selected
products.


PROMOTION SCHEDULE AND TESTS:

March:              List Timer Module package; P&K customer base

April through
September:          Energy Program Module, mail monthly to test
                    seasonality (6 months)

May:               Audio Intercom Module mailing to customers;
                    include Video Intercom as deluxe option

September:         Phone Answering Module to P&K customer list

November:          Outbound Phone Alarm Module to customers; test
                    list strategy
```

Project	Start	Copy	Keylines	Print	Drop	Receipt
Light Timer	10/21	11/29	12/24	2/4	2/20	3/1
Energy Program	11/12	12/28	1/29	3/18	4/1	--
Audio Intercom	1/18	2/4	3/4	4/10	4/20	5/1
Phone Answering	5/6	6/10	7/9	8/7	8/20	9/1
Outbound Phone Alarm	6/19	7/23	8/22	10/7	10/20	11/1

they help things get done because nobody likes to be embarrassed in front of his or her peers.

CHECK THE DETAILS   My old boss, W. Clement Stone, swore by the maxim, "Never expect what you don't inspect." Make sure someone checks all art boards and proofs before you approve them. A veteran proofreader taught me to double-check the obvious—headlines, firm names, addresses, and phone numbers. Did anyone fold a paper dummy and make sure it fits into its intended envelope? Ask to see a sample print-out of every list to make sure it's what was ordered. Vigilance can prevent all kinds of disasters.

HAVE CONTINGENCY PLANS IN MIND   What if response is substantially lower—or higher—than forecast? What if a new product that's an important part of your plan performs better or worse than budgeted? What if a competitor does something not anticipated? Odds are, one of these things *will* happen. Spend a little time thinking about what you'll do and emergencies won't capsize your program.

HOW TO ENSURE YOUR PROJECTS COME IN ON BUDGET

USE A REALISTIC ESTIMATE SYSTEM   Clients often ask their agency for an advance estimate before a project is even started. But an accurate estimate must be based on a given format—and until it's decided, estimates can range all over the lot. Maybe that's why they're called ballpark estimates. I wrestled with this problem for many years in the agency business before finally developing a two-quote system that has saved us—and our clients—time and trouble.

In the first stage of the process we only estimate the cost of developing a creative concept, with layouts and headlines. Once the concept is approved, the format is established, and we provide a second estimate. Instead of guessing what size the ad or mailing components will be, or how many photos or colors are needed, we can now accurately estimate the final production costs. For a real sense of the costs involved in your project, ask your agency or creative department to try this two-step approach.

♦

OPERATE ON A "NO SURPRISES" BASIS WITH YOUR AD AGENCY AND SUPPLIERS
Insist that anyone about to go over an approved budget should let you know about
the overrun *before* it happens. This should cut down on the number of times you
have to give the boss the bad news . . . and ask for more money.

GET COST STATUS REPORTS BY PROJECT ON A REGULAR BASIS As work pro-
gresses, monitor the costs. You can't assume you're still on budget unless you
ask. Suppliers and staff people get so involved in meeting production schedules
that cost recaps usually take a back seat. Ask, and you shall receive.

HAVE A CONTINGENCY FUND . . . JUST IN CASE Build an extra 10 to 20 percent
into your budget—but don't tell your agency or suppliers. Then, if the inevitable
changes occur, you can absorb an overrun and still come in on budget.

ESTABLISH THE VALUE OF A CUSTOMER

AS NOTED IN CHAPTER 5, YOU CAN'T decide how heavily to invest in new customer
acquisition until you know what kind of repeat business to expect. Too many
direct marketers still concentrate on their revenue and costs for the initial sale
and assume that if they at least break even, they'll make some money on repeat
business.

Businesspeople who use this breakeven approach should have a profitable operation. But, on the other hand, they are not maximizing their growth,
simply because they are only willing to proceed with ads or mailings where they
can at least break even. In so doing, they are automatically excluding other
publications, other lists, or other media that don't quite reach the breakeven point
on the first sale but can be profitable in the long run.

For a basic discussion of the subject, I recommend Julian Simon's book
How to Start and Operate a Mail Order Business. Simon says, "It is amazing and
sad to see how much profit mail order firms forego by not correctly estimating
and using the value of a customer." Here's the approach he recommends for
calculating the value of a customer:

1. Take a fair random sample of the names of
customers—active   and   inactive—who   first

bought from you about three years ago. (Simon recommends 300 customer names but I suggest you use at least 1000.)

2. Add up the total dollar amount they have purchased in the three years since the date of their first purchase.

3. Divide by the number of customer records in your sample.

4. Multiply by the percentage that represents your average profit margin.

Sounds simple enough, doesn't it? Let's try it out. Suppose you have a catalog operation selling gifts and household items. You randomly select 1000 three-year-old customers and get a computer print-out of their buying history. They have placed 1775 orders during this period with a total value of $89,300. Dividing that figure by 1000 gives you an $89.30 average per customer. Naturally, some customers have bought a lot more; some a lot less. But what you want is the average.

You have a 20 percent profit margin, which means the value of each new customer is $17.86. That's what the average customer you acquired three years ago was worth to you in terms of future profits. And if you really want to grow and expand, you should be willing to invest up to $17.86 to get a new customer instead of just trying to acquire customers on a breakeven basis.

To help dramatize the value of repeat business, let's suppose you somehow manage to double it. For our purposes, it doesn't really matter whether customers place more orders, larger orders, or a combination of the two. The 1000 customers now account for $178,600 in total sales. If you go through the rest of the calculations, you'll find you can now afford to spend twice as much for a new customer, $35.72 instead of $17.86.

You should also take into account the cost of your capital, since, with the example above, you will be effectively investing your money for up to a three-year period. And if your list rental income is substantial, that revenue should also be considered in calculating the value of a customer.

◆

THE IMPACT OF A GROWING CUSTOMER LIST

KNOWING THE VALUE OF A CUSTOMER IS half the battle. The other half is to understand the importance of a growing customer list on your bottom line. It comes down to very simple economics. The cost of mailing to a group of customers and a same-size group of prospects is almost identical (the customers are actually cheaper to mail because you don't incur list rental expense); yet your response from customers is much greater.

Let's look at an example I think is pretty realistic. We'll take a firm that uses direct marketing to sell collectibles. Its first offering is a limited edition series of five china plates. We do a P&L calculation, taking into account all direct costs. It shows that, allowing for attrition, the series would produce net sales of $173.81 per order. The gross profit, before promotion costs, would be $93.46 per order. Here are some more assumptions:

◆ The expected response rate from prospect lists is 0.5 percent, which would generate 500 customer names from every 100,000 pieces mailed.

◆ The P&L statement shows that this response rate would give us a profit of $167.30 for every thousand pieces mailed.

◆ There are 500,000 prospect names available for such an offer.

◆ We have product resources sufficient for development of twelve similar collectible offers a year. To simplify our example, we'll assume that all future offers would have a response rate and P&L identical to those of the plate series.

The first chart shows a five-year plan for *prospect* mailings (see Exhibit 18.2). As you can see, the plan calls for 12 mailings a year to the full prospect universe. Our profit percentage is a consistent 19 percent. And our promotions will bring in a total of 30,000 new customers a year.

EXHIBIT 18.2   Prospect mailings

YEAR	MAILINGS PER YEAR	QUANTITY PER YEAR	TOTAL SALES	TOTAL PROFIT	PERCENT PROFIT
1	12	500,000	$5,214,300	$1,003,800	19
2	12	500,000	5,214,300	1,003,800	19
3	12	500,000	5,214,300	1,003,800	19
4	12	500,000	5,214,300	1,003,800	19
5	12	500,000	5,214,300	1,003,800	19

Note: At a response rate of .005, each mailing produces 2,500 new customers. Therefore 12 mailings produce 30,000 customers per year.

The second chart (Exhibit 18.3) shows a five-year plan for *customer* mailings. The 12 mailings a year would be the same as those used for prospects. But there are two important differences. First, the size of the customer list is growing year-by-year as we generate new names from the prospect mailing program. Second, we assume a response rate of 3 percent instead of 0.5 percent, which reflects the higher response expected from a firms' own customers. As a result of the higher response rate, the customer list can be expected to produce a consistent profit of 46 percent.

The third chart (Exhibit 18.4) simply combines the totals of the first two, to reflect *both* the prospect and customer mailings. The dollar amount of sales and profits grow steadily year by year. Even more significant is the growing profit percentage. This, of course, is a reflection again of the increasing customer list with its higher and more profitable response rate. As the years go by, a higher percentage of the total mailing volume is concentrated on the customer list and, therefore, the profit percentage grows accordingly.

IMPORTANCE OF NEW PRODUCT DEVELOPMENT

NEW PRODUCTS ARE THE LIFEBLOOD of any business. It's a rare company indeed whose product mix will be the same five years from now as it is today. So new

♦

EXHIBIT 18.3   Customer mailings

YEAR	MAILINGS PER YEAR	CUSTOMERS MAILED	TOTAL SALES	TOTAL PROFIT	PERCENT PROFIT
1	12	15,000*	$ 938,574	$ 433,890	46
2	12	45,000	2,815,722	1,301,670	46
3	12	75,000	4,692,870	2,169,450	46
4	12	105,000	6,570,018	3,037,230	46
5	12	135,000	8,447,166	3,905,010	46

*Based on 30,000 customers acquired by the end of the year. The number 15,000 is used to represent an average for the year.

product development is essential, not only to sustain your present sales volume but also to meet the growth goals established by most businesses. Just one solid new product can have a big impact on the sales and profit picture.

Most firms are always on the lookout for new product ideas. Some use a new product committee that meets regularly to review the possibilities open to them. Others charge one person or department with the responsibility for generating new product ideas. For most, however, this is a function that marketing management has to oversee on a part-time basis, along with all other management responsibilities and current activities.

The key factors are that management makes a formal commitment to developing new products or services, establishes a budget for development and testing, and sets up some mechanism or reporting system to ensure that this area gets attention on a regular basis.

A STRUCTURED NEW PRODUCT PROGRAM

One of the most exciting new product development programs I've participated in was for the mail order division of Encyclopaedia Britannica. This was a joint effort on the part of the client and its ad agency. And the yearlong effort was a highly structured program to initiate, evaluate, and develop suitable ideas. Here are the ten steps that were followed:

1. BRAINSTORMING   Encyclopaedia Britannica's present product line, reputation, and editorial strengths were reviewed. Then through a series of brainstorming meetings and individual assignments, the agency began developing new product ideas. The result: Fifty-eight product ideas were presented to the client with a brief one-paragraph description of each concept.

2. IDEA EVALUATION AND REFINEMENT   A committee of six people—three from the agency and three from Britannica—then reviewed and voted on each product idea. From this review, 16 ideas were judged as suitable for further exploration.

3. CONCEPT MARKETING PLANS   For each new product idea, a two- or three-page mini-marketing plan was written which briefly explained the concept, the rationale behind it, the market segment it was aimed at, the competition faced in the marketplace, the proposed offer and operation (e.g., one-shot sale, monthly shipment plan), the suggested pricing, any problem areas anticipated, and a rough indication of the investment required to launch the product.

EXHIBIT 18.4   Prospect and customer mailings combined

YEAR	TOTAL SALES	TOTAL PROFIT	PERCENT PROFIT
1	$ 6,152,874	$1,437,690	23
2	8,030,022	2,305,470	29
3	9,907,170	3,173,250	32
4	11,784,318	4,041,030	34
5	13,661,466	4,908,810	36

4. IDEA EVALUATION AND REFINEMENT The concept marketing plans were then reviewed by the agency-client team. Four ideas were eliminated for one reason or another, and then there were 12.

5. FOCUS GROUP RESEARCH Visual presentations of the 12 remaining new product ideas were prepared, along with a brief description. A total of five focus groups were then conducted using the visual presentations. Some groups consisted of only women and some of only men, with all participants carefully selected to represent the potential market segments. Each product idea was exposed to at least two of the focus group sessions.

6. IDEA EVALUATION AND REFINEMENT Based on this qualitative research, five more product ideas were either completely eliminated or sent "back to the drawing board" for major revision. While most of the remaining ideas had been enthusiastically received in the research sessions, some suggested refinements were made in a couple of them to strengthen the product concepts.

7. PROFIT PROJECTIONS The agency then developed estimates for testing the seven remaining products, which included creative costs, production, and direct mail or space media cost. These were used by the client to develop profit and loss statements covering the test, as well as a five-year expansion program for each product idea.

8. IDEA EVALUATION AND REFINEMENT As a result of the profit projections, three of the ideas were approved for immediate testing, three were "tabled" for various financial considerations, and one was recommended as a possible joint venture with another company.

9. DEVELOPMENT OF CREATIVE MATERIALS Direct mail and space advertising were then created for the three ideas initially approved and a joint venture was set up for the fourth. Tests were planned. Media was scheduled. Ads and direct mail materials were created and produced.

10. MARKETPLACE MEASUREMENT The final evaluation of the new product ideas came from consumers who cast the critical votes by sending in the respective ad coupons and reply cards. One product was a failure, despite the encouraging

research results. Another showed some life but not enough to be profitable. The other two were winners.

In any type of new product development, whether in general advertising or direct marketing, the success ratio is usually pretty low. Most firms believe they're doing quite well if they get one winner out of every five products actually tested. This structured program for new product development produced two winners for Encyclopaedia Britannica. So our batting average was excellent.

NEW PRODUCT CONSIDERATIONS

When thinking about new products, don't limit your scope. How you define your business often has an important bearing on the range of product ideas that will be considered. A good example is the Franklin Mint, which started with commemorative coins. If the firm had limited its business definition to commemorative coins, it would not have enjoyed such tremendous growth. Instead executives regarded themselves as being in the collectibles business and have branched out from coins to a wide variety of other collectible products.

Also worth considering is how a proposed new product fits your existing distribution plan. For example, I know a firm selling home security products by mail that wanted to add an auto alarm system to its product line. But whereas its existing security products were all easy to install, the company couldn't find an auto alarm system with this same consumer benefit. It was decided to abandon the idea rather than set up a dealer installation network. Perhaps the company could have solved the problem by providing a video cassette, which would give step-by-step instructions for self-installation.

Another key consideration to think about is whether a new product or service can be sold to your existing database. A company that sells desk diaries might successfully sell a time management product to its database; it might find selling clocks and watches more difficult. On the other hand, a different type of product could lead the company into an altogether new business. I call this a *break-out* or *lead product* because it gets you into a new category. It's potentially a good idea if you are willing to build a new database and develop profitable follow-up offers.

Most of these issues can be resolved by careful strategic planning. Before you consider any potential new product, measure it against your company's goals—and your competition. Does your current product line have any holes in it? Are there market niches that your competitors are overlooking? Will the proposed new product help your company get where it wants to be in five years?

A REVOLVING REVIEW OF EXISTING PRODUCTS

While it's exciting to be involved in the birth of a successful new product, management should not overlook the opportunity for revamping or improving existing products. Very often, once a product has become established, it gets promoted regularly along with the rest of the product line.

But seldom does management make a full-scale review of existing products. One client I've worked with has recognized this shortcoming and has done something about it. The company has established a product audit committee. It meets every other month for an in-depth review of one product. The review includes product features, pricing, recent promotion efforts, results, and how the product is paying out. The committee members then brainstorm ideas ranging from product improvements to new promotion ideas. Decisions are made. Actions are taken. As a result, many existing products have been substantially improved and product life lengthened.

START YOUR OWN COMPETITION

HOW DO YOU SUBSTANTIALLY INCREASE sales when you think you might already be saturating the market with your present product line? Or when you have so many competitors it's difficult to win a bigger share of the market?

One possibility is by competing with yourself—establishing a second company name to sell the same type of products. This idea might seem far-fetched, but it's really what the big soap companies, breweries, cigarette companies, and auto manufacturers have been doing for years to increase their share of market. Some gift and clothing catalogs have had success with this technique. I've worked with a couple of direct marketing firms that have successfully started their own competition.

In the first case, the objective was to meet a competitor head-on. The client concerned had a successful premium-priced product for the business market. Suddenly it was "knocked off" by another firm selling a similar but much less expensive version of the same product. So the company started its own lower-price version, which was marketed under a different name.

In another case, a firm selling the school market had a dual buying influence. Some purchases were made by principals and faculty, others by students. This firm had a good share of the total market, but executives believed they weren't getting as much of the student business as they should. Maybe their catalog was too conservative, they reasoned. So they started another catalog under a different name. The product line was almost identical, but they gave the catalog a more youthful feel.

The results? In both cases, the second companies have brought in "plus" sales without hurting the original product line. In the second example, the new catalog operation has been growing much more rapidly than the original one. And there are some obvious economies. By utilizing the same office space, shipping facilities, and personnel, you can increase your volume with an effective decrease in overhead—because you're actually spreading those costs across two operations instead of one.

FOREIGN MARKETS ARE INCREASINGLY ATTRACTIVE

ANOTHER WAY TO GROW SALES AND PROFITS when you think you've saturated your market is by expanding beyond national borders. Response rates on direct mail in foreign countries are generally higher than in the United States, probably because consumers there see less of it. (Most U.S. households receive three to four times as much mail as households in European countries.)

List availability is still not nearly as widespread as it is in the U.S., but it is improving steadily. Lists are usually more expensive abroad, although expect this to change as the choices proliferate. In some countries, like the United Kingdom, the use of space advertising to bring in new customers is more prevalent.

At my former agency, I initiated the chart in Exhibit 18.5 so clients could readily compare European markets with the States. Generally, the percentage of retail sales made by mail order is the best indicator of potential. As Europe becomes a true Common Market, it should continue to see strong growth.

♦

And don't overlook the direct marketing potential in the Far East, which is multiplying more rapidly than the U.S. or Europe.

Overseas expansion is certainly worth pursuing, despite the language problems. For direct marketing leaders like Time-Life Books and Franklin Mint, who have been selling globally for some time, international sales usually account for 40 to 50 percent of total revenues.

TWELVE OVERLOOKED PATHS TO SALES AND PROFITS

AS I HAVE DEVELOPED MARKETING RECOMMENDATIONS for numerous clients and analyzed the present operations of others, I've noticed a lot of commonality. Following are some techniques that seem to apply equally well to a wide variety of companies in different types of businesses. You might call them activities most direct marketers don't do enough of.

1. MAIL YOUR CUSTOMER LIST HEAVILY   Some firms hit their customers only a few times a year. But, unless you have a seasonal operation and assuming you have enough different products available, customers can generally be profitably mailed at least six times, often twelve times, and sometimes even more frequently.

2. USE TELEMARKETING   Telemarketing is especially good for large ticket items, continuity offers, and renewal efforts to previous buyers. One large consumer direct marketer has been steadily building its telemarketing department and now has over 2000 people making outbound calls. That's not a typo, just a lot of bodies.

3. DEVELOP SPECIAL EFFORTS TO GET NEW CUSTOMERS   It's obviously easier to send the same mailing or catalog to customers and prospects alike. But it's not always the smartest approach. Sometimes prospects require a more complete or elaborate selling story. Or a special introductory offer. Customers, on the other hand, often respond best when your copy acknowledges a previous purchase.

4. SELL IN CANADA   Since it's so close to home, it's a good way to get your feet wet with foreign markets. Sales volume is about one-tenth of the U.S. for most companies. While there are duties and customs to contend with, response rates tend to be higher than in the U.S.

EXHIBIT 18.5   Key U.S./European figures indicate mail order potential

COUNTRY	POPULATION†	GROSS NATIONAL PRODUCT*†	RETAIL SALES*†	RETAIL SALES DOLLARS PER CAPITA*	MAIL ORDER SALES*†	MAIL ORDER AS A % OF RETAIL	MAIL ORDER DOLLARS PER CAPITA*
United States	235	4,488,000	1,507,000	6,412	77,300	5.1	329
West Germany	61	897,000	233,940	3,832	11,467	4.9	187
Great Britain	57	731,237	190,793	3,347	6,032	3.2	106
France	55	510,300	225,957	4,079	5,876	2.6	106
Finland	5	70,350	23,474	4,773	612	2.6	122
Switzerland	7	142,000	33,354	5,128	778	2.3	111
Sweden	8	105,500	40,991	4,897	716	1.7	89
Netherlands	15	175,000	50,248	3,349	735	1.5	49
Belgium	10	115,000	37,607	3,794	414	1.1	41
Norway	4	68,000	21,637	5,190	230	1.1	57
Denmark	5	79,000	20,887	4,079	210	1.0	42
Italy	57	743,000	153,609	2,684	852	.6	14
Spain	39	227,000	72,831	1,883	143	.2	3

*In U.S. dollars   †In millions

Source: Direct, January 10, 1990. Based on a 1988/89 study.

◆

5. USE ENOUGH LEVERAGE WHERE IT COUNTS In an inquiry-producing situation or a two-stage selling method, the heaviest effort is devoted to getting the initial inquiry or response. Often the conversion or follow-up effort doesn't get enough attention. Because the quantity of names in this second stage is small, a few added dollars well spent can mean a big improvement in the final profit picture.

6. CULTIVATE HIGH-VOLUME CUSTOMERS I've seen it so often I'm no longer surprised. But the old 80/20 rule—or some variation of it—usually holds true. The 20 percent of a firm's customers who account for 80 percent of its sales should get special attention, whether by mail or phone, to keep them buying. And the more you learn about them, the better the chance of finding more like them.

7. DEVELOP CUSTOMIZED PRODUCTS FOR NICHE MARKETS I have found that some markets can best be tapped by a product that seems to be tailor-made for their needs. This might be as simple as changing the product name or a few minor features or it might require a whole new product approach. A number of niche or specialized markets are large enough to be worth cultivating in this way. It can be more effective than trying to sell the same thing to everyone.

8. TRY FOR MULTIPLE-UNIT SALES The idea is to sell more units on each order by mailing to individuals, firms, or groups who represent a multiple market for the product. Those who receive the mailing can act like middlemen or agents to multiply product distribution and sales. This works well in the school market, for example, where the teacher gets students to sign up for magazine or book programs. In other situations, you can use "twofer" prices and volume-order discounts.

9. HAVE ENOUGH FOLLOW-UPS IN A SERIES For example, someone arbitrarily decides there should be three mailings in a conversion or renewal series. The firm tries it and all three pay out. The odds are that the series could and should be expanded to four, five, or more mailings—so long as each mailing continues to pay its own way.

10. USE MGM PROGRAMS The initials stand for *member get a member,* which is a fancy way of saying, go after customer referrals. Satisfied customers can be

your best salespeople. You can merely ask for referral names or provide a small gift as an incentive. Best proof of how well this works are the music and book clubs who constantly feature MGM programs.

11. DEVELOP A CATALOG   While many direct marketers rely entirely on catalog selling, many other marketing situations exist in which a catalog could provide supplementary sales, even if it's used only for the customer list or after-market sales. Catalogs provide an opportunity to offer a wide variety of products, and consistently get better readership and retention than solo mailings.

12. PROMOTE LIST RENTAL   Most firms with a list on the market leave the sales up to a list broker. But it's such a profitable area that it should get more promotion, either from a list manager or yourself. And the universe of potential list users is so small that a nominal budget can have a big impact.

THE LAST WORD ON MANAGEMENT AND MARKETING IMPROVEMENTS

THE BEST WAY TO CONTINUALLY improve your direct marketing program is by keeping your eye steadily on the future. If your organization expects to be in business for more than a year or two, it should have a laundry list of growth and expansion ideas. Ideas for future products, services, and markets to be explored. And some of them should be under active consideration right now.

19

DATABASES AND BACK-END MARKETING

♦

BACK IN CHAPTER 2, I POINTED OUT that the classic direct marketing success formula is to build a list of satisfied customers and then go back to them for repeat sales. In Chapter 5, I stressed that back-end marketing is where you maximize the value of your customers. It's what you do *after* the first sale that determines how profitable a return you get on your advertising investment. Your database is what allows you to do this.

THE DATABASE CONCEPT

THE PREMISE OF THE DATABASE CONCEPT is an old one—that knowledge is power. The more you know about your customers' purchase history and demographics, the more successful your advertising and sales efforts will be. Your marketing database helps you transform that knowledge into the ability to act before your competitors react.

What is a database? A collection of interrelated customer and transactional data that allows timely retrieval or use of that data to capitalize on marketing opportunities. In other words, you can use it to segment customer or prospect lists, identify and predict purchasing trends, and personalize your marketing communications to them to ensure the greatest possible response.

Here's another definition we often use in presentations at my agency. Database marketing is:

♦ Marketing to individual, known customers or prospects . . .

♦ Using purchase history and lifestyle data . . .

♦ To target relevant offers and rewards . . . .

♦

♦ That increase response or brand loyalty. . .

♦ More efficiently than with other media alternatives.

Exhibit 19.1 shows how a database processing system works. The database on the left stores information on customers, merchandise items, and transaction data. As the information moves through the system, it can be used to segment customer lists, fulfill orders, and update the accounts receivable system for billing. The results are summarized in a series of reports on buying history, order processing, and merchandise movement—and the customer name and address records are updated.

By the way, the customers tracked in a database can be individuals *or* establishments. Database marketing works just as well for business direct marketing efforts as it does for consumer.

EXHIBIT 19.1   How information moves through a database processing system.

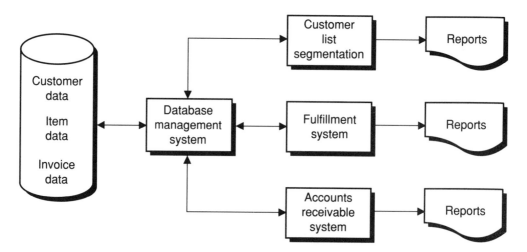

ADVANTAGES AND USES OF DATABASE MARKETING

DATABASE APPLICATIONS ARE CONSTANTLY growing and evolving as new marketing concepts are developed. But today, databases are commonly used to:

♦ Find out who's buying a product or service, so you can identify and reach more prime prospects like them.

♦ Generate and track leads for salespeople.

♦ Build relationships: welcome new customers, increase purchase frequency from light users, give heavy users special treatment, and reactivate former buyers.

♦ Identify opportunities for new products, services and businesses.

♦ Track the long-term cost-efficiency of advertising efforts by measuring repeat purchases of newly acquired customers.

♦ Protect the customer base by timely reactions to competitive promotions.

Let's look at how a few prominent marketers are using their databases.

The airlines are a good place to start. It's estimated that 50 million travelers are enrolled in their Frequent Flyer programs and that the top ten U.S. airlines spend over $100 million annually on them (Exhibit 19.2). After industry deregulation in the 1970s sparked competitive price wars, customers stopped requesting a favorite airline and chose flights primarily on price. To combat this, the Frequent Flyer programs were developed to stimulate brand loyalty among the airlines' best customer: The business traveler.

Frequent Flyer programs help airlines capture key database information they can use to develop customer profiles. Besides rewarding all regular customers with mileage or points, they can offer special benefits to the best ones. American Airlines maintains highly personalized profiles on the top two or three percent of its frequent flyers, so it can provide the seat, car rental, and hotel preferences of these priority passengers.

A recent traveler survey showed that 81 percent of respondents altered travel patterns to collect more miles and would wait up to three hours for a flight, while 97.5 percent would request a specific airline if a choice were available. In an age when time is a precious commodity, I find it incredible that people will go to such lengths to earn free fights. But they do. And that's why the programs work.

EXHIBIT 19.2   Frequent Flyer programs help airlines build customer databases and reward customer loyalty.

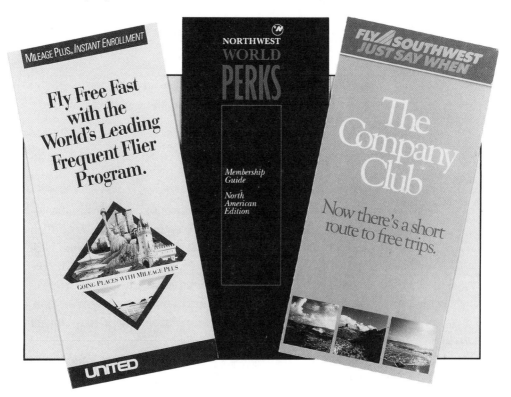

A database can also mean the difference between the success or failure of a new product. To extend its medical education efforts, Minnesota's prestigious Mayo Clinic decided to publish a health newsletter (see Exhibit 19.3). Its database of five million former patients was an ideal place to begin testing.

EXHIBIT 19.3   The Mayo Clinic used its database of former patients to test and launch its *Mayo Clinic Health Letter*.

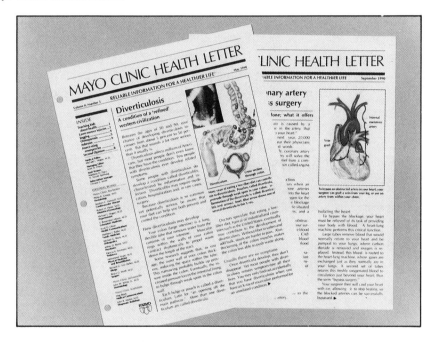

To find the most receptive target audience, a package containing a letter, a product brochure, a small folder about Mayo Clinic, and an order form and return envelope was tested to the Mayo Clinic database as well as selected rented lists. The overall mailing was quite successful, and the response rate from the Mayo database was five times greater than rented lists! Thanks to that kind of response, the *Mayo Clinic Health Letter* is now one of the largest-circulation newsletters in the country. It channels millions of dollars to medical research. And it generated so many new patient inquiries that Mayo has opened two new clinics in other parts of the country.

♦

Consumer products companies are discovering the benefits of database marketing, too. A major dog food company wanted to build a database of dog breeders—all heavy dog food users—so it could target special promotions to customers and non-customers. The company developed a survey that asked 19 key questions on breeder activities and dog food usage. The 21,000 breeders who responded were more than double what was projected. This customized database was built for less than $7.50 a name—a small amount to pay for the sales potential this group represents.

The list goes on and on. Traditional direct marketers, like Norm Thompson, send inexpensive solo mailings to their best catalog customers. When a former buyer neglects to order anything for a year, Damart mails an "anniversary letter" with a special offer. Omaha Steaks uses telemarketing to remind its best customers to keep their freezers stocked with its gourmet meat products. All these activities are triggered by database purchasing history.

Private or Custom Databases

A custom database is one you build yourself. Because it's proprietary, it can be used as a private advertising medium—even a "private marketplace," as some experts have dubbed it. A custom database, like the dog breeders database just mentioned, lets marketers identify, reach, and communicate with their best prospects—all without alerting competitors to their promotional activities, as would happen with TV or print.

Because cigarette advertising is not permitted on broadcast media, tobacco companies have quietly turned to direct marketing. R.J. Reynolds reportedly spends over $100 million a year marketing to its private database of smokers, which it builds through special coupon offers like the one in Exhibit 19.4. When they respond, smokers also provide information on their regular brand. Testing has shown which competitive users are most likely to switch, and future marketing efforts are targeted accordingly.

When National Liberty first began promoting life insurance to veterans, it couldn't find a big enough list of prospects to mail. So it built its own by mounting an inquiry campaign that invited veterans to call and find out about the benefits they qualified for. Their custom database now allows them to target an audience that couldn't be reached cost effectively before.

EXHIBIT 19.4   R.J. Reynolds builds its database with coupon offers like this one.

BUILDING A DATABASE

AS THE THE USE OF COMPUTERS EVOLVED in direct marketing, different business functions often wound up in separate systems—customer history in one, inventory in another, billing and collection in a third, and so on. Today it is becoming more common to try to link such files together so that an entry in one will update the others as well. As you enter and process an order, the system will automatically adjust inventory and update customer history.

But marketing is still what drives the business. And a marketing database should allow you to track four main areas: Customers and/or prospects (including date of first activity); promotions (who got what, when); transactions (when they bought, what they spent); and products or services (what was purchased). If you have a limited product line, you can capture data for each item; a catalog firm with an extensive product line will usually record purchases by category.

Computer costs have decreased so dramatically over the years that you can create and maintain an extensive database at a fraction of what it used to cost. Database experts like to use a Rolls Royce analogy to drive home the point. They claim that if automotive improvements had equalled data processing gains in the last 40 years, you could buy the car for $2.50 and get two million miles to the gallon! Whatever, you can now afford to not only maintain transactional data about your customers, but to add demographic and psychographic information.

Trying to analyze so much information to make promotion decisions can be both time-consuming and frustrating. Fortunately, new *relational* database software is making it easier for sophisticated direct marketers to perform complex, multi-dimensional queries very rapidly—greatly enhancing the actionable value of the stored data.

The more information you have to work with, the more "what if" questions you can ask. If your database system is "on line," you can even get instant answers to those questions with your desktop computer. It lets you make marketing decisions at the stroke of a key, rather than waiting a week for another department or an outside service bureau to get back to you with the data, and then realizing there's another question you should have asked.

PUTTING YOUR DATABASE TO WORK

THE ADVANTAGE OF ALL THIS INFORMATION obviously depends on how you use it. A good database system can become a priceless corporate asset. It helps you manage the buyer/seller relationship, develop effective contact strategies for each buyer segment, and serve your customers better.

But all too often, we barely scratch the surface of our database information. I did an informal survey of database experts in preparing for a recent

♦

speech. They overwhelmingly agreed that the technology is far ahead of the marketing.

It's almost as though we keep our great database knowledge in one department and our marketing and creative types in another. The latter have always realized that the more they know about the people they're targeting, the better job they can do to sell them. But they're not clamoring for more customer insight from the database people. Or even using the information they have. Did someone forget to build a bridge between the two departments?

In most cases, we're using our database knowledge and technology to make a simple, binary decision: To mail, or not to mail. We're not using it to plan promotions or design offers that appeal to people in a certain category.

My partner, Pierre Passavant, shares my views on this subject. He believes that we need to invent offers that use *more* of our databases rather than *less* of them. He notes that the typical approach to database marketing quickly weeds a file of 100,000 new book club members down to the 25,000 "best" members. Not enough attention is devoted to the other 75,000 names and how to get them to become regular book buyers.

If you're going to make the investment to build a database—and it does take time and money—it should be viewed as a strategic weapon. Squeeze all the marketing information you can out of that computer. Use it to develop database-driven creative programs. And it will be one of the best marketing investments you've ever made.

Back-end Marketing

In the old days, only a handful of experts really recognized the importance of the back-end marketing effort. One of these was mail order pioneer Max Sackheim, who liked to admonish clients to "make customers, not sales." He understood that a business can't be built on one-time sales. It must be built on repeat business—on customers who like your products, who are pleased with your service, and who are therefore likely to buy from you again and again.

In the last few years, our business has acknowledged the importance of good fulfillment and customer service, which is an integral part of back-end marketing. In the mid 1980s, I was fortunate to be part of the DMA's Task Force on Consumer Acceptance, which developed the industry's first guidelines for fulfillment and customer service. Since then, the DMA has developed seminars and other educational efforts to train people in this important area.

Stan Fenvessy, who heads Fenvessy Consulting, has long been the acknowledged expert on the subject. He describes fulfillment as "the full circle of handling an order from its initiation by mail or telephone until the customer is fully satisfied."

Fenvessy has identified eight elements or steps that are part of fulfillment:

1. Ordering tools and techniques including the product numbering system, order form design, and ordering instructions

2. Receiving mail and telephone orders

3. Processing orders

4. Checking credit

5. Maintaining inventory

6. Sending merchandise or subscriptions

7. Billing

8. Handling complaints

Fulfillment is important for two big reasons. First, to make the original order stick. The majority of direct marketing purchases are made on impulse, and virtually all carry a free trial or money-back guarantee. If fulfillment isn't handled promptly and efficiently, your returned goods rate can and will increase.

Second, good fulfillment builds customer satisfaction. As Fenvessy says, "Only a satisfied customer will order again. He or she must receive everything ordered, promptly, properly packed, the invoice must be clear and accurate, and the customer must have the assurance that any problems will be resolved fairly, quickly, and courteously."

HOW LONG ARE CUSTOMERS WILLING TO WAIT?

The FTC has established a 30-day rule for most mail order sales. In effect, it says that unless you tell the customer shipping will take longer in your front-end ad or mailing, you must either ship the order in 30 days or give the customer an opportunity to cancel his or her order. A similar rule is currently being considered to cover telemarketing sales.

About 20 years ago, a survey showed that most mail order buyers expected to receive their orders in two to three weeks. The industry has improved fulfillment time a lot since then. But a recent Gallup survey showed that about half of all consumers still find it difficult to order products by mail because of the time it takes to get them. In a world dominated by FAX and Federal Express, consumers naturally expect to receive their orders more quickly. It seems to me that all of our fulfillment efforts should be directed at meeting their expectations.

SLOW FULFILLMENT CAN COST YOU MONEY   I haven't seen a lot of testing on the back-end lately. But some years ago, when he was with Rapp & Collins, Walter Marshall did an article for *Direct Marketing* which cited some test results I think are still relevant.

Speed shipping. A music club was taking about five weeks to get its first shipment to new members. In testing the effect of getting the first shipment out sooner, 5000 orders from a single magazine insert were split into two groups. Half got standard fulfillment; the other half were handled under a "speed ship" plan that got the first shipment to new members in about two and one-half weeks.

Six months later a computer analysis was done on both groups to measure two key factors. First, the payment of the invoice that came with the initial shipment. The "speed ship" group had a 17 percent higher payment rate than the control group who got standard fulfillment. Second, what's known as the "take per member" was measured, i.e., the number of club selections purchased during the first six-months. The "speed ship" group won again with a "take" that was over 20 percent higher than the control group. The test was later

♦

verified in even larger quantities and, as a result, the club's entire fulfillment operation was streamlined.

Acknowledging orders. Knowing that customers had to wait a few weeks to get their first shipment, a major book club wanted to test the addition of an acknowledgment mailing to let new members know their order had been received and was being processed. The mailing used contained a personalized thank you letter and an eight-page booklet that described the club's operations.

The test group received this acknowledgment mailing, which was sent first class. The control group merely received its introductory shipment. And both groups got their introductory shipment at the same time. The results showed that the test group, who received the acknowledgment, came out ahead on all three scores being measured: 10.4 percent more converted and purchased additional books, the bad debt rate was reduced 18.7 percent, and the returned goods rate on the introductory shipment was 44 percent lower.

Handling inquiries. Still another test Marshall cited was for a direct marketing firm who advertised to generate inquiries for their catalog. Management wondered if they could save money by sending out their catalog via third class instead of first class, knowing the former method would add about a week to the delivery time. They tested and found their percent of catalog sales was 19 percent lower for the third class group.

Good Service Helps, Not Hurts

In addition to speedier fulfillment, other tests have shown that good customer service also pays out. Years ago executives of mail order companies were scared to death to put anything in their shipping cartons about how to send back merchandise because they felt it would increase their returns. Some even kidded about trying to develop self-destruct cartons so that, once opened, the carton couldn't be used to send the merchandise back. Finally, one of the giant catalog firms made a test. On the back of the packing slip, instructions were given on how to return merchandise the customer was unhappy with. There was no increase in returns and the normal returns were easier to process because customers followed the instructions given them.

Still another tack was taken by a firm selling camera outfits on a free trial basis. The firm was experiencing an abnormally high returned goods rate.

Research disclosed that many returns were being made for very minor reasons. If the customer couldn't figure out how to work the camera, he or she would just pack up the complete outfit, ship it back, and forget the whole thing.

To solve the problem, a card was inserted in all shipments telling customers to call the company toll-free if they had any questions or problems. The return goods rate was cut by about 25 percent, and the phone expense turned out to be a mere fraction of the sales and profits that were saved.

Fulfillment can be critical for the continuity marketer, too. Insiders attribute the success of a couple recent direct marketing continuity programs to their more sophisticated, customer-driven fulfillment programs.

When Johnson & Johnson began selling its child development toys through the mail, it had to surmount the problem of very high levels of returned goods. Through research, J & J learned that too many toys were reaching babies at the wrong age. In other words, before or after the child was ready for them. To solve this, it began a system of "variable entry." Now, customers indicate the birth date of their child, and Johnson & Johnson makes sure it provides the right toy at the right time. This customized fulfillment reduced the return shipment rate by 35 percent (see Exhibit 19.5).

Similarly, the feedback slip that Gevalia Coffee includes with each shipment makes it easy for customers to change the type of coffee, the quantity, or the delivery date of the next shipment. They can either send the slip back with their payment or call a customer service 800 number. It's obviously easier for the company, Kraft General Foods, to repeat the same shipment at regular intervals. But I'm sure the flexibility of this customer-driven process increases the average "take" per member.

ORDER CONVERSION AND RENEWALS: KEY LEVERAGE POINTS

Many direct marketing situations call for a series of mailings to get conversions or renewals. Most insurance companies, for instance, have to convert policyholders who inquire or accept an introductory offer to pay their first regular premium. Magazines have to renew subscriptions, usually annually. Both provide great leverage opportunities because a small percentage increase can mean big dollars.

In my experience, it's important that a conversion series be given enough efforts. Most firms I know use a five- to seven-piece series, though some use as

◆

many as a dozen efforts and many include some telemarketing later in the series as a clean-up effort. The series should have a lot of variety in format and copy approach so each effort has a good chance to get opened and produce action. In addition, it helps if you improve or "sweeten" the offer later in the series, perhaps by adding a free gift or reducing the down payment.

———

EXHIBIT 19.5   Johnson & Johnson ads now request baby's age so the firm can send the right Child Development Toys.

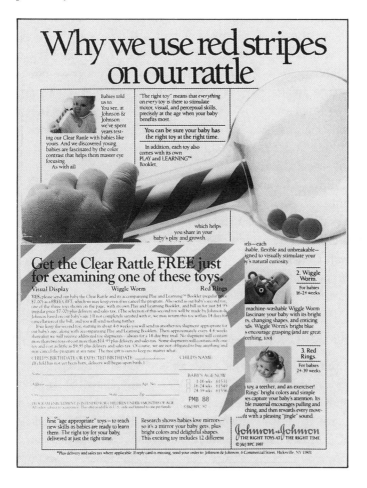

When you're developing a new inquiry conversion program, you don't need to create the whole series upfront. A series usually doubles the results of a single effort. In other words, if you get a six percent conversion rate with a single mailing, experience shows a series will convert about twelve percent. So you can start by only creating and testing the first effort—and hold off on creating and producing the rest of the series until you analyze the test.

Once you have a complete conversion program in place, you can also test the creative strength of each piece in the series. In a series mailing, where you maintain the same offer, the results of each piece should decline somewhat from the previous step. But if results fall off too sharply on one mailing, it's safe to assume that effort is weak and that new creative should be tested against it.

Getting that Second Order

Another key leverage point for most direct marketing firms is the second order. Yet, companies often treat all customers alike. They make no special effort to get an individual to order a second time, ignoring the fact that a two-time buyer is much more likely to become a good long-term customer.

Let's consider some figures to prove the point. One firm sells a gift item with an annual repeat factor. Out of 100 new customers, 49 will buy again the following year. But of those who place a second order, 68 percent will buy again the third year, and 76 percent of these will also buy the fourth year. Once a buying pattern is established, customer loyalty and repeat purchases remain high.

The same principle applies in fund raising. Officials of one charity found that they lost 53 out of 100 new contributors the following year. But, of the 47 who donated a second time, 85 percent were still contributing four years later!

The message is clear: Getting that second order is important. Special renewal or promotion efforts directed to first-time buyers can pay big dividends. Even a simple note acknowledging a first-time order can increase the likelihood that someone will order again. Yet too often, this kind of simple effort is overlooked. In an informal study of back-end efforts, catalog consultant Dick Hodgson placed 119 catalog orders to study fulfillment and customer service practices. Only two firms sent a note acknowledging that he was a new customer and thanking him for his business.

Continuity marketers generally work harder to get a second order. When customers receive new selections on a monthly basis, you have a built-in opportunity to pre-sell—not only the second shipment, but every future shipment. Many publishers use what is sometimes called a "running resell." They enclose a letter or flyer with each shipment that previews what's coming next month. It can not only increase the acceptance rate or "take" of the next selection, it can cut down the expense of processing returns from customers who decide that they don't want the selection after they've received it.

Are you Maximizing Customer Value?

Virtually all direct marketers will acknowledge that their customer list or database is their greatest asset. But varying degrees of sophistication are shown on how well they utilize that asset. Most have learned the basics, of course. They keep their list segmented by year of last purchase because they know the most recent buyers perform better than the older ones. And, through testing and experimentation, they've gained some idea of how many times a year they can profitably mail each group.

But those really are the elementary methods. The more advanced direct marketing practitioners go well beyond this. They know that some two-year old customers are better than others, maybe because their last order was a large one or because they had purchased frequently for some time and temporarily have become inactive. They adjust their contact strategy accordingly to concentrate as much mail as possible on the customers whose past history proves they are most likely to buy again.

They normally do it by using a *recency/frequency/monetary* formula, or RFM, which we touched on in Chapter 8. Let's look at how an RFM system is actually set up, using an example that Bob Stone provided in an *Advertising Age* column:

In its simplest form, a point system is established with purchases broken out by quarters. A typical formula might be as follows:

Recency points: 24 points—purchased in current quarter
12 points—purchased 4 to 6 months ago

6 points—purchased 7 to 9 months ago

3 points—purchased 10 to 12 months ago

Frequency points: Number of purchases times 4 points

Monetary points: 10 percent of each dollar purchase with a ceiling of 9 points (ceiling avoids distortion from an unusually large purchase)

The points allotted vary among those using RFM formulas, but the principles are the same. Once the system is established and point values are confirmed, the opportunities for maximizing profits are phenomenal.

APPLYING THE RFM FORMULA

Using Stone's typical formula as a guide, let's see how it might be applied by a catalog marketer. We'll assume that the firm puts out eight catalogs a year and has 100,000 names on its customer file. The firm assigns RFM points as indicated above and finds that its customer file breaks out as follows:

Points	Number of names
75 or more	13,000
50 to 74	22,000
25 to 49	46,000
0 to 24	19,000

At this point, judgment and testing come into play. But a typical mailing plan might call for an annual catalog frequency like this:

Points	Number of names	Catalogs
75 or more	13,000	12
50 to 74	22,000	8
25 to 49	46,000	6
0 to 24	19,000	3

As you can see, the top two categories would get all eight catalogs. The top group, in fact, would get a remail of the four strongest books, ideally with a

♦

different cover. The bottom two groups, however, would get less than eight catalogs. The lowest group might get a book only in the best months—perhaps January, August, and October—when they have the best chance of paying out.

The above plan calls for a total mailing of 665,000 catalogs. If, on the other hand, the firm were to mail all eight catalogs to its entire 100,000 list, it would be mailing 800,000 books. In our example, we would end up mailing 135,000 less catalogs and probably do as well or better in total sales.

This is, of course, an over-simplified example. Many RFM formulas become quite complicated. Some publishers and catalog firms have over 100 identifiable segments. The example, however, shows that the same system can be applied on a smaller scale by any direct marketer with a substantial list. And it's not unusual for the better segments of a list to perform six to ten times as well as the poorer segments.

Pretend You're a Customer

Everyone likes to think their firm is doing a good job on fulfillment and customer service. But are your orders really shipped as fast as you think they are? Are all the correct forms and enclosures being used? Do complaints get handled efficiently? Are inquiries processed promptly?

I've always made it a practice to answer ads or mailings and check up on the fulfillment of the clients with whom I have worked. I've seen a number of surprises or "things nobody happened to think about." Many potential problems were quickly corrected. Try it yourself. Send in the coupons or order cards from your own ads or mailings. Under a decoy name, of course. Or have a friend do it. See how long it takes to get a shipment. Find out if the merchandise is received in good condition and can be easily repacked for returning it. Learn whether returns are acknowledged. Find out what it takes to get a problem straightened out and how many past due invoices you get in the meantime. Learn whether the form letters being used convey the proper customer service attitude. You may be surprised.

Eight Tips for Better Customer Service

In this chapter, I hope I've made the point that good customer service is good business. But the FTC, Better Business Bureaus, and newspaper "action line" columnists still receive an alarming number of mail order complaints every year. That's too bad—because everyone in the direct marketing industry suffers when a customer has a bad experience buying by mail. To make sure your company provides the best service it can, consider taking these steps, if you haven't already.

1. SIMPLIFY YOUR GUARANTEE A leading mail order nursery did this recently. The firm dropped the confusing legal terms. The refund and replacement policy was explained in simple, everyday language. The result was a sharp drop in customer complaints and correspondence.

2. ACKNOWLEDGE ORDERS Many customers probably wouldn't mind waiting a little while for merchandise delivery if they at least knew their order had been received and was getting your careful attention. If you can't ship immediately, send a postcard acknowledgment. While sending a card will add somewhat to your ordering processing cost, it should greatly reduce customer inquiries, look-ups, and correspondence expense.

3. SHIP MERCHANDISE MORE PROMPTLY Stan Fenvessy says your goal should be to get your order into the customer's hands the calendar week after the one in which the order was placed. It may not always be possible. But the closer you can come, the better.

4. DON'T BILL BEFORE YOU SHIP This must be near the top of a mail order buyer's "pet peeve" list. He or she sends an order, waits a couple of weeks, then receives an invoice before the merchandise arrives. If there's even a slight chance that the invoice will arrive before your shipment, enclose a note explaining that the order has been shipped and should arrive shortly. And by all means, point out that payment need not be sent until after the order has been received.

5. ACKNOWLEDGE RETURNS AND CANCELLATIONS If the average customer sends back merchandise, he or she wants to know you received it. And when the next statement arrives, he or she might be a little irritated that the returned goods haven't been credited yet. Or wonder why he or she gets another monthly club mailing after telling you to cancel. Easy solution: Send an acknowledgment card telling the customer you got the returned goods or cancellation request, explain that it may take a couple of weeks to process it, and don't be alarmed if you get another invoice or mailing in the interim.

6. ANSWER CORRESPONDENCE PROMPTLY How many stories have you heard about people writing a book or music club two, three, or four times before they got a problem straightened out? What happens to all those first letters that never seem to get answered? Use a form letter with check-off boxes, if necessary, but give the customer the courtesy of a reply. And then follow through to get the problem straightened out so he or she doesn't have to write you again—with copies to the BBB, FTC, and anybody else he or she can think of.

7. MAKE COMPLAINT RESOLUTION A PRIORITY One recent study showed that customers who have a complaint or problem satisfactorily resolved become *better* long-term customers than those who have never had a problem. To really show your commitment to solving customer problems, handle serious complaints by phone. When you consider the high cost of a personal letter today, you may actually save money. And the goodwill you'll generate by calling is nothing short of amazing.

8. APPOINT YOUR OWN CONSUMER AFFAIRS MANAGER You may prefer to call him or her a customer service manager. But their job is to act as an ombudsman for the consumer. They are charged with keeping customers happy, seeing that orders go out promptly and that complaints are handled properly. Then encourage customers to direct their inquiries to that person. Psychologists tell us that customers would much rather write to a real person than to a corporation.

Finally, stop and think about what it cost you to get those customers in the first place. It naturally makes good dollars-and-sense to keep them happy, and keep them coming back.

THE LAST WORD ON DATABASES AND BACK-END MARKETING

THE MAIN POINT OF ALL DATABASE activities—and of all back-end marketing efforts—is to build and keep a list of customers. But customers, like products, have life cycles. They don't buy forever. Their purchases eventually slack off. Good service and back-end marketing can lengthen the customer life cycle by encouraging satisfied customers to keep buying.

Not long ago I visited a company whose walls were plastered with signs reading "OMO"—one more order. There's no better battle cry for people in database and back-end marketing. The ultimate goal of all of our activities should be getting one more order from every customer—an attainable goal with tremendous potential for the bottom line.

PART V

SPECIALIZED APPLICATIONS

20

BUSINESS DIRECT MARKETING

♦

THE BUSINESS WORLD TODAY ACKNOWLEDGES direct marketing as an effective bottom-line marketing tool. In fact, it is a profit center of major proportion for thousands of companies.

The Postal Service estimates that 30 percent of all direct mail advertising is directed to business firms. That means direct response accounts for over $7 billion in marketing expense to the business community.

Business marketers have traditionally relied on three strategies to reach their market: Direct sales, trade show participation, and advertising in trade journals. But the cost of making a business sales call has continued to rise sharply. As mentioned in Chapter 1, the latest figures available put the cost of a single face-to-face sales call at over $250. So more and more business advertisers are relying on direct marketing to pinpoint and sell their specialized and selective markets.

MAYBE BUSINESS DIRECT MARKETING ISN'T SO DIFFERENT

SOME BELIEVE THAT BUSINESS OR industrial buyers can't be sold the same say as customers. They reason that the business buyer is only interested in nuts-and-bolts facts. He or she can't be persuaded with flashy four-color brochures. The buyer doesn't have time to play with involvement devices. Yet my experience with clients like Hewlett-Packard and Xerox has proven otherwise.

Several tests helped dispel the myth that a business audience needs only technical product information to make a buying decision. In mailing to engineers and scientists for Hewlett-Packard, we saw that consumer-like techniques—such as four-color brochures, multi-page sales letters, and illustrated envelopes—repeatedly produced much better results than more traditional business mailings.

I guess we need to remember that a person doesn't change that much when he or she takes off a jogging outfit, puts on a business suit, and heads to the office. The main difference is business buyers are spending company money, not their own. And in the case of many small businesses where the owner is the decision maker, they are also spending their own money in an office setting.

Differences Beyond the Basics

Many of the basics of direct marketing covered in other chapters—things like offers and testing—apply equally well to the business field. But there are some differences. First, the audience is usually smaller. There are only about nine million business firms you can reach by mail, compared to about 85 million households on consumer mailing lists. It's also a universe that is dominated by small businesses: All but roughly 350,000 of those firms have fewer than 50 employees.

Second, less testing is generally done with business direct marketing. To some extent, this is a function of the more limited universe. Let's say you have only 25,000 prospects and four mailing packages you want to split test. If you test them with 5000 pieces each, that only leaves 5000 names to come back to with the winning package.

While you have to approach testing somewhat differently, it doesn't mean you should ignore it altogether. Roy Ljungren, formerly Advertising Manager of NCR Corporation, has extensive experience with business direct marketing. As he pointed out in *Business Marketing* magazine, "We can learn something from every mailing we make." Ljungren feels there should be some testing aspect as a by-product of the regular mailings we make. He says, "If you make enough meaningful tests, you will build up a fund of knowledge that will give you the edge when betting on the success of future mailings."

Third, still another difference is that most business purchases entail a bigger ticket or unit of sale. Just as in personal selling, it often takes more than one mailing to get an order. In fact, studies show that an average of 4.3 calls are needed to close a business sale. When you combine the bigger unit of sale with the limited universe available, it becomes obvious that most business direct marketing involves repeated efforts aimed at the same market segments.

Finally, business marketing uses complex and varied selling channels. Some firms distribute their products entirely through dealers, distributors, and wholesalers. Other firms might have their own offices and salespersons in some geographic areas, with dealers in others. Still others rely on a different combination of sales channels for each product line. The sales channel must be taken into account in planning a business direct marketing strategy. In lead-getting mailing programs, for example, you often have to "sell" dealers on participating in the program.

THREE MAIN APPLICATION AREAS

AS IN THE CONSUMER FIELD, MANY specialized ways exist to use business direct marketing. But the "big three" are to get leads, to make direct sales, and to reinforce the sales effort. Let's take an overview look at each area before going into more detail.

1. TO GET SALES LEADS   While there may be a great many potential prospects for your product or service, there's usually a smaller and more select number who represent the prime prospects. These may be the ones who are disenchanted with a present supplier; or the ones who are most receptive to new methods and new ideas.

Direct marketing can help you identify and separate these prime prospects by generating sales leads for your salespeople or the salespeople of your dealers or distributors. Regardless of whom he or she works for, a good salesperson should be able to close a higher percentage of calls when working leads than when making cold calls. In fact, it's not unusual for the closing percentage to be twice as high—and that can mean a dramatic reduction in your sales costs.

2. TO MAKE DIRECT SALES   Some people still don't realize that business products can be sold by mail, with no involvement from the sales force. But many of them are, including ad specialities, furniture, corrugated file boxes, printed products, office supplies, and maintenance items. Many are also expendable products that are suited to repeat business.

Actually, business mail order is quite flexible. You can sell a single product, aftermarket supplies and accessories, or have a full-line catalog. Some firms sell entirely by mail. Others use direct marketing to cover small and geographically distant territories where it is too expensive to maintain a sales force. Still others use direct marketing for lower-priced products that don't have sufficient margin to justify normal selling costs and commissions.

3. To REINFORCE THE SALES EFFORT Sometimes you know your salespeople are covering their markets and calling on most of the right prospects. They know who their prime targets are and really don't need sales leads. You can, however, still use direct marketing to reinforce their sales effort, to deliver background information on the company and its products, and to make sure your message gets through to everyone who influences the buying decision.

Reinforcement efforts can take the form of pre-approach mailings. Or a sales call can trigger an automatic follow-up mailing series. Or you can develop a special high-impact series of mailings for only a small group of top prospects. Even such devices as institutional mailings or house organs fall in this category of supporting the sales effort.

Other more-specialized applications of business direct marketing include bringing prospects to you (such as building attendance at a trade show exhibit), signing up new dealers, or getting needed information through research mailings. But let's concentrate the balance of this chapter on some things you should know about getting leads, making direct sales, and reinforcing the sales effort.

LEAD DEVELOPMENT PROGRAMS

AS WAS POINTED OUT IN CHAPTER 4, inquires themselves are easy to get. But you have to decide what kind of leads you want and then structure your offer accordingly. To get a lead, you usually have to offer something in your ad or mailing. That something might be a free booklet, a free gift, or just more information. Or it might be something the salesperson will *do,* like a free survey, free estimate, or free demonstration.

The late Ed Mayer, a great student and teacher of direct mail, once wrote a booklet for National Business Lists called the *Q Concept.* Here's how he explained the title: "The Q Concept is just a phrase, of course. But it is one that puts all the power you can muster right where it belongs: On Quality and Quantity. By developing direct mail support for the salesperson in the field with the Q Concept as a guiding principle, you'll be directing your energies toward the essential need: The right quality of sales leads, in the right quantity."

What's the right quality or quantity mix for your firm? That's something only you can decide. It might depend on your competitive position, the size of your sales force, or even its level of sophistication. For a relatively young and inexperienced sales force, many sales managers believe in providing salespeople with a good *quantity* of leads. This gives plenty of face-to-face selling experience. On the other hand, if you have a staff of higher-paid and more experienced sales representatives, you probably don't want to waste their time chasing down loose leads.

Remember, what it boils down to is this: The more you promise to send or give away, the more leads you will get—but the lower the *quality* of leads. Conversely, you can get a smaller number of better-qualified inquiries by just making your offer less generous.

DON'T BE FOOLED BY COST-PER-LEAD

You naturally have to keep in mind that getting leads or inquiries is only the first step in the selling process. Making the sale is the real payoff. And how you vary the quantity/quality mix has a real bearing on your cost-per-sale.

As an example, let's say you test two different direct mail offers. The first is a free gift offer and pulls a two percent response. The second merely offers free information and the response rate is one percent. To simplify matters, let's assume that both mailings cost the same $400 per thousand—and that the cost of the gift itself is nominal. The first chart (see Exhibit 20.1) shows the cost-per-lead from the two mailings. The free gift mailing is the clear winner with a $20.00 cost-per-lead compared to $40.00 for the free information offer.

But let's go a step further. Let's now assume that the sales force closes 15 percent of the free gift leads, while with the better quality free information leads, they close 20 percent. The second chart (Exhibit 20.2) takes these closure rates into account, as well as the cost of the sales calls and mailings. While the second mailing results in one less sale, the cost-per-sale is only $1458 versus a comparable cost of $1811 on the more generous offer.

EXHIBIT 20.1   Cost-per-lead

	QUANTITY MAILED	PERCENT RESPONSE	NUMBER OF LEADS	COST OF MAILING	COST PER LEAD
Mailing A Free gift offer	1,000	2	20	$400	$20.00
Mailing B Free information offer	1,000	1	10	$400	$40.00

These response rates and closure figures are purely hypothetical. But they illustrate the dynamics of the quantity/quality equation, as well as the effect the closure rate and the cost of sales calls have on the end result.

HOW TO IMPROVE LEAD QUALITY

In launching a new lead-development program, I've found it's usually best to start off aiming for quantity. That way you establish that you can get leads and you gain some experience with closing ratios.

It's then relatively easy to tighten up the leads to improve the quality. The main way to do this is by making the offer itself less generous, such as switching from a free gift to free information. But you can also make it harder to respond. In space advertising, for example, you can ask the prospect to write you for more information instead of supplying a coupon in the ad.

You can also use a self-qualification offer in which you give the prospect a choice of options. Your reply card, for instance, might provide a choice of "send me more information" or "have a salesperson phone me for an appointment." Those who select the latter are obviously better-quality leads and should be worthy of a sales call, while the free booklet requests might simply be fulfilled by mail.

The telephone is another great qualification tool, as Chapter 11 explained, and can help you turn suspects into prospects. On a basic level, it might simply mean sale reps call respondents and ask a few key questions to determine

Exhibit 20.2   Cost per sale

	NUMBER OF LEADS	COST OF SALES CALLS*	TOTAL SELLING COST†	PERCENT CLOSURE	NUMBER OF SALES	COST PER SALE
Mailing A Free gift offer	20	$5,033	$5,433	15	3	$1,811
Mailing B Free information offer	10	$2,516	$2,916	20	2	$1,458

*Based on $251.63 as average cost per business sales call.
†Includes cost of mailing and sales calls.

their level of interest before scheduling an appointment. Or a more sophisticated approach is lead scoring, which is usually done by a telemarketing center. In effect, this changes your lead development program to a three-step process: The ad or mailing which generates the inquiry, the qualification, and the sales call.

THE SYSTEMS APPROACH

A sound lead-getting system has many characteristics that have to be monitored and coordinated for optimum results. The flow chart in Exhibit 20.3 shows how the elements of the system interact and provide feedback to fine-tune the program. Some key points:

♦ Determine how many leads your sales force should be able to handle within certain time parameters.

♦ The marketing team needs to be aware of the entire selling process. Have your advertising people spend a few days in the field and get first-hand selling experience.

◆ Communicate with the sales force to sell them on the value of the leads they receive. Point out the science of testing and explain that while they might occasionally get a few unqualified leads, those are a necessary evil of the testing process that will lead to more sales.

◆ To ensure tight control, leads should always come back to a central location, like the home office, to be recorded and distributed.

◆ Following up a direct response lead may require special sales techniques. If you have a loose offer, like a free booklet, a prospect may not really expect a sales call. So the salesperson needs to have a full repertoire of door openers.

◆ A list of unsold inquiries should be set up for future promotions and used regularly.

CHECKING UP ON THE SYSTEM

Finally, any system like this must be monitored to control both lead flow and lead accounting. Monitoring is somewhat simpler now thanks to commercial software that helps management track leads through the sales process. But care must still be taken to control flow, so salespeople are neither drowning in leads or starving for them.

Too many leads boost the cost-per-sale because the sales force begins to treat them too casually or lets them get cold before they follow up. Too few leads can result in salesperson downtime and is harmful to morale. You must continually review the size of your active lead pool to determine whether mail and media promotions need to be stepped up or held back.

EXHIBIT 20.3   Lead generator system.

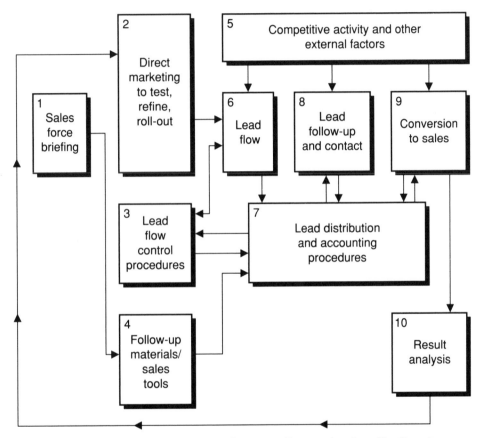

Adapted from the Components of Lead Generator System developed by Russ Lapso.

The other monitoring device is lead accounting. The objective is to keep tabs on all leads received and follow them through the selling process. This enables you to get a feeling for lead quality and salesperson efficiency. You can calculate the cost-per-sale by individual salespeople and by source of lead.

While a lead-generation system requires some effort to establish and monitor, it can also provide handsome dividends. One business client I've worked with carefully analyzed all the expenses and results of their program and found that every dollar they invested in lead-getting promotions had generated $24.00 in additional sales.

GUIDELINES FOR INQUIRY HANDLING

While inquiry handling procedures vary widely from company to company, here are the basic steps that I've found are important.

1. HAVE A SYSTEM   Keep it as simple as possible. Try to process the inquiry and record and capture the data you need without getting too complicated. If you have a large sales force, it probably calls for some type of computer-based system. But smaller firms can use a multiple-copy lead form. Or even staple an inquiry card or coupon to a simple 8-1/2 × 11 inch form and make photocopies for distribution and follow up (see Exhibit 20.4).

2. ANSWER INQUIRIES PROMPTLY FROM THE HOME OFFICE   You can't control how quickly a salesperson will follow up an inquiry in person, but you can at least acknowledge the inquiry from the home office. A well-done letter should be used, indicating the name and phone number of the local salesperson or dealer. If the prospect can't wait for a sales call, he or she can contact the rep directly. If your promotion has offered a free gift or booklet, most salespersons prefer to deliver it in person and use it as a door opener. But your letter can still acknowledge the request and promise that the gift or booklet is on the way.

3. REMIND THE PROSPECT OF HIS OR HER REQUEST   If you send out literature by mail, make sure the envelope is marked with copy like, "Here's the information you requested." This reminds the reader of his or her interest. And if a secretary sorts out important mail from advertising, it will usually get into the priority stack.

4. PAY ATTENTION TO THE QUALITY AND MESSAGE OF YOUR SALES MATERIAL Prospects who are responding to an ad, a direct mail promotion, or publicity are already interested in your product or service. They may know a little or a lot

EXHIBIT 20.4   Simple inquiry follow-up form.

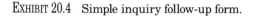

| | PAYROLL LEAD PROGRAM | |

Lead No.

Sales Rep.

Date Lead Received

No. of Employees

Free! Pocket Executive Planner for 1976! Handiest way to manage your time. Removable phone index, lie-flat pages, many other deluxe features. You'll receive this get-acquainted gift along with your free copy of the booklet on *Payroll Management.*

Please return this certificate for your complimentary copy of

PAYROLL MANAGEMENT: Asset or Liability?

Gentlemen: I would like to receive a copy of *Payroll Management: Asset or Liability.* I am interested in learning how my company can turn its payroll system into a flexible, information-generating tool for management, while lowering the overall cost of payroll preparation. Of course I will be under no obligation whatsoever.

Signature _____

(If the following information is not shown on the label at right, or is incorrect, please indicate below.)

Print name _____

Title _____

Phone _____

I am also interested in receiving information on the following Stat.Tab program(s):

☐ Accounts Payable   ☐ Accounts Receivable   ☐ Inventory Control   ☐ General Ledger

	TYPE OF CONTACT			RESULT		
Date of Contact	Meeting Held	Meeting Scheduled*	Other	Sale Closed	Sale Effort Continuing	Sale Effort Discontinued

about what your firm has to offer. But they are above-average prospects who deserve materials with above-average sales appeal. Make sure that every piece of sales and product literature your office distributes helps move key prospects a step closer to a buying decision.

5. KEEP ACCURATE RECORDS   Inquiries should be recorded by individual promotion key numbers. And the same key number should be recorded on any lead control forms so that sales closures can be tracked back to the inquiry source. A follow-up system should be used for the sales force. This can be a simple card or form that's returned to report the results of each lead they receive. Or you can use a weekly or monthly lead accounting form that asks salespeople to report the status of all active leads. Records may be maintained manually, or in a computerized tracking system—whichever makes more sense for your budget.

♦

BUSINESS MAIL ORDER

BY COMPARISON WITH THE NUMBER of firms who use lead-getting programs, business mail order activity is probably not as widespread. However, I think there's a lot more of it around than most people realize, since many efforts are directed at specialized market segments without wide exposure.

Some business mail order promotion is done through space advertising. But most is done with direct mail and governed by essentially the same factors that affect consumer mail order efforts.

There are a few differences for the business market, however, that are worth noting. First, the envelope is probably less important. Because the majority of executives have their mail opened or screened by a secretary, many do not even have a chance to see envelopes or teaser copy. Plain, businesslike envelopes appear to have a better chance of getting by the secretary than more elaborate ones.

The most common formats used are number 10 envelopes and 9 × 12 envelopes. Both usually employ standard 8-1/2 × 11 inch components that are comparable to normal business correspondence. Report formats are often effective, using a booklet-style piece that simulates a regular business report. Self-mailers also tend to work somewhat better in the business market than they do for consumers. Most business seminars, for example, are promoted with some type of self-mailer format (see Exhibit 20.5).

There also is less four-color printing in the business market. Not because it isn't effective, but because the smaller market segments mean that the cost of photography and separations add a larger percentage to the in-the-mail cost. On the other hand, sampling seems to be more widely used in the business market, especially for ad specialities and printed products. Many firms selling these items enclose samples in their mailings.

Business copy tends to be more fact-heavy and objective, with less use of emotional appeals. It recognizes that potential buyers are often experts in their specialty and need sophisticated information to make a purchase decision. They may also need details on how much time or money the product will save to justify the purchase decision to their boss. So business copywriters must be well-versed about the product they are writing about. And know enough about product applications to describe how it will meet the prospect's needs. But copy should still be written in simple sentences with short, easy-to-skim paragraphs.

Catalogs for Business Selling

With about 30 percent of business direct marketing budgets spent on catalogs, it's clear that many firms have found the catalog an ideal way to sell the business market. Catalogs can carry a firm's full line of products or be used for aftermarket supplies and accessories. Many general advertisers who provide catalogs for their

---

EXHIBIT 20.5   Business seminars are usually promoted with self-mailers like this one.

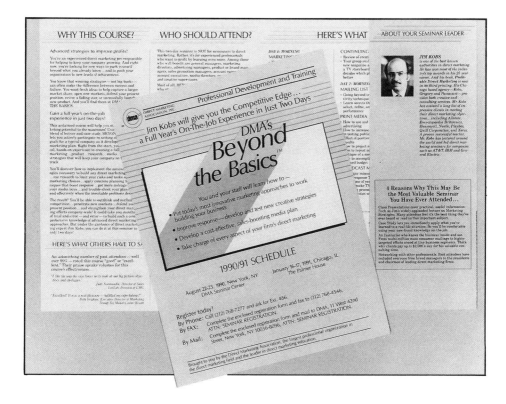

sales force make the mistake of thinking they will be acceptable for direct marketing. They usually are not.

One reason is that a salesperson's catalog ordinarily doesn't carry enough copy to do a complete selling job. It may, for example, just provide the product specs and rely on the salesperson to explain how the product works, describe the benefits it provides, and answer questions. Many such catalogs don't even include prices because the salesperson always carries a separate price list. A good mail order catalog, by contrast, usually has attractive product illustrations, tells a complete selling story on each item, and has the price right near it.

Many business mail order catalogs have started with a single product line, met with success, and been expanded into related product areas. Fidelity Products in Minneapolis is a good example. The firm was started as a direct marketing subsidiary of a corrugated box firm to sell storage files for business correspondence. Today, the firm issues four different catalogs that offer a wide variety of products for both office and plant use.

Aftermarket catalogs have a built-in audience. Namely, those who have bought the firm's equipment or system. But they still have to compete with outside sources and/or other distribution channels to get the aftermarket supplies and accessories business. And management often requires them to carry a complete product line. So an aftermarket catalog has to be carefully planned and skillfully executed to maximize its potential. The *AT&T Sourcebook,* which offers telephone products and accessories for small and medium-size firms, does a nice job on both counts (see Exhibit 20.6).

REINFORCEMENT SELLING PROGRAMS

AS WAS NOTED EARLIER, REINFORCEMENT efforts can take the form of pre-approach or sales call follow-up. These are often direct mail efforts that are used at the discretion of the salesperson, not the home office.

Many salespeople, however, don't do as much of this as they should, primarily because they would rather be out on the street making sales calls than sitting in the office writing letters. Recognizing this, some firms supply salespeople with a manual of stock letters that can just be turned over to a secretary for typing and mailing.

EXHIBIT 20.6   AT&T Sourcebook sells aftermarket supplies and accessories to owners of AT&T phone systems.

But some progressive companies are going even further. They get the sales force involved by having them submit a list of top prospects in their territory. then a pre-approach letter goes out, personalized with the name of the prospect's sales rep. Copy often states that "John Jones will be calling you to arrange an appointment." Salespeople are then obligated to follow up.

♦

This kind of approach almost guarantees that salespeople will integrate direct mail into their selling strategy. And reinforcement mailing programs like this do pay off by improving the sales rep's productivity per call. For example, IBM has used them to help its sales force reduce the time involved in making a typewriter sale from seven hours to less than two.

THE PLACE FOR SHOWMANSHIP MAILINGS

Another type of reinforcement selling program is a series of showmanship mailings. They're sometimes called impact mailings, dimensionals, or spectaculars. They're usually done as a series of efforts aimed at a small group of top prospects. And each mailing has a gift or dimensional enclosure of some type.

A few years ago, *Business Week* magazine employed a nine-step showmanship mailing series to attract a bigger share of tobacco advertisers' budgets. The *Business Week* Tobacco Farm Contest invited tobacco advertisers to enter a contest to raise the biggest office-grown tobacco plant (see Exhibit 20.7). As the series went on, *Business Week* sent prospects seed, soil, pots, garden tools, fertilizer, and finally, a yardstick—each item keyed to a different message, such as "Tobacco advertising needs good rich soil for growth." Seventy-three percent of the 450 targeted prospects participated in the lively contest and the publication's tobacco advertising revenue jumped from a paltry $60,000 to nearly a million dollars.

Mailing campaigns like this certainly cost more than normal direct mail efforts. For example, the *Business Week* program had a budget of $26,000 or about $6.40 per mailing. But when you compare that expense with the $250 or more cost of a single sales call and take into account the potential sales a group of top prospects can represent, the cost can be viewed as quite reasonable.

BUSINESS LIST AND MEDIA CONSIDERATIONS

FOR OPENERS, YOU MAY WANT TO review the section in Chapter 8 on the types of business lists available. In this section we'll start off with how to get your mail to the right individual at those firms.

A long-standing debate persists in business direct mail circles on whether it's better to mail to executives by name or title. Some claim that mailing

EXHIBIT 20.7 This *Business Week* showmanship mailing helped boost tobacoo advertising revenues to nearly a million dollars.

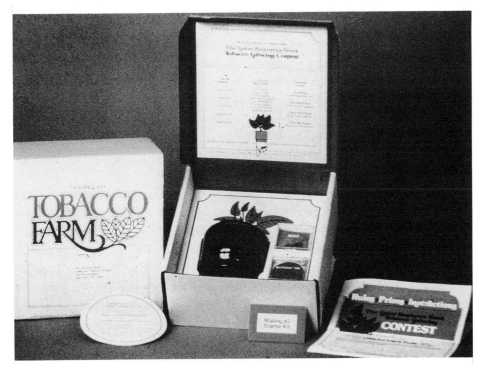

by name gets a little better readership and response. Others believe that the turnover of job changes and promotions is so high you have a better chance of getting your mail to the individual you really want with title addressing. Lists with individual names are more expensive to rent and maintain and are not always up to date. I've seen test results where title addressing has pulled better than individual names and vice versa. So this is an area I suggest you test for yourself.

Related to this is the importance of finding the right position or title to mail. Sometimes several persons within a firm can influence the buying decision and it's often necessary to mail more than one title. Response can also vary widely by title. In one recent test for a client selling financial services, two seemingly logical titles were tested and keyed accordingly and one pulled 69 percent better than the other.

♦

Three Ways to Get Your Mail to the Right Person

It's nice to have a situation where the product or service you're selling is always purchased by somebody with a specific title, like office manager or treasurer. But sometimes the buying decision for certain products or services is made by a person with one job title in firm *A,* another title in firm *B,* and still another in firm *C.* This is especially true in small- to medium-size firms.

One way to solve this problem is to address by functional title, such as "To the executive who buys Christmas gifts," or "To the person in charge of office supplies," or "Top financial executive." These are not titles that appear on business cards, but they generally get your mail delivered to the right person, regardless of his or her actual title.

Another approach that catalog mailers have found effective is to print a buck slip or "Route to" box near the address area. They normally preprint two or three different titles and leave a couple of blank spaces so the recipient can fill in specific names at their organization.

Still another way to solve this problem is to write a personalized "we need help" letter to company presidents. Tell them you have important information available on a specific subject, like planning meetings, but you don't know who in the firm makes decisions about such meetings. Ask for the name and title of the individual who's responsible and provide a stamped card or envelope for the reply. It's not unusual for a well-done *identifier mailing* like this to get a response as high as 50 percent, and you'll often get the name of more than one individual to contact at the firm.

How Often Should You Mail?

Jack Miller, President of Quill Corporation, says, "Very few companies are on top of mailing frequency. They simply don't know what is best." Surveys show that the number of mailings made to the average business customer varies widely. About half of all business mailers solicit their house list 25 or more times a year; 25% mail them between 12 and 24 times a year; and the balance send less than a dozen mailings annually.

House list mailing frequency naturally differs by product category. How often is someone likely to be in the market for your product or service? Office supply companies, like Quill and Reliable, mail customers as often as three times a month. But they have the advantage of a highly consumptive category and a broad product line.

With prospects, the rule of thumb is to mail a successful list twice a year. However, I do know some firms that annually go back to their best business lists three or more times.

Helpful Services for Business List Users

Thanks to today's computer technology and the sophistication of the SIC numbering system, major list compilers or service bureaus can provide important services to help you in targeting your business direct marketing program. Here's a sample of the types of services available.

♦ Customer profile analysis showing the number of customers you have in each SIC area and the percent of penetration.

♦ Availability reports, indicating the number of firms available in the specific SICs and geographic areas you want.

♦ Dealer marketing programs that provide counts and prospect listings, with names and addresses, broken down by each dealer's territory.

♦ Prospect record cards that provide salespeople with a complete file of all prospects in their area.

♦ Customer or prospect list enhancements that add phone numbers or SIC codes to name and address records.

TRADE JOURNALS AND BINGO CARDS

SOME BUSINESS OR TRADE JOURNALS have paid subscribers, while others are made available on a no-cost or controlled-circulation basis. Publishers claim the latter get just as high readership as paid circulation books, and maybe they do. But when you're looking for a direct response, such as an order or inquiry, my experience is that paid circulation books usually pull somewhat better.

Also, many business publications offer "bingo" cards as a reader service. Instead of filling out coupons or writing letters to get advertised information, the reader simply fills out a single card, circles the numbers that correspond with the ads he or she wants to reply to, and mails it back to the publication. The publication, in turn, forwards the inquiries to the advertisers specified.

A study by the Center for Marketing Communications estimated that bingo cards generate more than 50 million requests annually for information. But a survey the Center made of business publication readers showed that 43 percent of the respondents receive material too late to be useful.

Perhaps the length of time it takes publications to process and forward these inquiries helps explain why their quality is usually not as high as coupons returned from ads. A large business direct marketer I worked with tested the pulling power and conversion of bingo-card inquiries versus coupons. The marketer used an attractive full-page ad with a coupon offering more information. Below the ad the publications inserted the bingo card number to be used to get the same information. The conversion rate on coupons was 5.5 percent compared to less than one percent for the bingo card inquiries. So if you want better-quality leads from your space advertising, use a coupon in your ads instead of a bingo card number.

Finally, when considering print ads for the business market, don't overlook card decks, which were discussed in Chapter 12. They can be very effective, especially for lead generation.

THE LAST WORD ON BUSINESS DIRECT MARKETING

BUSINESS DIRECT MARKETING CONTINUES to be one of the fastest-growing segments of the direct marketing field. Whether you use it for getting sales leads, generating orders, or reinforcing your sales efforts depends on your particular marketing situation.

While the size of your market might impose some restrictions, try to do as much testing as practical. You'll gain information by which you can continually refine and fine-tune your promotion efforts. And don't be afraid to apply some of the offers and selling techniques you see being used for consumer direct marketing. You may be surprised to find they work equally well in the business market.

21

CATALOGS

♦

PEOPLE LIKE CATALOGS. Most don't even think of them as advertising mail. A catalog is considered something special and catalog shopping is a favorite pastime for many consumers. And they're almost as popular in the business market, where catalogs are often used as buying guides.

What explains their great popularity? I like to think of catalogs as stores that never close. They fit today's busy lifestyles. Their round-the-clock sales presentation lets you browse through merchandise, complete an order form, or call an 800 number whenever you want—even in the middle of the night.

Besides convenience, catalogs offer another important service. Almost any catalog can provide better, more complete product information than the shopper is likely to find in today's self-service retail environment.

The average U.S. household gets about 75 catalogs a year. Over 80 percent of all consumers at least look through catalogs; and research shows that roughly half of all adults have bought something from a catalog in the last twelve months. This kind of consumer acceptance has made the catalog category one of the fastest-growing areas of direct marketing. In 1980, about 5.8 billion catalogs were mailed; by 1990, 13.6 billion. They include full-line retail catalogs, business or industrial catalogs, and consumer specialty catalogs. With catalogs literally selling everything from soup to nuts, this last category is by far the largest.

Economics is another reason for the growth in catalogs. It's estimated that launching a catalog requires about one-sixth the start-up capital it takes to open a store. Catalog profits are comparable to retail, sometimes higher. And if the economic climate grows sour, catalog marketers can cut back circulation. Retailers have no choice but to close an outlet.

Much has been made of the "kitchen table" success stories that pepper the catalog field. But success isn't automatic. Whether you're thinking about your first catalog, expanding a catalog division, or trying to improve the return on an existing book, there are eight key areas to address. I call them "Eight Steps to a Successful Catalog."

♦

STEP 1: POSITIONING THE CATALOG

WHEN I FIRST GOT INTO THE direct marketing business, every catalog had to have a "reason for being"—an identifiable, unique niche it could fill in the marketplace. Of course, catalogs should still know why they exist, but now that multiple catalogs fill formerly unique market niches, it's usually how a catalog is positioned that sets the stage for success or failure.

Positioning a catalog combines three things:

1. What you say and show on the cover.

2. What you offer in the way of merchandise.

3. The personality you create for your book or "store."

If combined properly, these three elements get your catalog off to an excellent start.

The Norm Thompson catalog provides a good example. It offers apparel, home accessories, and gifts—a field with a lot of mail order competition. Every catalog cover includes the theme line: "Escape from the Ordinary," and portrays an unusual merchandise item in an attractive setting. Inside, the upscale merchandise is displayed in an uncluttered way with longer-than-normal body copy to romance the products and bring out unusual features and benefits.

When Demco, a leader in library supplies, wanted to enter the competitive business supplies market, it brainstormed to carve out a unique position. Because librarians are known for their organizing skills, Demco positioned the catalog as a business organizer filled with "ideas to help you organize, file, locate and protect." Supporting copy pointed out that "We've been helping librarians organize for over 70 years."

If you leaf through a group of catalogs in the same category—say, food, gifts, or women's fashion—you'll find some that use a theme on the cover, others that don't. But all convey a position by their cover design and what it shows. Some catalogs make a positioning statement just by their choice of illustration. A computer supplies catalog, for instance, might show people rather than products on its covers, both to humanize its product line and set itself apart from competitors.

Deciding the position of your catalog means defining the concept of your business. As catalog consultant Lawson Hill notes, "How you define the business sets the merchandise limits for the catalog. Merchandise that falls within those limits is sought; products that land outside are excluded." The broader your definition, the greater the number of unique items you'll be able to sell. But don't get carried away. My experience shows it's a mistake to define the concept too narrowly or too broadly.

STEP 2: DETERMINING CATALOG SIZE AND FORMAT

HERE'S WHERE A NUMBER OF IMPORTANT decisions have to be made: How many pages to include, what size they should be, and how many products to show per page.

Let's start by looking at the norms. Kate Kestnbaum's CatalogSCAN℠ database tracked trends in over 600 catalogs for a number of years. Her analysis showed that 58 percent of all catalogs are between 21 and 52 pages, split roughly in half between 21–36 pages and 37–52 pages. Only five percent are less than 21 pages, because consumers tend to regard them as fliers, skimming and tossing them rather than shopping and saving. In terms of size, about 25 percent of all catalogs are digest size; about 45 percent are 8-1/2″ × 11″; about 20 percent are in between; and the rest (about 10 percent) are smaller or larger.

The format and size you choose should fit the merchandise you carry and how much space you need to sell it. Also, it should complement, not detract from, the image you are trying to project. For example, a catalog of high-end merchandise should have an open, uncluttered look. Generally speaking, the higher the price points, the more space or square inches an item requires. Medium-price catalogs average about six or seven items per page, but item density per page is higher in a catalog selling less expensive goods. Just compare the two page treatments in Exhibits 21.1 and 21.2. Spiegel's page tastefully displays a limited number of jewelry items, while the Service Merchandise catalog crowds the page with jewelry bargains.

A bigger or fatter catalog is more likely to pay out when it is mailed to customers rather than prospects. If your catalog starts at 24 pages but grows

◆

EXHIBIT 21.1 In keeping with its image, Spiegel displays a limited number of jewelry items per page.

with your business, you might consider adding pages to your customer catalog and retaining the 24-page version as a prospecting tool.

Adding pages does have a positive impact on overall sales. Sales usually go up in proportion to the pages you add—but only by about half. In other words, if you increase the number of pages by 20 percent, you can expect a 10 percent sales increase. And your promotion cost will probably only increase about five percent. But contrary to what you might expect, a larger catalog won't yield a higher average order. Instead, adding pages increases percent response. It's more likely that prospects or customers will find something they want, but they won't necessarily buy more items.

EXHIBIT 21.2   Service Merchandise creates a bargain feeling by crowding the page with over two dozen items

For various reasons, it's best to use standard page sizes. You'll save on production and paper costs if your catalog can be cut from standard-sized sheets or rolls and be printed economically. And if you are creating an industrial or business catalog, your catalog is more likely to be retained if it's a standard size suitable for filing.

If you're starting a catalog and don't have enough products yet, consider going to a smaller size. Twelve 8-1/2″ × 11″ sheets might feel skimpy and insubstantial. Twenty four 5-1/2″ × 8-1/2″ sheets use the same amount of paper to gain greater heft and importance.

In an established catalog with a heavy mailing frequency, you can vary your size throughout the year. Consider using a smaller catalog most of the year, to keep costs down. But switch to a larger page size or add more pages during your best season, when strong results allow you to carry more items.

Color is also a format consideration, but not a decision that catalog executives labor over these days. Virtually all consumer books have gone to four-color printing. While it's not as critical to show most business or industrial merchandise in full color, it has become much more common in recent years. And, if affordable, it helps convey a quality image.

STEP 3: MERCHANDISING THE CATALOG

"THE MERCHANDISE IS THE MESSAGE," says Roger Horchow. "No matter how well presented, beautifully described or specially priced—if the customer doesn't have a need or can't figure one out, you won't make a sale." Deciding what merchandise or items to offer and how much space to give them is a key factor in a catalog's success—just as deciding how many square feet to devote to a line or department can affect a retailer's profitability.

First, you must establish a merchandising strategy. Will you offer the best products or the best value? The lowest prices on acceptable merchandise or exclusive, hard-to-find items? Does it make sense to offer a broad range of choices, so you will have the best selection in each category? Your merchandising strategy will not only determine your product mix, it will also influence your creative execution. A catalog offering great values shouldn't look as classy as one offering high-end items.

As you select products, keep in mind the "four plus one" product selection formula mentioned in Chapter 3. However, not every item has to be unique. In most catalogs, some basic bread-and-butter items are necessary to round out the product line—egg beaters and rolling pins in a cooking catalog, for example, or file folders and pencils in an office supplies book.

ORGANIZING FOR MAXIMUM SALES

Once the overall merchandising strategy is set, you must determine how to organize the book. In what order will your products appear? How much space will each item get? To determine the pagination and space allocation, most catalogers use some type of form like the one in Exhibit 21.3. It's divided into

EXHIBIT 21.3 Catalog planning forms are best filled out in pencil so they can easily be revised. A blank sample is in the Appendix.

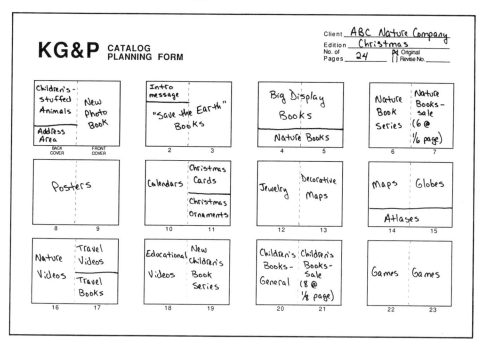

spreads so you can view the merchandise as the consumer sees it. You'll probably create several versions, juggling and rearranging items a number of times before you determine your final pagination.

A few general principles can help you organize the presentation of your merchandise. It's a good idea to lead with your best-selling item or category, so browsers will quickly see something they might want and decide your catalog is worth "serious shopping." Of course, best-selling products—or in a new book, those *expected* to sell best—should also get the most space.

Catalog "hot spots" like the cover, first inside spread, order form spread, inside back cover, and back cover should be used to play up strong items. You want to put the good stuff where people will spot it. The order form itself is a catalog's "checkout counter." Low-price, high-impulse items should be placed on or near it, just as candy bars and magazines are prominently placed near a supermarket checkout.

♦

The real key to space allocation is sales results. If a product doesn't sell well or pay out, more space won't usually help. Don't be sentimental: Drop or replace it. On the other hand, more space will usually help a hot item. Exhibits 21.4 and 21.5 show how Sharper Image pushed a hot-selling product at different stages of its sales life. After an oak file cabinet introduced in an early summer catalog took off, it was given a full-page treatment in September. In October, it appeared on the cover and in a double-page spread. By November, it was off the cover but still highlighted in a double-page spread. As sales finally tapered off, the file cabinet was returned to less than a page of space, something more like its original size.

Business catalogs almost always departmentalize their items—grouping stationery, computer supplies and such so buyers can quickly find what they need and compare the choices.

EXHIBIT 21.4   The Sharper Image catalog tested oak file cabinets by giving them two-thirds of a page.

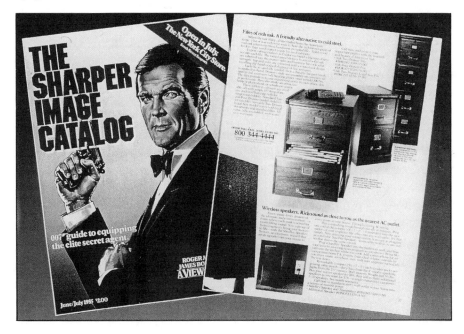

EXHIBIT 21.5 After strong sales, oak file cabinets are featured on the cover and inside spread of a later Sharper Image catalog.

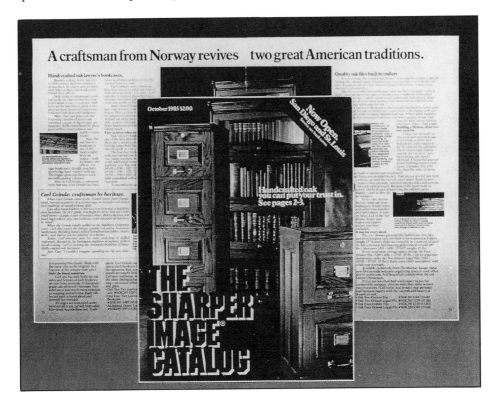

Departmentalizing makes sense in a business catalog, but it makes no difference in a consumer catalog. I know of just one firm that went to the considerable expense of split-testing departmentalization against random order in a consumer book, only to find the results were the same. So most consumer catalogs opt for random order, which gives them greater merchandising flexibility—and encourages more extensive browsing. It makes sense, of course, to cross reference related products that appear in other sections.

STEP 4: CREATING GRAPHICS THAT WORK OVERTIME

IT'S THE GRAPHIC TREATMENT THAT makes one catalog really stand out from the crowd. What graphics do is twofold: They showcase the merchandise and they establish the image of your "paper store" as vividly as layout and design create Neiman-Marcus or Macy's. That's why in catalog marketing, unlike any other print medium, graphics play the music and copy marches to it.

CREATING A CATALOG IMAGE

The graphics you select should reflect the image of your firm or the image you are trying to convey. For example, a catalog can look modern, like the sleek and sophisticated catalogs from the Museum of Modern Art, or traditional, like the cozy country catalogs from Yield House and Sturbridge Yankee Workshop. Other catalogers intentionally seek a somewhat cluttered look to suggest a complete merchandise assortment or create a promotional look to imply low prices.

The goal of your graphic treatment is to entice customers to enter your "store" and spend as much time shopping there as possible. The longer they stay, the more likely it is they'll find something to buy. Retailers spend time on store design for the same reason—focusing first on their windows or "curb appeal." In a catalog, that's the cover.

DESIGNING AN INVITING COVER

The cover of your catalog should suggest to the right customers that it's the kind of store they want to shop in, filled with merchandise they can't wait to buy. There's more than one way to convey this message. In fact, from working with lots of catalogs, I know that selecting or designing a cover is a very subjective process.

One way to entice customers is to *show* a new or hot item on the cover, as Sharper Image did with the file cabinet. A photo showing the product in use often works well; studies show that photos which include people draw the most attention. A montage of merchandise is another approach. It allows you to portray the range of products inside.

Using the cover to *sell* merchandise, especially if the cover includes body copy and pricing, gives a catalog a more promotional, downscale feel. A cover that

♦

features a special illustration or design instead of merchandise may sometimes be appropriate, especially when you want to convey a holiday theme. Some companies vary their approach. Orvis found through testing that it gets best results by sending a product cover to prospects and a pictorial cover to current customers. Apparently, prospects who haven't yet been in their "store" need to know more about its merchandise before they decide to shop.

Don't overlook the design of the back cover. One catalog readership study found that 20 percent of all consumers don't read a catalog from front to back, a surprising fact I've had confirmed in focus groups.

Make Each Spread Interesting

Unless you are starting a new section or department on a right-hand page and finishing off another section on the left-hand page, facing pages are usually treated as spreads.

In designing a spread, it's important to consider how the reader's eye flows across each page or spread. If every item on a spread is the same size, nothing will "stop" the reader's eye. Making one of those items much larger than the others will invite the eye to slow down and examine it. There are design tactics to direct the eye to continue reading the page or spread. Such as having a model who's wearing the featured dress look in the direction of a blouse on a facing page. Props can also subtly "point" the eye toward other items. A common background color helps visually tie the spread together.

Some solid advice on directing eye movement through page composition and the arrangement of merchandise can be found in *The S.D. Warren Catalog of Catalog Design,* written, designed, and produced by Jo-Von Tucker, a leading catalog consultant.

Visual Change of Pace

It's not enough to make each spread interesting. A department store with identical clothing, accessory, cosmetics, and furniture departments would be too boring to spend much time in. Likewise, prospects will race through a catalog that looks the same from start to finish—and they'll never stop to shop.

♦

To encourage the rapid page-turner to browse more slowly, you need to provide a change of pace without destroying your catalog's overall design theme. You can vary the layout format by rotating three or four basic page designs. Or switch from a grid format with twelve items per spread to one that features a few strong sellers. Or you might make a more dramatic design or color change every so many pages. The trick is to design a catalog whose rhythm changes often enough to keep prospects "in the store."

In business catalogs, it's often a good idea to open each section or department with a separate introductory page. It's another way to provide a visual break and let customers know they are moving from one merchandise category to another.

GIVE THE MERCHANDISE THE "STAR TREATMENT"

The best graphics are designed to show products off to their best advantage—to make every product a hero. Good photography goes a long way towards accomplishing this, whether it takes place in a studio or in glamorous location setting.

The best way to make the product a hero is to make it large enough for prospects to see it clearly. Say you're selling a sofa and you're illustrating it in a living room arrangement. Unfortunately, all too many beginners show the entire arrangement instead of cropping the photo tightly so the sofa will be as large as possible.

Models and in-use shots humanize a catalog, especially in the business market, which tends to focus on merchandise. But people shouldn't overwhelm products, either. In fact, all of the techniques that can make a catalog visually interesting—backgrounds, props, models, or borders—are the "supporting cast." The merchandise plays the lead role.

EASY READING BOOSTS READERSHIP

This isn't double talk. Pictures are important, but the picture alone doesn't close the sale. If your book is a chore to read, readership will decrease. More catalog eye tracking studies have been conducted outside the U.S. than within. But all show that readership is higher when catalogs avoid sans serif, cursive, or script type, all caps, and reverse type. One major cataloger compared results generated by two layouts and found that type reversed out of a colored background reduced sales by 33 percent!

A pet peeve of catalog readers is having to search or hunt for the copy block that goes with the picture. If an item looks interesting, they want to read about it—not play detective to find out where you hid the details. Research clearly shows that the closer the copy block is to the illustration, the better the results.

Of course, if we design a catalog for high readership, we better make sure its copy is worth reading . . . which just happens to be our next step.

STEP 5: WRITING COPY THAT TELLS AND SELLS

LIKE GRAPHICS, COPY HAS A DUAL ROLE. It describes the product, providing enough details to make a rational buying decision possible; and it creates desire for the item, encouraging an impulse purchase. Or, as creative expert Tom Collins says, "Catalogs bowl you over with a beautiful, emotional depiction of the product. And then they nail down the buying decision by giving you solid, logical, factual reasons why you should obey that impulse."

Good catalog copy is hard to write. It must be concise, compelling, and squeeze into a space dictated by the art director. "Great catalog writers compress years of direct marketing know-how and understanding of human psychology into single paragraphs," says Denison Hatch, editor of *Who's Mailing What.* It's a discipline that has taught many writers their craft.

Good copy is also one of the strongest benefits offered by catalog shopping. When we shop at retail, we prefer to deal with informed sales clerks who know their merchandise. You know how frustrating it is to ask a simple question, then stand around and wait while the clerk disappears to try and get you an answer. Ideal catalog copy is like the best-informed sales clerk, standing by, ready to give you the details on any item in the store.

DETERMINE A KEY SELLING BENEFIT

Before you start writing, you need to list your product's benefits and decide which one matters most—not to you, but to your customers. It's easier to determine the key selling benefit if you have a feel for your audience. If your catalog is aimed at busy, professional women, the time-saving convenience of a certain product might

◆

be hailed as a key benefit. The same product aimed at homemakers might lead you to select a different key benefit.

Once it has been determined, the key selling benefit belongs in the opening of the copy block. As you'll see in a second, it may also belong in the headline, so it's the first thing the prospect reads about the product.

Headlines Come in Three Flavors

There are three main types of catalog headlines. A label headline includes a product name or description; a selling headline skips the name and goes straight to the benefit; and a combination head combines the two.

Let's suppose we're selling a top-of-the-line hunting boot. It's made by Beaver Dam and it's similar to the one that was L.L. Bean's first product. What makes it unique is a waterproof rubber bottom, like duck shoes. We know that hunters often go out in damp or snowy weather and we reason that being able to keep your feet dry is the key benefit. Since all our catalog products are sold with a money-back guarantee, it can give our key benefit some support. Here are examples of the three types of headlines.

Label:	Beaver Dam Hunting Boots
	(or) Our Best Hunting Boots
Selling:	The Hunting Boot That's Guaranteed to Keep Your Feet Dry
Combo:	BEAVER DAM HUNTING BOOTS
	Guaranteed to Keep Your Feet Dry

By the way, I checked the L.L. Bean catalog and found it uses a combo heading for this product (see Exhibit 21.6). But the rest of the catalog uses a mixture of combo and label headlines.

One direct mail expert compared the presentation of the same item, a solar-powered outdoor garden light, in six different catalogs. Three of the catalogs used label headlines; two used selling statements; one used a combination head. He felt every one of the label headings missed the main benefit and Brookstone's selling headline was best.

EXHIBIT 21.6   L.L. Bean uses a combination headline for its original Maine Hunting Shoe.

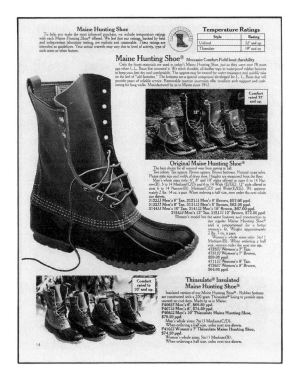

His conclusion inspired me to spend some time studying Brookstone's headlines. Whether Brookstone is selling solar lights ("Light patios, walkways without wiring") or door sealers ("Make your front door as tight as a refrigerator door"), its selling/benefit heads are vivid and specific.

BODY COPY: SELL THE STEAK AND THE SIZZLE

Catalog body copy is almost always tight. Sometimes it's necessary to sell a product with only two or three sentences. Worse, every copy block must include certain "ordering basics," such as sizes, color choices, catalog number, and price. If your layout gives you seven lines of 42 characters each in which to sell our Beaver Dam Hunting Boots and ordering basics take up two lines, then you only have five left for tangible, persuasive benefits.

♦

For that reason, it usually isn't possible to squeeze all of a product's benefits into a copy block. Consult your list of key selling benefits and sequence the most pertinent. Cover as many as possible in a concise writing style, remembering that your copy must work in tandem with the graphics. If the accompanying picture doesn't make the product's size or use absolutely clear, then your copy must do so.

In spite of space limitations, the best catalog copy succeeds in helping a prospect feel and taste the product or visualize using it. For its magnetic tool rack, Brookstone promises that "The heaviest tools cling securely to these powerful barium ferrite magnets." Damart sells insulated undergarments by inviting the purchaser to "Surround yourself with pure cashmere-like softness and luxurious warmth." Copy like this has "pizazz." It uses specific, evocative words and phrases to make a product's benefits irresistible.

Catalog experts know good copy when they see it, but they don't always agree on how to do it. In preparing an article for *Catalog Age,* Tom Collins wrote three dozen leading catalog firms for their copy guidelines. As it turned out, many didn't have any written guidelines and, among those that did, there was little unanimity on how best to persuade catalog readers to buy.

From this informal study we can conclude that catalog copywriting isn't an exact science. But most do agree that it's essential to lead with the strongest benefit, either in a headline or at the outset of your body copy.

STEP 6: MAKING IT EASY TO ORDER

ONCE YOU'VE FILLED YOUR CATALOG with can't-lose merchandise and must-buy prose and pictures, make sure that the ordering process isn't a roadblock.

Your order form should include devices that make ordering literally "as easy as 1, 2, 3." Simple and logical instructions, legible type, ample room, perhaps a sample line filled in as a guide—all make an order form user friendly. But just to make sure, try filling it out yourself.

In general, a combination order form/envelope that is bound into the middle of a catalog pulls better than an on-page order form. Customers won't have to search for an envelope. And a pre-formed envelope is more secure than asking customers to just fold up an order form and put a stamp on it.

While a bound-in order form is worth the extra cost, it *isn't* worthwhile to pre-pay the postage. Numerous tests have shown that once customers have shopped a catalog and filled out the order form, they will find a stamp to mail it. Customers sometimes complain about paying shipping and handling charges. But this, too, has been tested. Unless the charges are excessive, they're not a serious deterrent to ordering.

Instructions for telephone orders should also be clear and the order number prominently displayed. Fine-print information about customer service, guarantees, returns, and refunds should appear near the order form, but not on it. Customers should be able to reach you if a problem arises.

Actually, your entire catalog should be easy to use—now and later. Consumer books are primarily designed for impulse sales, but many business books are "keeper" catalogs that are filed away for later use. Including a thorough index and/or table of contents will help the business buyer find a specific item or category of merchandise quickly.

STEP 7: PROMOTING THE CATALOG

CATALOG PROMOTIONS OFFER PLENTY of possibilities. They range from advertising strategies that entice new customers to incentives which are included in the catalog itself.

Not every audience needs incentives. Regular customers don't necessarily need special offers to entice them to buy, although such offers may help increase response rate or average order size. A catalog used for prospecting, on the other hand, may need a boost by offering a free gift with any order, an incentive for early or large orders, sweepstakes, or discounts.

The catalog format offers some promotional opportunities, the most common being an overwrap. It's a four-page "outer cover" that wraps around a catalog and lets you call out a promotional offer without detracting from the design impact of the regular cover. The four pages you gain with an overwrap give you ample room to play up a special offer, add a letter or memo, inexpensively test new products, and add a second order form. You can also use a wrap to vary the promotional message for different audience segments, such as sending a "last chance" message to inactive customers. Overwraps can also include involvement devices and personalization. Breck's does a nice job with overwraps that reassure me every year that its flower bulbs will look spectacular in "the Kobs garden."

Most catalog companies use remails to maximize a catalog's sales. By merely changing the cover or replacing the outer eight to 16 pages, a catalog can achieve an entirely different look. The customer reads it like a new book, while the advertiser saves production costs. It's not uncommon for a remail book, mailed a month or so later, to get 75 percent of the response that came in the first time around. And if you only send it to your best-pulling names, it's usually quite profitable.

Space ads are especially suited for attracting new catalog customers. You can feature a best-selling item, just offer the catalog, or combine the two. Most catalog firms run small space ads, like one-sixth of a page. I've had good experience with a couple of techniques. One is offering a catalog subscription, which sounds a lot more generous than a single issue. The other is making a nominal charge for the catalog or subscription, which is refundable on the first order. I've seen order starters like this double the conversion rate.

Obviously, the objective of every promotional effort is persuading a prospect or customer to make a purchase. According to consultant Dick Hodgson, one-third of all first-time buyers will become "actives" simply by being offered additional buying opportunities, while another third won't order again, regardless of how many catalogs you send them. but the remaining third can be encouraged to buy again with special promotions. That's a big enough group to be worthy of your best efforts.

STEP 8: ANALYZING RESULTS

THE FINAL STEP IN BUILDING A successful catalog is determining its performance. For the most part, that means deciding which items to repeat, which to drop, which to play up, and which to minimize.

In deciding the fate of a product, it's important to carefully compare not just sales but *profit* per item. You do this by taking the production expense of a catalog and allocating an advertising cost-per-page. In the examples that follow, I assumed it costs $432,000 to print and mail a 48-page catalog, which is $9,000 per page. I then divided that figure by two or three (the number of products per page) to get the advertising cost for each item. Here's how the P&Ls turn out:

	Item A	Item B
Space	1/2 page	1/2 page
Sales	$10,500	$15,000
Advertising cost	$4500	$4500
Product cost	$5250	$7500
Profit	$750	$3000

In this example, the overall page shows a profit of $3750. Analyzing it by product, however, reveals that B was four times as profitable as A. Increasing the space allotted to Item B would be a good idea.

In the next example, we'll look at a page with three products, and use the same production costs cited above:

	Item A	Item B	Item C
Space	1/3 page	1/3 page	1/3 page
Sales	$6750	$2250	$16,500
Advertising cost	$3000	$3000	$3000
Product cost	$3375	$1125	$8250
Profit	$375	($1875)	$5250

Once again, the whole page shows a profit. But it looks like Item A should get the same amount of space, B should be dropped, and C should get more space.

These examples are over-simplified. Sophisticated catalogers would also allocate the cost of non-selling space, like the front cover and order form. And they'd analyze costs more precisely on a square-inch basis, which is akin to the retailer's measure of sales per square foot. Analyzing results by category, not just by page or item, can also help you make merchandising decisions, as can analyzing performance by price point.

A good way to study results is to mark up an actual catalog with the number of orders and sales for each item. This mark-up book will let you visually compare results with the item presentation, making it a useful companion to the numbers-oriented reports your computer generates.

Obviously, successful products should be repeated and losers dropped— no excuses! But don't let the fear of losers keep you from testing new merchandise

♦

and categories. A typical catalog will have 20 to 30 percent winning items and 20 to 30 percent losers. The rest will be anywhere from around breakeven to marginally profitable. It requires patience to find out which is which . . . since it usually takes about six weeks to get 50 percent of a catalog's orders.

To judge the overall results of your catalog, you need to look at more than just the response rate. Because a catalog is, by nature, a multi-product offer, the average order size will vary from one list segment to another. The key yardstick or measurement to use is *sales per thousand pieces mailed,* which automatically takes into account both the percentage of response and the average order size. Here's an example:

	List A	List B
Response	3%	2.2%
	or 30 per M	or 22 per M
Average order	$50	$85
Sales per M	$1500	$1870

Examining the response rate alone might lead you to conclude that list *A* performed better than list *B*. But looking at sales-per-thousand shows that list *B* clearly did better, because its average order size was significantly higher.

THE LAST WORD ON CATALOGS

DON'T EXPECT A NEW CATALOG TO SUCCEED overnight. It takes time to find the best items, test and segment the best lists, determine the reorder rate, and build a strong customer database. Most experts assume it will take two or three years for a catalog business to get in the black.

Unfortunately, I can't promise that the eight steps we covered in this chapter will shorten that period. But I do know, based on many years of experience in catalog marketing, that they will increase your odds for success.

22

PACKAGE GOODS, FUNDRAISING, FINANCIAL SERVICES, AND RETAIL APPLICATIONS

◆

THERE ARE MANY SPECIALIZED WAYS to use direct marketing. And these increasingly important, rapidly growing applications are pushing the industry beyond its traditional focus. In this chapter, we'll cover the most prominent, concentrating on package goods, direct marketing philanthropy, and financial services direct marketing. All three have grown tremendously in the past decade.

As package goods marketers have shifted from mass marketing to niche markets, they have come to understand how direct marketing can help them reach customers cost effectively. And as the billions contributed to causes through the mail have doubled in the last ten years, so have the efforts of direct marketing fundraisers. Financial services marketers have found that direct marketing helps them get the right product to the right market at the right time to make a sale.

As we go through each application, we'll sprinkle in some mini case histories so you can see what leading marketers are doing.

PACKAGE GOODS DIRECT MARKETING: HOW TO WIN SHARE AND INFLUENCE PEOPLE

LET'S START WITH AN EXAMPLE, so we can contrast what's normally done with what could be done. We'll use a dog food manufacturer with a full line of products and broad retail distribution. A line like this is usually marketed through trade promotions that induce retailers to give the products greater display exposure, with consumer advertising and sales promotion to encourage trial use.

Cents-off coupons distributed a few times a year via FSIs and other mass media are wasted on the 60 percent of all households that don't own dogs. And when they do reach dog owners, a large percentage of the coupons will be

♦

redeemed by people who already use that brand—not, as was intended, by dog owners who use a competitive product. Self-liquidating premium offers—like flea collars or identification tags—might help induce trial. But typically, the manufacturer will fulfill the offer—and then throw away the names of respondents!

These sales promotion efforts are backed up by heavy advertising designed to build awareness and brand image. At one time, two-thirds of all marketing dollars went to image advertising. But as advertisers have grown more "coupon dependent," most companies have reversed, allocating almost 60 percent of their dollars to sales promotion and the balance to image advertising.

This is the traditional approach. There's nothing wrong with it, except that its emphasis on short-term sales and promotion keeps consumers at armslength. The brand manager tries to sell as many cases of the product as quickly as possible, but isn't developing any kind of long-term relationship with users. Nine times out of ten, the company doesn't even know the names of its customers. And even though pet owners buy dog food week in and week out, nothing special is done to induce repeat sales or reward their loyalty.

THE DIRECT MARKETING FRONTIER

Now, let's paint the rainbow. How could our dog food manufacturer use direct marketing to build customer loyalty and increase sales?

First, it could use coupon redemptions, special offers in or on the dog food package, and consumer survey list services to build a database of dog owners. Ideally, that database would include information on the dog's breed, its name and age, and the dog food brands it consumes.

Using the information in the database, the manufacturer could spend the majority of its ad budget on mailings to competitive users. Heavier mailing schedules could be developed for prospects with the most potential—i.e. owners of large dogs rather than small ones or owners of two or more dogs. Coupons could help induce trial among this market and follow-up mailings would help convert respondents to steady users.

Present customers could be acknowledged through regular mailings that would build a real relationship between the company and the dog owner. Mailings tied into a canine's life cycle would let the firm market products at the right moment—say, by promoting an adult dog food when it's time for a puppy to switch. And line extensions or related new products such as dog treats could be "exclusively" sampled to present customers first.

The marketing possibilities are almost endless. Special products and services—such as a premium dog food line or special health and diet foods not widely available through mass outlets—could be developed for direct sale. An automatic shipment plan could even deliver large sizes of regular dog food right to the owner's door every month. A certain percentage of dog owners would surely pay for this convenience instead of lugging a 25-pound sack home from the store. I think you'll agree the what-could-be-done scenario is quite a contrast from the norm.

One firm that is already doing many of these things is Carnation Company. Its Perform brand pet food is sold direct to dog and cat owners; it has built a multimillion name database; and it even owns a minority interest in a pet supply catalog. Carnation's senior vice president, John L. Dintman, recently said: "Direct marketing to pet owners is a fast-growing means of distribution of pet products, with significant future and potential."

EARLY DIRECT MARKETING ATTEMPTS

Actually, package goods manufacturers have been quietly experimenting with direct marketing for quite some time. A lot of programs have not been publicized, however, because of the traditionally competitive nature of the package goods category.

A company's interest in direct marketing often starts with a sales promotion manager who sees similarities between direct marketing and sales promotion. Plenty of similarities do exist, but there's one big difference.

Sales promotion and direct marketing are both offer-oriented, measurable, and focused on immediate sales. But direct marketing doesn't stop with short-term response. It builds a database and accumulates information about customers from coupons, premium offers, and other promotions.

Instead of developing a database and building customer relationships, sales promotion managers tend to move from one promotion to another, and use specific mailings as tactical weapons. But the occasional company does venture into a full-scale direct marketing program like the Kraft General Foods mailing in Exhibit 22.1—something I think we'll see more of in the future.

EXHIBIT 22.1   Kraft General Foods multi-mailer includes over a dozen coupon offers and a sweepstakes.

STRATEGIC DIRECT MARKETING FOR PACKAGE GOODS

To tap that future potential, we have to look beyond short-term, tactical thinking. Here's how direct marketing can strategically support package goods:

1. DIRECT MARKETING CAN CONCENTRATE ADVERTISING ON KNOWN PROSPECTS   If you want to reach dog owners, why speak to them through a medium that also reaches people who don't own dogs and probably never will? If you're launching a new vitamin, why not try to reach consumers with the greatest interest in health and fitness? Direct marketing can take your message directly to an interested party without wasting money on circulation or viewership that is not interested in your product category.

Similarly, direct marketing will allow you to reach the competitive users you want to persuade. Especially people who use brands very similar to yours—someone who buys another healthful breakfast cereal, for example. Or a competitor's heavy users. Tests show you can send them a coupon or a sample and get 20 or 30 percent to switch brands. With targeted direct marketing, you can stop subsidizing purchases by your present customers with costly coupons. And you can avoid sending them to non-users.

2. DIRECT MARKETING LETS YOU COMMUNICATE WITH CUSTOMERS TO MAINTAIN OR INCREASE MARKET SHARE FOR A PRODUCT   You can identify your own customers, build a database, and start a relationship. Consumer survey list services can help you identify the users of your brand (see Exhibit 22.2). And chances are, you already have some rebate and self-liquidating premium respondents whose names are gathering dust in your warehouse. When you communicate with your customers on some regular basis, you'll stop treating them like prospects or strangers. They'll notice—and you'll notice an increase in brand loyalty.

Concentrating on heavy users is another way to make direct marketing pay out. Large families probably consume more breakfast cereal than small ones. Target great dane owners instead of someone who has a chihuahua. Send your message to the guy who consumes a six-pack of beer a night instead of once-a-week drinkers.

3. DIRECT MARKETING HELPS YOU KEEP IT IN THE FAMILY   The light users of your brand aren't necessarily light users. Often a dual "brand set" exists in the same household. Certain family members may drink regular pop, while others prefer diet; or perhaps deluxe beer or coffee is reserved for company, while less expensive brands are consumed every day. You can use direct marketing to cross-sell other product lines—unless you insist on thinking like a brand manager and limit your focus to one brand or product.

4. DIRECT MARKETING LETS YOU CULTIVATE SPECIAL MARKET SEGMENTS   You can focus on influencers—dentists, dieticians, dermatologists, veterinarians, or whoever might recommend your product to others. You can also target volume users, such as dog breeders, schools, and nursing homes. Or you can use direct marketing to introduce new products to the retail or wholesale trade.

♦

EXHIBIT 22.2   Consumer surveys like this can help identify users of your own or competitive brands.

Direct marketing can also be used to bolster weak markets. Perhaps a brand is doing well overall, but—for whatever reason—has not gained the share you would like in a few specific markets. Direct marketing could be used to target prospects in that area with special offers designed to pull the product through the distribution channel.

Just as easily, direct marketing can be used to fight and discourage competition in strong markets. If a competitive product is being introduced in one of your market strongholds, you can flood loyal customers with coupons.

Somebody is less likely to try a new soft drink when the refrigerator is already filled with your brand.

These first four strategies use direct marketing to build business through existing distribution channels. The next two strategies use direct marketing to build a "side business" with mail order as the distribution channel.

5. DIRECT MARKETING CAN ENLARGE YOUR FRANCHISE   In the world of package goods, nothing is more valuable than an established brand name. (That's why package goods companies were the takeover targets of the '80s.) Brand identities that have been strengthened by years of image advertising can help sell related products through mail order. Pepperidge Farm's reputation contributes to its specialty gift foods business (see Exhibit 22.3). Other food products companies could sell cookbooks, recipe cards, or baking utensils.

EXHIBIT 22.3   Pepperidge Farm's reputation helped make its gift catalog a success.

Viewed this way, your database becomes a profit center. At the very least, selling related products will help offset your database cost. Not to mention that your primary brands will get "free advertising" every time your catalog or direct mail package is read—even if some consumers don't respond.

6. DIRECT MARKETING LETS YOU PROFITABLY SELL PRODUCTS THAT ARE RETAIL MISFITS Supermarkets and drug stores are geared to high-demand, heavy-turnover products that can be sold without sales help. Special products that don't fit this mold may sell better direct. General Foods successfully markets its Gevalia premium coffee, which didn't do well at retail, through the pages of upscale magazines. L'eggs started by selling white hosiery to nurses, then offered imperfect pantyhose by mail, and now has a 68-page catalog of hosiery and undergarments. And if oversize Hefty bags aren't stocked in the supermarket, a package slip with the regular-size bags encourages leaf rakers to order them direct from the manufacturer.

THE ECONOMICS OF DIRECT MARKETING FOR PACKAGE GOODS

Direct marketing can be costly and package goods are often inexpensive. Using a multi-brand approach can spread the costs. Ideally, a database should be a corporate asset, funded by the corporation at large rather than a single brand or brand manager. After all, your customer may only spend $20 a year on your shampoo, but $250 to $500 on your family of products.

But don't rule out direct marketing for a single product if it has regular and heavy consumption. Soft drinks, snacks, paper products, pet foods, breakfast cereals, coffee, salad dressing, baby food and diapers are a few examples that come to mind. Many households buy these products weekly, or at least monthly, and their annual expenditure can be substantial. The same is true for a brand's heavy users.

A self-funding approach can also stretch your direct marketing budget. Mattel has a Barbie Club that asks girls to send a $2 initial membership fee and pay a $6 annual subscription charge. Can you transfer this idea to the package goods category? You may be surprised to find how many consumers are willing to pay a small fee for useful information and services.

PACKAGE GOODS CASE HISTORIES

A number of package goods marketers have already made their mark in direct marketing. Here's a round-up of some leaders.

PROCTER & GAMBLE'S PAMPERS The world's largest diaper supplier has quietly rolled out the Pampers Baby Life Cycle program. This elaborate mailing series includes product samples, free gifts, discount coupons, self-liquidating premiums, sweepstakes, a catalog, and even a complimentary subscription to *Pampers Baby Care Magazine* (see Exhibit 22.4).

Along the way, P&G has built its own maternal database and maintains a personalized dialogue with mothers from the birth of a child until toilet training. It's estimated that P&G is spending as much as $25 million on this program

EXHIBIT 22.4 *Baby Care Magazine* delivers special offers as part of the Pampers Baby Life Cycle program.

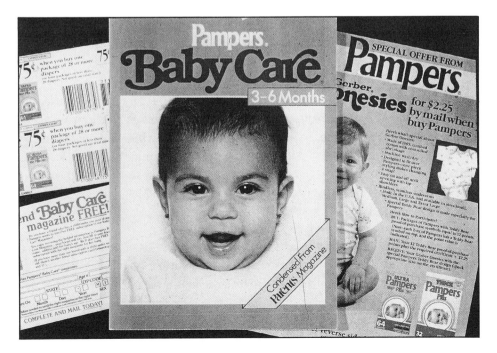

in the U.S. alone and has recently expanded it throughout Europe and the Far East.

KRAFT GENERAL FOODS General Foods committed itself to direct marketing in 1985 when it launched a company-wide campaign to "bring direct marketing disciplines into our mainstream marketing." By 1990, the company (now Kraft General Foods) had a database of 20-million households and was spending over $6 million a year on several flourishing direct marketing programs, including a mail order continuity business.

On products sold through traditional retail channels, GF programs have ranged from the Crystal Light frequent buyer club to a TV spot offering a *free* sample of a new frozen entree. Its *What's Hot* magazine included variable discount coupons for Jell-O, Kool-Aid, and Post cereals with sales increases on individual products as high as 41 percent. Dr. Lorraine Scarpa, GF's Vice President of Marketing Services, recently reported that direct marketing has exceeded company objectives with current users, in attracting brand switchers *and* in building brand equity.

TOBACCO GIANTS Tobacco companies started experimenting with direct marketing in 1971, when TV ads were banned. Today, the $450 million they spend annually on direct marketing is more than they spend on magazines and newspapers combined. And the giants understandably do it in a big way.

R.J. Reynolds has built a custom database of 25 million smokers to target their direct mail efforts, many of which are aimed at competitive users. Competitor Philip Morris has used a Blind Taste Test to persuade people to try its Merit brand, sending respondents two packs of unmarked Merits, which weren't identified until a later mailing. Almost two million smokers participated. A point increase in cigarette market share is worth over $300 million and Merit reportedly gained well over a point from this campaign.

STASH TEA You don't have to be big to benefit from direct marketing. Oregon-based Stash Tea uses its four-color foil pouches to tell restaurant tea drinkers that they can order directly from the company (see Exhibit 22.5). Stash receives 3000 requests a month for its catalog, which sells premium tea and accessories for tea drinkers. About 30 percent of those requests become catalog customers and now account for ten percent of the firm's total sales.

EXHIBIT 22.5   Stash Tea sells directly to consumers, and uses its list to build retail distribution in new markets.

When it seeks retail or restaurant distribution in a new market, Stash uses its proprietary mailing list as a sales tool to convince food brokers and distributors that a built-in market already exists. A final step wins friends among new retail clients: Stash sends a personal letter to mail order customers in that market telling where Stash Tea can be bought locally—and lists new retailers in the next issue of the catalog.

The above case histories just scratch the surface of what's going on with package goods direct marketing. Bufferin offered a free sample to competitive users and its 38 percent response was four times higher than projected. Carnation is able to triple the redemption of its cat food coupons when it mails established product users. Dove Soap has been sending a sample bar to qualified prospects and its repeat purchases are up 110 percent. The better you can target your promotions, the better the results will be.

Raising Funds by Mail

WHETHER YOU ARE RAISING FUNDS for a welfare organization, a national health fund, a religious organization, or an educational institution, the problem is the same. There is a great deal of competition for the donor's dollar. And you are asking donors to give money to help others rather than to get something specific for themselves.

That's why in direct marketing fundraising, the offer isn't the most important element; the appeal is. "If you are to touch your prospect's pocketbook, you must first touch his heart," note fundraising experts Margaret M. Fellows and M.H. Koenig. The fundraising writer has to be able to capture on paper the feeling of satisfaction and happiness we all get from helping others.

Guilt helps, too. A recent Gallup survey revealed that a good 43 percent of the population feel guilty when they toss out letters from charities requesting a donation. To turn that guilt into action, the writer must be able to paint a grim picture of what things will be like for an impoverished child, an endangered species, or an embattled constitutional right *without* funds to protect them.

A good mailing package must convey the knowledge that one's contribution is helping to make the world a better place. It's often a good idea to include a nominal token of appreciation, such as a membership card, name and address labels, or a decal. Tangibilizing your donation request also helps. What respondent won't feel better knowing that $10 will feed a starving child for a day or that $50 will send a boy to camp for a week?

The formats and executions used in fundraising are usually not elaborate. They either include a simple two-color brochure or omit a brochure altogether. The overall execution should be decent and presentable, but not slick. The best fundraising package is modest and middle-of-the-road: Not too poor, not too fancy.

THE TRUMAN LIBRARY When Truman Library Institute, the fundraising arm of the Harry S. Truman Library and Museum in Independence, Missouri, decided to broaden the base of its financial support, it turned to direct marketing to build a $1-million endowment fund. Institute directors felt that widespread mailings would ensure a large number of donors and help increase visitors to the Truman Library.

Almost every fundraising mailing program is based on the premise that getting the first contribution from a new donor costs more than future contributions. Once you have built a mailing list of donors or members, you can secure those future contributions at a very favorable expense-to-income ratio. The Truman Library Institute decided to develop a membership-type appeal, where the annual renewal provides a structured program for repeat giving—instead of just asking for a one-time, no-commitment contribution.

In securing new members for its Honorary Fellows Program, which required a $25 annual contribution, the Institute determined it would try to acquire them on a breakeven basis. Thus, there would be no net income from prospect mailings. But a positive cash flow was projected over the five-year life of the campaign, as the quantity of new member mailings decreased and renewal mailings increased.

An effective renewal program begins laying the groundwork for renewals as soon as a new member is signed up. The Truman Library Institute sent new members a presidential medallion, a personalized membership card, and a welcome letter pointing out that all memberships expire on May 8, the date of President Truman's birthday (see Exhibit 22.6). A year later, a three-step mailing urged members to continue their support. The renewal rate was 56 percent, which brought the expense-to-income ratio of acquiring and renewing new members to less than 50 percent. As renewal contributions continued to flow in, the Institute reached its five-year fundraising goal almost a year ahead of schedule.

DISABLED AMERICAN VETERANS On a larger scale, DAV has six million active donors, mails over 20 million pieces a year, and raises more than $45 million annually. DAV carefully tests premiums, like personalized name stickers, both to acquire new donors and increase contributions from existing ones.

DAV has found that including these inexpensive items in solicitation mailings to potential donors can produce three times as much response as a

EXHIBIT 22.6 Truman Library new member welcome package includes presidential medallion.

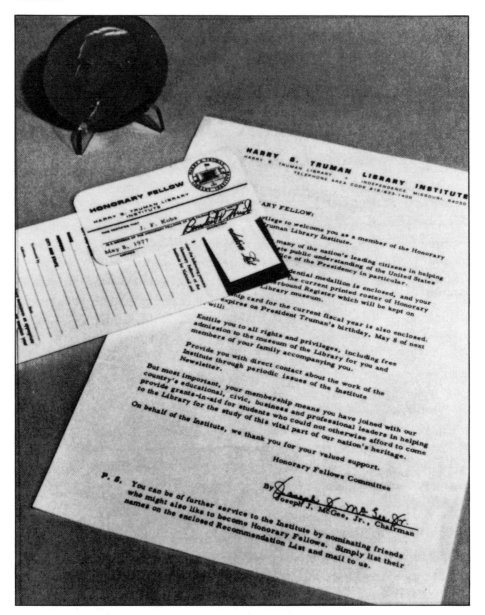

straight, no-premium appeal. When going back to its donor file, which is segmented by dollar amount, premiums have helped upgrade the average contribution by as much as 60 percent. Overall, DAV's sophisticated testing program has boosted its fundraising gross revenue 94 percent in the last ten years.

Direct Marketing for Financial Services

IF YOU'VE BEEN CHECKING YOUR MAILBOX, you might feel as I sometimes do that this must be the fastest-growing category of direct marketing. Mailings for credit cards, insurance, investments, and other financial services just keep coming. Why are these offers so widespread? Let's see if we can identify some common principles behind this surge in activity.

To begin with, financial services are private matters. Studies show many people prefer dealing with them independently, in the privacy of their own homes, rather than having to face a stranger in a high-pressure selling situation. This is particularly true when the consumer wants to compare and select from a host of competing products.

Then, too, buying financial services is usually a complicated business. It takes time to evaluate the benefits and drawbacks of a typical offer. Because the sale of most financial services is highly regulated, solicitation mailings must spell out all the details and choices pertinent to a product. But that's actually an advantage for direct marketers. Experienced copywriters are very good at telling the whole story—and making it clear enough for the prospect to reach an informed decision.

Direct marketing works better for some products than others. Health and accident insurance usually does better than life insurance, although there are some exceptions. Likewise, it's easier to get someone to try a new credit card than to move their checking account and upset a long-standing banking relationship.

Timing can be critical to the success of an offer. It's tough to get a driver to switch auto insurance if existing coverage doesn't expire for five months. It usually requires a two-step effort, with the first step directed towards finding out the expiration date of the current policy. The actual selling effort comes later, shortly before renewal time. Similarly, Medicare supplement policies sell best to people who are nearing 65 and just becoming eligible for the government's basic coverage.

It's the highly targeted nature of direct marketing that makes these audiences—so difficult to reach at the right time through mass media—so receptive to financial services sold by phone or mail. Let's look at a couple of examples.

AARP/SCUDDER Suppose you wanted to get senior citizens to part with their hard-earned savings and invest them by mail. It helps if you have a good name and reputation, like the American Association of Retired Persons. The

EXHIBIT 22.7 The AARP/Scudder program attracted $3.9 billion in investments from AARP members.

association launched the AARP Investment Program from Scudder in 1985 with a multi-media program. One of the neat things it did was sensitivity training for the telemarketers. It included putting cotton in their ears and smearing their glasses with Vaseline to simulate the hearing and vision problems common to older people.

This carefully planned marketing program concentrated on helpful educational materials (see Exhibit 22.7) and conservative investments. And it really paid off. After only two years, over 300,000 AARP members had already invested in this family of seven mutual funds. To the tune of $3.9 billion in assets!

ALLSTATE UNIVERSAL LIFE   Direct marketing success isn't always automatic. Even when you have a unique product like Allstate's Universal Life, which combines traditional insurance death benefits with a "cash account" that pays high interest rates comparable to a money market fund. Allstate agents weren't selling many of these policies. So Allstate asked its general agency to develop some lead generation ads. The ads showed potential, but didn't produce nearly enough leads to be cost effective.

At this point, Allstate dumped the problem in the lap of a direct marketing agency. It developed and tested five new ads and one of them turned out to be a big winner. In fact, it pulled so well that Allstate's cost-per-lead was reduced to 28 percent of what it was in the first campaign. To make sure the winning ad would convert well, the agency also developed new fulfillment materials, which were sent to respondents before the sales call. The combination of a strong new ad, reinforced with the back-end sales materials, resulted in a highly successful program.

RETAIL DIRECT MARKETING

IF DIRECT MARKETING FOR PACKAGE GOODS or financial services had the biggest growth in the 1980s, many experts think the retail field has the greatest growth potential in the 1990s. Considering that there are over 1.8 million retail outlets in the U.S., that wouldn't be surprising. And it's underscored by a recent DMA survey which showed more than 75 percent of retailers expected their use of direct marketing to increase.

◆

In the past, attention has often focused on retailers who have built a successful mail order business. Like Neiman-Marcus, with its well-publicized Christmas gifts, or Bloomingdale's by Mail, whose sales now represent its second largest "store," next to their flagship store in New York City. But in many cases, it's worked better the other way around. Victoria's Secret, Eddie Bauer, and Hammacher Schlemmer are all good examples of stores whose retail success was enhanced, thanks to the loyal audience and high name recognition built by their catalogs.

I believe the greatest growth potential will probably come not from getting retailers to understand mail order (which is a different business with a different orientation), but from using direct marketing to build traffic and sales for existing stores. The key will be the retailer's ability to match Universal Product Codes, or UPCs, with what I call UCCs, for Unique Customer Codes. UPCs can now capture large amounts of important data at the supermarket check-out counter. Once retailers learn to capture the same important data about their customers, they will be able to turn these private databases into powerful marketing tools. And you don't have to be a giant retailer to do it, as the next example shows.

THE MEN'S SHOP IN GORDON'S ALLEY This store in Atlantic City has a secret weapon: It's headed by direct marketing guru, Murray Raphel. One of his many successful promotions was establishing a Gold Card program for his best customers . . . those who spend at least $1000 a year. He only has 500 of them, but they represent more than a million dollars worth of annual business for Gordon's. These Gold Card customers get a personalized monthly promotional mailing (see Exhibit 22.8) that routinely brings in $12,000 in additional store business. The cost? About $500 a month.

The Power of Direct Marketing

DIRECT MARKETING CAN BE A POWERFUL tool in any category. These final mini-cases illustrate how it can fuel sales forces, sell business equipment, and build a cable network.

EXHIBIT 22.8   Gordon's Gold Card rewards the store's best customers.

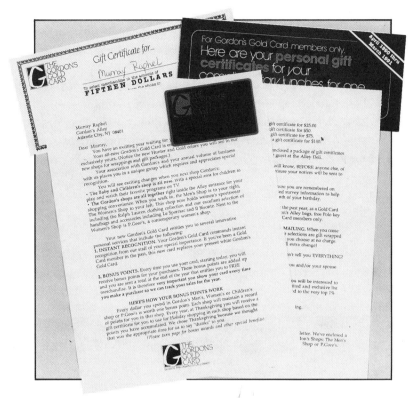

ENCYCLOPAEDIA BRITANNICA   Britannica's lead machine never stops. When virtually every school and public library has a set of encyclopedias available for reference, it takes a pretty aggressive selling program to convince families they should have their own set at home. That's why Britannica has over 2000 U.S. salespeople.

One of the secrets to Britannica's success is a highly sophisticated lead-development program. It includes direct mail, magazine ads, and television. It may well be the largest lead program in the country. Based on its spending level, industry sources estimate that Britannica generates almost three-quarters of a million sales leads a year!

♦

XEROX   Another organization with a big sales force, estimated at more than 4000 bodies. But it wasn't big enough to cover the rapidly growing number of small businesses that needed low-priced copying capability. So Xerox began testing direct marketing, not for sales leads, but to sell copier supplies.

It worked so well the company started selling copiers the same way, with mail and telemarketing—and mailed millions of pieces a year (see Exhibit 22.9). Before long, Xerox was selling over $40 million worth of copiers and typewriters annually. All without any face-to-face selling contact. At its peak, the program sold more copier and typewriter units than the whole Xerox sales force!

EXHIBIT 22.9   Xerox used direct mail and telemarketing to sell over $40-million of business equipment annually.

HOME BOX OFFICE In the mid 1980s, HBO's annual budget for direct marketing was under $1 million. By 1988, HBO was sending out over 100 million mailing packages a year, using four-page inserts in *TV Guide,* making up to 300,000 telemarketing sales calls a month, and running three TV flights a year in over 120 markets. One source estimates their annual direct marketing budget now surpasses $35 million.

The pay off? Continual growth for HBO, even though the cable market has tightened. With 17.6 million subscribers, it's estimated that HBO leads the next-largest pay TV channel by ten million! J. Richard Munro, former Chairman of HBO's parent company, once admitted, "Direct marketing is the lifeblood of this company. This is where our strength lies, and our future."

THE LAST WORD ON DIRECT MARKETING APPLICATIONS

THE THREE CASE HISTORIES WE'VE JUST reviewed, and the dozens of others sprinkled throughout this book, show where direct marketing is at today. It's being used to target business and consumer prospects, generate highly qualified sales leads, and move mountains of merchandise. Direct marketing is already being employed to promote everything from fast foods to luxury automobiles.

And the future world of direct marketing will be even brighter, because it will be shaped by people like you. I think it was Sir Isaac Newton who suggested the future gets better because its players have the benefit of "standing on the shoulders" of those who have gone before them. I hope my shoulders and the collective wisdom of the many experts I've cited in these pages have been helpful.

APPENDIX: THE MATHEMATICS OF PLANNING PROFITABLE MAILINGS

◆

Author's Note: This section was written by the late Virgil D. Angerman, when he was Sales Promotion Manager for Boise Cascade. I first reprinted it over fifteen years ago in a booklet I wrote for Dartnell Corporation. Just recently somebody came up to me after a West Coast speech to tell me how useful he has found this worksheet. So we've reprinted it again and have updated Virg Angerman's original figures to reflect current costs.

One of the questions asked frequently at direct marketing meetings is, "How many orders per thousand can I expect?" Obviously, no one can give an accurate answer to that question; there are too many variables involved.

The response from a mailing depends upon the nature of the proposition offered; the copy used; the offer—whether cash, billed, or sold on time payments; the mailing list used; the appearance of the envelope; whether you use first- or third-class postage; the date of mailing; and the general economic condition of the country at the time of mailing.

Any one of these factors or variables can influence the pull of a mailing. It's not a question of how many orders per thousand can I expect, but how many orders per thousand *must* I get to break even.

To determine the breakeven point, you must know the actual cost of obtaining and filling an order. We have prepared a worksheet to show you how to do it. The figures used in the worksheet example are those experienced by several mailers of the offer.

Once you know the breakeven figure, you can proceed with your tests. The following worksheet and explanation show you how to calculate your breakeven point (See Exhibit A.1). There's also a blank worksheet you can reproduce to analyze your own costs (Exhibit A.2.).

HOW TO USE THE WORKSHEET

Let's take a hypothetical mail order proposition and go through the various steps to see what costs must be included to determine how many orders per thousand you must get to break even. First, the Worksheet should carry the date, name of the proposition, and the key number for that particular mailing. You need this for future reference.

EXHIBIT A.1

WORKSHEET FOR PLANNING PROFITABLE MAILINGS

Date: *Date*

PROPOSITION *4 Val Set "Practical Mathematics"* . KEY *64*

1 - Selling Price of Merchandise or Service	**$100⁰⁰**	
2 - Cost of Filling the Order		
a) Merchandise or Service	**24 00**	
b) Royalty	**none**	
c) Handling Expense (Drop Shipping & Order Processing)	**3.80**	
d) Postage and Shipping Expense	**2.40**	
e) Premium, including Handling and Postage	**1.20**	
f) Use Tax, if any (1 x **6** %)	**6.00**	
TOTAL COST OF FILLING THE ORDER		**37.40**
3 - Administrative Overhead		
a) Rent, Light, Heat, Maintenance, Credit Checking, Collections, etc. (**10** % of # 1)	**10·00**	
TOTAL ADMINISTRATIVE COST		**10·00**
4 - Estimated Percentage of Returns, Refunds or Cancellations	**10%**	
5 - Expense in Handling Returns		
a) Return Postage and Handling (2c plus 2d)	**6·20**	
b) Refurbishing Returned Merchandise (**10** % of # 2a)	**2·40**	
TOTAL COST OF HANDLING RETURNS	**8·60**	
6 - Chargeable Cost of Returns (**10** % of $ **8·60**)		**.86**
7 - Estimated Bad Debt Percentage	**10%**	
8 - Chargeable Cost of Bad Debts (# 1 x # 7)		**10⁰⁰**
9 - Total Variable Costs (# 2 plus # 3, # 6, and # 8)		**58·26**
10 - Unit Profit after Deducting Variable Costs (# 1 less # 9)		**41·74**
11 - Return Factor (100% less # 4)	**90%**	
12 - Unit Profit Per Order (# 10 x # 11)		**37·57**
13 - Credit for Returned Merchandise (% of # 2a)		**2·40**
14 - Net Profit Per Order (# 12 plus # 13)		**39·97**
15 - Cost of Mailing per 1,000	**402·00**	
16 - NUMBER OF ORDERS PER 1,000 NEEDED TO BREAK EVEN		**10·10**

Form No. 8-9

Exhibit A.2

WORKSHEET FOR PLANNING PROFITABLE MAILINGS

Date:_____

PROPOSITION _____ KEY _____

1 - Selling Price of Merchandise or Service _____

2 - Cost of Filling the Order

    a) Merchandise or Service _____

    b) Royalty _____

    c) Handling Expense (Drop Shipping & Order Processing) _____

    d) Postage and Shipping Expense _____

    e) Premium, including Handling and Postage _____

    f) Use Tax, if any (1 x ____%) _____

    TOTAL COST OF FILLING THE ORDER _____

3 - Administrative Overhead

    a) Rent, Light, Heat, Maintenance, Credit Checking,
       Collections, etc. (____% of # 1) _____

    TOTAL ADMINISTRATIVE COST _____

4 - Estimated Percentage of Returns, Refunds or Cancellations _____

5 - Expense in Handling Returns

    a) Return Postage and Handling (2c plus 2d) _____

    b) Refurbishing Returned Merchandise (____% of # 2a) _____

    TOTAL COST OF HANDLING RETURNS _____

6 - Chargeable Cost of Returns (____% of $ ____) _____

7 - Estimated Bad Debt Percentage _____

8 - Chargeable Cost of Bad Debts (# 1 x # 7) _____

9 - Total Variable Costs (# 2 plus # 3, # 6, and # 8) _____

10 - Unit Profit after Deducting Variable Costs (# 1 less # 9) _____

11 - Return Factor (100% less # 4) _____

12 - Unit Profit Per Order (# 10 x # 11) _____

13 - Credit for Returned Merchandise (____% of # 2a) _____

14 - Net Profit Per Order (# 12 plus # 13) _____

15 - Cost of Mailing per 1,000 _____

16 - NUMBER OF ORDERS PER 1,000 NEEDED TO BREAK EVEN _____

Form No. 8-9

Item #1. We start with the retail selling price of the merchandise or service. In this case, let's say we are selling a four-volume set of books, *Practical Mathematics,* for $100.00 on ten days' free examination with a premium, a Calculating Chart, included as a "look-see" introduction. The customer keeps the chart whether he or she buys or returns the books. Post $100.00 in the box opposite Item #1.

Item #2. We enter in 2-a your cost of the books, including shipping carton, which is $24.00. This gives over a four-to-one mark-up, which is an ideal selling margin.

The next consideration is Royalty (2-b). If you are publishing a book or selling an item on which a royalty is paid to the author, manufacturer, or inventor, this expense should be included as a part of the total cost of the merchandise or service. The author's royalty on books sold by mail is usually five percent to ten percent of the retail price. In this hypothetical case there is no royalty, as the books are purchased from another publisher.

The Handling Expense (2-c), which includes the opening of the mail and processing the order for fulfillment, amounts to $3.80. Postage and shipping expense (2-d) is $2.40. As we included a "look-see" premium in this offer (Calculating Chart 2-e), we must add this item ($1.20) as a part of the expense of filling the order. If your state has a Sales or Use Tax (2–f), this must also be added. Let's take six percent as an example. Multiply Item #1 by six percent and you have $6.00 tax. Adding all the expenses under Item #2, it costs $37.40 to fill an order.

Item #3. But there are other costs that must be included. How about administrative costs such as rent, light, heat, use of equipment, maintenance, expense of checking credit, collection follow-up, office supplies, etc.? Many firms make a flat charge of 10 percent to 20 percent of the Retail Price (#1) to cover these expenses. Let's use ten percent of $100.00 or $10.00 and enter this under Item #3-a as the total administrative cost.

Item #4. The next question is what percentage of your customers will return the merchandise if sold on a free examination offer? Suppose we take ten percent as an average and post this under Item #4.

Item #5. How much does it cost to handle returns? It certainly costs as much as it did to ship the books. So let's charge $6.20 (2-c plus 2-d) for this item. Of course, some customers will prepay returned merchandise, but let's not count on it. Some of the books may be damaged in shipping, so allow ten percent of the cost of the set (10% of $24.00) or $2.40 for refurnishing (5-b). This brings the Total Cost of Handling Returns (Item #5) to $8.60 per order.

Item #6. As we are figuring that ten percent of the orders will be returns, refunds or cancellations (Item #4), the Total Cost of Handling Returns will be ten percent of $8.60 (Item #5), or 86 cents per order.

Item #7. Bad debts are another expense that must be considered. This percentage will vary from about 5 percent to 25 percent, depending upon the proposition, the way the offer is presented and the list used. Let's take ten percent as an average figure and enter it in Item #7.

Item #8. The Chargeable Cost of Bad Debts is ten percent (Item #7) times $100.00 (Item #1). This amounts to $10.00 that must be allowed for the cost of bad debts. Enter $10.00 opposite Item #8.

Item #9. The Total Variable Costs are Item #2 ($37.40) plus Item #3 ($10.00), Item #6 (.86) and Item #8 ($10.00) amounting to $58.26.

Item #10. After deducting the total variable costs (Item #9) amounting to $58.26 from the selling price (Item #1) of $100.00, this leaves a Unit Profit of $41.74.

Item #11. But there is a return factor of ten percent (Item #4) that must be accounted for. Deducting item #4 or ten percent from 100 percent leaves 90 percent of the unit profit that is left. Post 90% opposite Item #11.

Item #12. Taking 90 percent (Item #11) times $41.74 (Item #10) leaves a unit profit of $37.57 per order. Post this amount opposite Item #12.

Item #13. Any merchandise that is returned after examination will be sent back to the manufacturer or put back into your inventory if you are the manufacturer. *This represents a credit against the original cost of the merchandise.* Since we estimate the returns to be ten percent (Item #4), we would have a *credit* of ten percent of our cost (Item #2-a, $24.00) or $2.40. This amount should be added as Item #12.

Item #14. Adding the credit per unit profit due to returned merchandise as explained above, we have a *net* profit per order (Item #12 plus Item #13) of $39.97.

Item #15. Suppose the cost of your mailing package—outer envelope, letter, brochure, order form, reply envelope, mailing list, lettershop labor, postage, etc., amounts to $400.00 per thousand. What about creative and production charges such as editorial preparation, artwork, advertising consultation, copy, engravings, and typesetting which must be paid for?

You have a choice of charging these expenses against the test mailing or amortizing them over your projected mailing possibilities. If charged in one lump sum against the test, it will show a distorted picture. This could kill the test before you give it a chance. It's better to spread the cost over the total quantity of a projected mailing. If the charges amount to $4,000.00 and you figure you can mail 2,000,000 names if the test pulls, you could charge $2.00 per thousand against the cost of the mailing (Item #15). If the test is a flop, you will have to absorb the expense anyway, so why not give it a reasonable chance to come through. So enter $402.00 under Item #15 ($400.00 plus $2.00).

Item #16. If you have a Net Profit per Order of $39.97 (Item #14) and the cost of mailing 1,000 pieces is $402.00, divide $39.97 into $402.00 and you need 10.1 orders per thousand, or 1.01% to break even.

Suppose your breakeven point on a test mailing is 10.1 orders per thousand pieces mailed (1.01%). How many orders more than 10.1 per thousand should you get to justify going ahead with a large mailing? It is generally considered safe if you get 33-1/3 percent (1/3) more orders. In this analysis, one third more than 10.1 would give us a total of 13.5 orders per thousand or 3.4 orders more than the breakeven point.

If the final mailing pulled 13.5 orders per thousand, 3.4 orders more than the breakeven point, and the unit profit is $35.97 per order, the net profit would be $135.90 per thousand (3.4 × $39.97). On a 100,000 mailing, the net profit would be $13,589.80; on 500,000, it would be $67,949; on one million $135,898.

A word of caution! The time elapsing between the date of the test and the date of the final mailing may affect results. For example, a test made in January that pulls 13.5 orders per thousand might pull only 10.1 or less if mailed in June. So test in the poor month, if possible, and mail in the good months to eliminate unprofitable mailings.

KOBS' 99 PROVEN DIRECT RESPONSE OFFERS

A review of tested, successful propositions that can improve your results.

BASIC OFFERS

1. **RIGHT PRICE** The starting point for any product or service being sold by mail. Consider your market and what's being charged for competitive products. And make sure you have sufficient margin for your offer to be profitable. Most products sold by mail require at least a three-time markup.

EXHIBIT A.3 This form can be used to plan the pagination and space allocation for a catalog. There is a filled-out sample in Chapter 21.

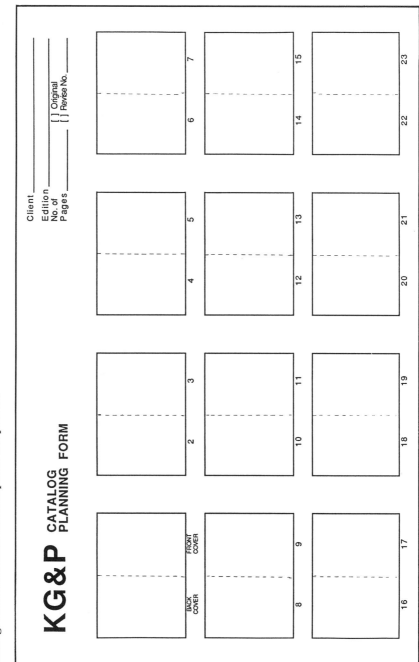

♦

2. Free trial If mail order advertisers suddenly had to standardize all their efforts on one offer, this would no doubt be the choice. Widely used for book and merchandise promotions. Viewed from the standpoint of a consumer, the free trial relieves the fear that you might get stuck buying by mail, because the advertiser is willing to let you try *his* product before he gets *your* money. Most free trial periods are 10 or 15 days. But the length of the trial period should fit the type of product or service being offered.

3. Money-back guarantee If for some good reason you can't use a free trial offer, this is the next best thing. The main difference is that you ask the customer to pay part or all of the purchase price *before* you let him or her try your product. This puts inertia on your side. The customer is unlikely to take the time and effort to send a product back unless he or she is really unhappy with it.

4. Cash with order This is the basic payment option used with a money-back guarantee. It's also offered with a choice of other payment options. Incentives (such as paying the postage and handling charge) are often used to encourage the customer to send his or her check or money order when the order is placed.

5. Bill me later This is the basic payment option used with free trial offers. The bill is usually enclosed with the merchandise or follows a few days later. And it calls for a single payment. Because no front-end payment is required by the customer, the response can be as much as double that of a cash offer.

6. Installment terms This payment option works like the one above, except that it usually involves a bigger sale price with installment terms set up to keep the payments around $10.00 to $20.00 per month. Usually this is a necessity in selling big-ticket items by mail to the consumer.

7. Charge card privileges Offers the same advantages of "bill me later" and installment plans but the seller doesn't have to carry the paper. Can be used with bank charge cards, travel and entertainment cards, and specialized cards (like those issued by the oil companies or large retailers).

8. C.O.D. This is the U.S. Postal Service acronym for Cash-On-Delivery. The postal worker collects when he or she delivers the package. Not widely used today because of the added cost and effort required to handle C.O.D. orders.

Free Gift Offers

9. Free gift for an inquiry   Provides an incentive to request more information about a product or service. Usually increases inquiries, though they become somewhat less qualified.

10. Free gift for a trial order   Sometimes called a "keeper" gift, because the customer gets to keep the gift just for agreeing to try the product.

11. Free gift for buying   Similar to the above, except the customer only gets to keep the gift if he or she buys the product or service. The gift can be given free with any order, tied to a minimum purchase or used as a self-liquidator.

12. Multiple free gifts with a single order   If one gift pays out for you, consider offering two or more. You may even be able to offer two inexpensive gifts and spend the same amount as one more expensive item. Biggest user of multiple gifts is Fingerhut Corporation. They currently offer three or more free gifts for a single order!

13. Your choice of free gifts   Can be a quick way to test the relative appeal of different gift items. But will seldom work as well as the best gift offered on its own. The choice probably leads to indecision on the consumer's part.

14. Free gifts based on size of order   Often used with catalogs or merchandise suitable for a quantity purchase. You can offer an inexpensive gift for orders under $25.00, a better gift for orders running between $25.00 and $50.00, and a deluxe gift for orders over $50.00.

15. Two-step gift offer   Offers an inexpensive gift if the customer takes the first step, a better gift for taking the second step. Such as a free cassette for trying a new stereo set, and a deluxe headset of you elect to buy it.

16. Continuing incentive gifts   Used to get customers to keep coming back. Book clubs often give bonus points to save up for additional books. Airline *frequent flyer* programs also fall in this category.

17. Mystery gift offer   Sometimes works better than offering a specific gift. It helps if you can give some indication of the item's retail value.

OTHER FREE OFFERS

18. FREE INFORMATION   Certainly an inexpensive offer, and a very flexible one. The type of information you provide can range from a simple product catalog sheet to a full-blown series of mailings. If the information is not going to be delivered by a salesperson, this should be played up.

19. FREE CATALOG   Can be an attractive offer for both the consumer and the business market. In the business field, catalogs are often used as buying guides and saved for future reference. In the consumer field, you can often attach a nominal charge for postage and handling or offer a full year's catalog subscription.

20. FREE BOOKLET OR VIDEO   Helps establish your company's expertise and know-how about the specific problems of your industry. Especially if the booklet contains helpful editorial material, not just a commercial for your product or service. A video brochure can be an effective way to show your product in action. The booklet or video should have an appealing title, like "How to Save Money on Heating Costs" or "29 Ways to Improve Your Quality Control System."

21. FREE FACT KIT   Sometimes called an Idea Kit. It's usually put together in an attractive file folder or presentation cover. You can include a variety of enclosures from booklets to trade paper articles to ad reprints.

22. SEND ME A SALESPERSON   This one is included here because the offer is actually a free sales call with wording like "have your representative phone me for an appointment." Normally produces more qualified inquiries than a free booklet or fact kit. Those who respond are probably ready to order or seriously considering it.

23. FREE DEMONSTRATION   Important for things like business equipment that has to be demonstrated to be fully appreciated. If the equipment is small enough, it can be brought into the prospect's plant or office. If not, the prospect might be invited to a private showing or group demonstration at the manufacturer's facilities.

24. FREE "SURVEY OF YOUR NEEDS"   Ideal for some business products or services, like a company that sells chemicals for various water treatment problems. Offering a free survey by a sales representative or technical expert is appealing and gives you the opportunity to qualify a prospect and see if your product or service really fits his or her needs.

25. FREE COST ESTIMATE Many large business or industrial sales are only made after considerable study and cost analysis. The offer of a free estimate can be the first step in triggering such a sale.

26. FREE FILM OFFER Many mail order film processing companies have been built with some variation of this offer. Either the customer gets a new roll of film when he or she sends one in for processing, or the first roll is offered free in hopes that it will be sent back to the same company later for processing.

27. FREE HOUSE ORGAN SUBSCRIPTION Many business firms put out elaborate house organs for customers and prospects which contain a good deal of helpful editorial material. You can offer a free sample issue or better yet, a year's subscription.

28. FREE TALENT TEST Popular with home-study schools, especially those that offer a skilled course, such as writing or painting. Legal restrictions require that any such test be used to measure real talent or ability, not just as a door opener for the salesperson.

29. GIFT SHIPMENT SERVICE This is one of the basic offers used by virtually all mail order cheese and gift-food firms. You send them your gift list, and they ship direct to the recipients at little or no additional cost.

DISCOUNT OFFERS

30. CASH DISCOUNT This is the basic type of discount. It's often dramatized by including a discount certificate in the ad or mailing. However, it should be tested carefully. In most cases, a discount offer will not do as well as an attractive free gift of the same value.

31. SHORT-TERM INTRODUCTORY OFFER A popular type of discount used to let somebody try the product for a short period at a reduced price. Examples include "Try 13 weeks of the *Wall Street Journal* for only $34.00" and "30 days of accident insurance for only $1.00." It's important to be able to convert respondents to long-term subscribers or policy-holders.

32. REFUNDS AND REBATES Technically, this is a delayed discount. You might ask somebody to send $5.00 for your catalog and include a $5.00 refund certificate good on a first order. The certificate is like an uncashed check—it's difficult to resist the urge to cash it.

33. INTRODUCTORY ORDER DISCOUNT A special discount used to bring in new customers. Can sometimes cause complaints from old customers if they're not offered the same discount.

34. TRADE DISCOUNT Usually extended to certain clubs, institutions, or particular types of businesses. Magazines sometimes offer a *professional courtesy discount* for doctors and dentists.

35. EARLY-BIRD DISCOUNT Designed to get customers to stock up before the normal buying season. Many Christmas cards and gifts have been sold by mail with this offer.

36. QUANTITY DISCOUNT This discount is tied to a certain quantity or order volume. The long-term subscriptions offered by magazines are really a quantity discount. The cost per copy is usually lower on a two-year subscription because it represents a quantity purchase—say, 24 issues instead of 12.

37. SLIDING-SCALE DISCOUNT In this case, the amount of the discount depends on the date somebody orders or the size of the order. Such as a 2 percent discount for orders up to $50.00, a 5 percent discount for orders over $50.00, and a 10 percent discount for orders over $100.

38. MYSTERY DISCOUNTS Most commonly used by retailers. Customers bring in a special ad or mailing, and a mystery spot is rubbed off to reveal their discount amount.

SALE OFFERS

39. SEASONAL SALES Such as a pre-Christmas sale or a summer vacation sale. If successful, they are often repeated every year at the same time.

40. REASON-WHY SALES This category includes inventory reduction, clearance sales, and similar titles. These explanatory terms help give the sale a reason for being and make it more believable to the prospect.

41. PRICE-INCREASE NOTICE A special type of offer that's like a limited-time sale. Gives customers a last chance to order at the old price before an increase becomes effective.

SAMPLE OFFERS

42. FREE SAMPLE If your product lends itself to sampling, this is a strong offer. Sometimes you can offer a sample made *with* or *by* your product. Such as a steel company who uses take-apart puzzles made from their steel wire. Or a printer who offers samples of helpful printed material it has produced for other customers.

43. NOMINAL CHARGE SAMPLES In many cases, making a nominal charge for a sample—like 50¢, $1.00, or $5.00—will pull better than a free sample offer. The charge helps establish the value of the item and screens out some of the curiosity seekers.

44. SAMPLE OFFER WITH TENTATIVE COMMITMENT This is also known as the "complimentary copy" offer used by many magazines. In requesting the sample, the prospect is also making a tentative commitment for a subscription. But if the prospect doesn't like the first issue, he or she just writes "cancel" on the bill and sends it back.

45. QUANTITY SAMPLE OFFER A specialized offer that has worked for business services and newsletters. Like a sales training bulletin where the sales manager is told to "just tell us how many salespeople you have, and we'll send a free sample bulletin for each one."

TIME LIMIT OFFERS

46. LIMITED-TIME OFFERS Any limited-time offer tends to force a quick decision and avoid procrastination. It's usually best to mention a specific date, such as "This special offer expires April 5th," rather than "This offers expires in 10 days."

47. ENROLLMENT PERIODS Have been widely used by mail order insurance companies who include a specific cutoff date for the enrollment period. It implies that there are savings involved by processing an entire group of enrollments at one time.

48. PRE-PUBLICATION OFFER Long a favorite with publishers who offer a special discount or savings before the official publication date of a new book. The rationale is that it helps them plan their printing quantity more accurately.

49. Charter membership (or subscription) offer Ideal for introducing new clubs, publications, and other subscription services. Usually includes a special price, gift, or other incentive for charter members or subscribers. And it appeals to those who like to be among the first to try new things.

50. Limited edition offer A proven way to go for selling plates, coins, art prints, and other collectible items. The edition may be limited by date or quantity.

Guarantee Offers

51. Extended guarantee or warranty Such as letting the customer return a book up to a year later. Or with a magazine, offering to refund the unexpired portion of a subscription any time before it runs out. Or extending the manufacturer's warranty if product purchase is made with a certain credit card.

52. Double-your-money-back guarantee Really dramatizes your confidence in the product. But it better live up to advertising claims if you make an offer like this.

53. Guaranteed buy-back agreement While it's similar to the extended guarantee, this specialized version is often used with limited edition offers on coins and art objects. To convince the prospect of their value, the advertiser offers to buy them back at the original price during a specified period that may last as long as five years.

54. Guaranteed acceptance offer This specialized offer is used by insurance firms with certain types of policies that require no health questions or underwriting. It's especially appealing to those with health problems who might not otherwise qualify.

Build-Up-the-Sale Offers

55. Multi-product offers Two or more products or services are featured in the same ad or mailing. Maybe you've never thought about it this way, but the best-known type of multi-product offer is a catalog, which can feature a hundred or more items.

56. Piggyback offers Similar to a multi-product offer, except that one product is strongly featured. The other items just kind of ride along or "piggyback" in the hope of picking up additional sales.

57. THE DELUXE OFFER A publisher might offer a book in standard binding at $19.95. The order form gives the customer the option of ordering a deluxe edition for only $5.00 more. And it's not unusual for 10 percent or more of those ordering to select the deluxe alternative.

58. GOOD-BETTER-BEST OFFER This one goes a step further by offering three choices. It's often used as part of a catalog's merchandising strategy.

59. ADD-ON OFFER A low-cost item related to the featured product can be great for impulse orders. Such as offering a wallet for $19.95 with a matching key case offered for only $5.00 extra.

60. WRITE-YOUR-OWN-TICKET OFFER Some magazines have used this with good success to build up the sale. Instead of offering 17 weeks for $14.45, which is 85¢ per issue, they give the subscriber the 85¢-an-issue price and let him or her fill in the number of weeks he or she wants the subscription to run.

61. BOUNCE-BACK OFFER This approach tries to build on the original sale by enclosing an additional offer with the product shipment or invoice.

62. INCREASE AND EXTENSION OFFERS These are also follow-ups to the original sale. Mail order insurance firms often give policyholders a chance to get increased coverage with a higher-priced version of the same policy. Magazines often use an advance renewal offer to get subscribers to extend their present subscription.

SWEEPSTAKES OFFERS

63. DRAWING-TYPE SWEEPSTAKES Many sweepstakes contests are set up this way. The prospect gets one or more chances to win. But all winners are selected by a random drawing.

64. LUCKY NUMBER SWEEPSTAKES With this type of contest, winning numbers are pre-selected before the mailing is made or an ad is run. Copy strategy emphasizes "You may have already won." And for those winning numbers that are not actually entered or returned, a drawing is held for the unclaimed prizes.

65. "EVERYBODY WINS" SWEEPSTAKES No longer widely used, but a real bonanza when this offer was first introduced. The prize structure is set up so the bottom or low-end prize is a very inexpensive or nominal one. And it's awarded to everyone who enters and doesn't win one of the bigger prizes.

66. INVOLVEMENT SWEEPSTAKES   This type requires the prospect to open a mystery envelope, play a game, or match his or her number against an eligible number list. In doing so, the prospect determines the value of the grand prize he or she wins *if* that entry is drawn as the winner. Some of these involvement devices have been highly effective in boosting results.

67. TALENT CONTESTS   Not really a sweepstakes, but effective for some types of direct marketing situations. Such as the mail order puzzle clubs, which offer a simple puzzle to start, so contestants will pay to play.

CLUB AND CONTINUITY OFFERS

68. POSITIVE OPTION   You join a club and are notified monthly of new selections. To order, you must take some positive action, such as sending back an order.

69. NEGATIVE OPTION   You are notified in advance of new selections. But under the terms you agreed to when joining, the new selection is shipped *unless* you return a rejection card by a specific date.

70. AUTOMATIC SHIPMENTS   This variation eliminates the advance notice of new selections. When you sign up, you give the publisher permission to ship each selection automatically until you tell the firm to stop. It's commonly called a "till forbid" offer.

71. CONTINUITY LOAD-UP OFFER   Usually used for a continuity book series, like a 20-volume encyclopedia. The first book is offered free. But after you receive and pay for the next couple of monthly volumes, the balance of the series is sent in one load-up shipment. However, you can continue to pay at the rate of one volume per month.

72. FRONT-END LOAD-UPS   This is where a music or book club gives you four records for $1.00, if you agree to sign up and accept at least four more selections during the next year. The attractive front-end offer persuades you to make a minimum purchase commitment. And the commitment usually has a fixed time period for buying your remaining selections.

73. OPEN-ENDED COMMITMENT Like the front-end load-up, except that there is no time limit for purchasing your four additional selections.

74. "NO-STRINGS-ATTACHED" COMMITMENT Like the above two offers, except it's more generous because you are not committed to any future purchases. The publisher gambles that you will find future selections interesting enough to make a certain number of purchases.

75. LIFETIME MEMBERSHIP FEE You pay a one-time fee to join—usually $10.00 or $20.00—and get a monthly announcement of new selections, which are normally offered at a discount. But there's no minimum commitment, and all ordering is done on a positive-option basis.

76. ANNUAL MEMBERSHIP FEE Here you pay an annual fee for club membership. It's often used for travel clubs where you get a whole range of benefits, including travel insurance. Also used for fundraising, where a choice of membership levels is often effective.

SPECIALIZED OFFERS

77. THE PHILANTHROPIC PRIVILEGE This is the basis of most fundraising offers. The donor's contribution usually brings nothing tangible in return but helps make the world a better place in which to live. Sometimes enhanced by giving gummed stamps, a membership card, or other tokens of appreciation.

78. BLANK CHECK OFFER First used in the McGovern presidential fundraising campaign. Supporters could fill out blank, post-dated checks which were cashed one-a-month to provide installment contributions. Later adapted for extending credit to charge card customers.

79. MATCHING CHECK Popular fundraising offer. A gift from a large donor is used to encourage and match contributions from individuals.

80. EXECUTIVE PREVIEW CHARGE A successful offer for such things as sales training films and videos. Executive agrees to pay $25.00 to screen or preview the film. But if he decides to buy or rent it, the preview charge is credited against the full price.

81. YES/NO/MAYBE OFFERS Asks the prospect to let you know his or her decision. In most cases the negative responses have little or no value. But by forcing a decision, you often end up with more "yes" responses. A "maybe" option is sometimes used to indicate a tentative commitment.

82. SELF-QUALIFICATION OFFER Uses a choice of options to get the prospect to indicate a degree of interest in your product or service. Such as offering a free booklet *or* a free demonstration. Those who request the latter qualify themselves as serious prospects and should get more immediate attention.

83. EXCLUSIVE RIGHTS FOR YOUR TRADING AREA Ideal for selling some business services to firms who are in a competitive business. Such as a syndicated newsletter that a bank buys and sends to its customers. You give the first bank that responds an exclusive for its trading area. The percentages that order are such that you seldom have to turn anybody down.

84. THE SUPER-DRAMATIC OFFER Sometimes very effective. Such as the offer to "Smoke my new kind of pipe for 30 days. If you don't like it, smash it up with a hammer and send back the pieces."

85. TRADE-IN OFFER An offer like "We'll give you $100.00 for your old typewriter when you buy a new electronic model" can be very appealing.

86. THIRD-PARTY REFERRAL OFFER Instead of renting somebody's list, you get the list owner to make a mailing for you—using their firm's name—and recommend your product or service. Usually works better than your own promotion because of the rapport a company has with its own customers.

87. MEMBER-GET-A-MEMBER OFFER Often used to get customers to send in the names of friends who might be interested. Widely used by book and music clubs who give their member a free gift if he or she gets a new member to sign up.

88. NAME-GETTER OFFERS Usually designed for building a prospect list. A firm can offer a low-cost premium at an attractive price.

89. SELF-LIQUIDATING PREMIUM A premium is offered at the advertiser's cost if you send proof-of-purchase from regular products.

90. PURCHASE-WITH-PURCHASE Widely used by cosmetic firms and department stores. An attractive gift set is offered at a special price with a regular purchase.

91. DELAYED BILLING OFFER The appeal is "Order now and we won't bill you until next month." Especially effective before holidays when people have heavy expenses.

92. POST-DATED CHECKS Similar to the above, advertiser promises not to cash your check or process a credit card charge until after a trial period. Air France has used in offering travel videos. You can watch and return the video at no cost, but if you don't return it by a deadline date, they automatically charge it to your credit card.

93. REDUCED DOWN PAYMENT Frequently used as a follow-up in an extended mailing series. If customer does not respond to the regular offer in previous mailings, you reduce the down payment to make it easier for the customer to get started.

94. STRIPPED-DOWN PRODUCTS Also used in an extended mailing series. If the prospect doesn't order the deluxe model featured in the first mailing or two, you switch emphasis to the standard model at a lower price.

95. SWEETEN-THE-POT OFFERS First used in TV support by CBS records. The commercial offered an extra bonus record if you write the album number in the "secret gold box" on the order form.

96. RUSH SHIPPING SERVICE An appealing offer for things like seasonal gifts and film processing. Customers are often asked to pay an extra charge for this service.

97. THE COMPETITIVE OFFER Can be a strong way to dramatize your selling story. Like Diner's Club offering prospects $10.00 to turn in their American Express card.

98. THE NOMINAL REIMBURSEMENT OFFER Used for research mailings. A token payment is offered to get somebody to fill out and return a questionnaire.

99. ESTABLISH-THE-VALUE OFFER With an attractive free gift, you can build its value and establish credibility by offering it in your catalog at the regular price.

BIBLIOGRAPHY

There are now over 200 books on direct marketing. The following are those mentioned in the text, which are still in print, and others the author can personally recommend. Most of these books can be ordered directly from the publisher or Hoke Communications. Many are also available in the business reference sections of public libraries. Naturally, these prices are subject to change.

Catalog Marketing
by Katie Muldoon
AMACOM
American Management Association
135 W. 50th Street
New York, NY 10020
$75.00

Concept of Direct Marketing
by Vin Jenkins
published by Australia Post
Hoke Communications, Inc.
224 Seventh Street
Garden City, NY 11530
$5.00

Direct Mail and Mail Order Handbook
by Richard S. Hodgson
3rd Edition
Dartnell Corporation
4660 N. Ravenswood Avenue
Chicago, IL 60640
$49.95

Direct Mail List Rates and Data
SRDS
3004 Glenview Road
Wilmette, IL 60091

Six issues per year for $317.00
Single issue is $139.00

The Greatest Direct Mail Sales Letters of All Time
by Richard S. Hodgson
Dartnell Corporation
4660 N. Ravenswood Avenue
Chicago, IL 60640
$91.50

How to Build Your Business by Telephone
by Murray Roman
McGraw-Hill
1221 Avenue of the Americas
New York, NY 10020
$47.95

How to Start and Operate a Mail Order Business
by Julian Simon
4th Edition
McGraw-Hill
1221 Avenue of the Americas
New York, NY 10020
$42.50

Integrated Direct Marketing
by Ernan Roman
McGraw-Hill
1221 Avenue of the Americas
New York, NY 10020
$33.50

MaxiMarketing
by Stan Rapp & Tom Collins
McGraw-Hill
1221 Avenue of the Americas
New York, NY 10020
$24.95

*The S. D. Warren Catalog of Catalog
Design*
by Jo-Von Tucker
S. D. Warren Company
225 Franklin Street
Boston, MA 02110
No Charge

Statistical Fact Book
Direct Marketing Association
1650 Blue Grass Lakes Parkway
Alpharetta, GA 30201
$89.95

Successful Direct Marketing Methods
by Bob Stone
4th Edition
NTC Business Books
4255 W. Touhy Avenue
Lincolnwood, IL 60646
$34.95

Tested Advertising Methods
by John Caples
4th Edition
Prentice-Hall, Inc.
Route 9W
Englewood Cliffs, NJ 07632
$9.95

A Whack on the Side of the Head
by Roger Von Oech
Warner Books
666 Fifth Avenue
New York, NY 10103
$12.95

Winning Direct Response Advertising
by Joan Throckmorton
Prentice-Hall, Inc.
Route 9W
Englewood Cliffs, NJ 07632
$18.95

Where to Get More Information

Magazines and Newsletters

Catalog Age
Hanson Publishing Group, Inc.
911 Hope Street
6 River Bend Center
Stamford, CT 06907
$64 per year
203-358-9900

The Delay Letter
Robert F. Delay & Associates
320 E. 54th Street
Suite 6G
New York, NY 10022
$145—published 22x a year
212-688-7559

Direct
Hanson Publishing Group, Inc.
911 Hope Street
6 River Bend Center
Stamford, CT 06907
$64 per year
203-358-9900

Direct Marketing Magazine
Hoke Communications, Inc.*
224 Seventh Street
Garden City, NY 11530
$52 per year
516-746-6700

DM News
Mill Hollow Corporation
11 W. 42nd Street
New York, NY 10036
$75 per year
212-741-2095

The Friday Report (Newsletter)
Hoke Communications, Inc.*
224 Seventh Street
Garden City, NY 11530
$165 per year—published weekly
516-746-6700

Target Marketing Magazine
North American Publishing Company
401 N. Broad
Philadelphia, PA 19108
$65 per year
215-238-5300

Who's Mailing What!
Denison Hatch
210 Red Fox Road
Stamford, CT 06903
$168—published 10 × a year
203-329-2666

*Hoke Communications is the oldest publisher in the direct marketing field, and also offers an extensive list of audio and video cassettes.

Associations and Clubs

Direct Marketing Association
6 East 43rd Street
New York, NY 10017
212-768-7277

The leading trade association in the field. Sponsors many conferences and trade shows plus numerous seminars. Has an annual awards competition. Maintains an information service center. Represents direct marketers in legislative and government affairs. Has councils to serve special interests of members.

The Direct Marketing Association also serves international members and can provide contact information for associations in other countries.

In addition, most major U.S. cities have a local direct marketing club, such as the Chicago Association of Direct Marketing. Clubs usually sponsor monthly meetings with guest speakers and an annual Direct Marketing Day seminar.

There are also groups which serve special interests, such as the Direct Marketing Creative Guild. A directory of the leading clubs and groups is included in *Target Marketing's* annual issue on "Who's Who in Direct Marketing."

Colleges and Universities

Over 100 colleges and universities now offer courses in direct marketing. Some also offer graduate programs. A listing of these schools can be obtained from:

Direct Marketing Educational Foundation
6 East 43rd Street
New York, NY 10017
212-768-7277

INDEX

♦